THE PRACTICAL
—GARDEN—
COMPANION

THE PRACTICAL
GARDEN
COMPANION

Select Editions

This edition published in 2000 in Canada by
Select Editions
8036 Enterprise Street
Burnaby, BC Canada V5A 1V7
Ph: (604) 415-2444 Fax: (604) 415-3444

© Anness Publishing Limited 1999

Produced by
Anness Publishing Limited
Hermes House
88-89 Blackfriars Road
London SE1 8HA

Publisher: Joanna Lorenz
Production Controller: Yolande Denny
Project Editor: Simona Hill
Design: Axis Design
Jacket Design: Ruth Hope

1 3 5 7 9 10 8 6 4 2

CONTENTS

Introduction

Gardening is more than a collection of plants in beds and borders – it is about creating an overall effect in which the plants and the hard landscaping both play a vital part. This book shows you how to stamp your own identity on every aspect of your garden, from the planning stage to the finishing touches, whatever the limitations of time and space.

The importance of comprehensive organisation is stressed in the opening sections on planning and designing the garden. With design ideas for even the most unpromising plots and differing lifestyles, these sections will enable you to make the most of the specific advice offered later in the book. With the plans in place, the task of creating the structure, adding paths, patios and ponds, planting a lawn and creating borders can begin. Expert advice guides you through the practicalities one step at a time. Beautiful gardens and inspirational ideas are pictured and there are many suggestions for beautiful planting schemes for every season of the gardening year.

Left: Rosa *'Cupid' trained on a rope.*

Planning the Garden

Thorough and realistic planning is the key to successful gardening. Whether you are starting from scratch or redesigning an existing plot, it is vital to have in mind an overall scheme and set of priorities before you begin to erect your fence or plant your border. Even if your garden is awkward in shape or situation, you can create the environment you want, provided you follow a few simple principles of design.

Left: *A small garden should not lack impact. Provided it is well planted and has strong focal points, it becomes easy to ignore the limitations of size.*

Above: *A sense of mystery and excitement can be created simply by adding ornaments and providing a hidden area of the garden to be explored.*

Initial Planning

With a few exceptions – such as wild gardens or those with an informal country cottage style, for example – the hallmark of a well-designed garden is that it has either a strong theme or detectable pattern. If your interest lies primarily in plants, then clever planting patterns, pretty colour themes, or contrast will be enough to give your garden that special look. Usually, however, it is the hard landscaping that gives a garden a strong sense of having been designed.

One way to guarantee impact in a small area is to mix paving materials and introduce small changes in level. The design here has a strongly rectangular theme, and because of the variety of textures and changes of level, it looks interesting. This professionally designed garden also shows the importance of foliage plants and the role of moving water as a focal point.

This combination a creative use of plants and strong hard landscaping has the indisputable hallmark of careful planning and design. Even in a small area like this, the impact is immediate.

Circular themes can be difficult to accommodate in a small garden, and where the circles leave awkward angles, they can be hard to manage. Here the problem has been overcome by the clever use of water, with bold plants to help mask transition points.

The choice of a single specimen plant with an almost spherical outline, off-set to one side of the decking, combines simplicity with a strong sense of design. Garden size is less important than how you use the space.

As a basic shape, gardens cannot be any simpler than this, but even a quick glance tells you that it has the stamp of a very experienced designer. The plants in this country garden have that magical English cottage garden look, yet they have been framed in a clearly modern setting.

Bricks and clay pavers are an excellent choice for this kind of informal planting as they have a mellowness that complements the plants. This very simple design works so well because the pavers have been laid in an interesting herringbone pattern with a crisp outline around the inner bed.

Focal points are very important, and even a potentially dull or boring corner of the garden can be transformed into an area of special charm with the imaginative use of a focal point. Before a focal point was introduced, this small path led between some shrubs to the boundary hedge, and was a very dull part of the garden that you would not want to show your visitors. A couple of slate steps and a Japanese lantern set in a small gravelled area were all that was needed to transform this area into a feature that seldom fails to attract favourable comment.

Improving your garden does not necessarily mean a major redesign. Often, only small changes or the clever use of focal points are all that are required.

Left: Multiple and linking circles always make a better design than individual or isolated circular areas. This design is particularly effective because the circular pond is reflected in the edging, the band of grass, and then the surrounding brick path, rather like ripples in a pool. By using the same bricks for the path leading to this part of the garden, the whole feature has been well integrated.

Above: If you take over a mature garden, with large trees and shrubs, you may feel that major reconstruction would be too demanding. Often, however, a few simple modifications will achieve a transformation.

The addition of a couple of formal beds edged with box is sufficient to transform a plain lawn into something more formal that seems appropriate for this style of older garden. But it still needs colour and a central focal point to create a sense of design, and here it has been achieved with a large and attractively planted urn.

To give your garden a strong appeal, it is not necessary to destroy most of what is there already. Sometimes it is sufficient to remove one or two features and perhaps create an area of strong visual appeal in their place.

Plan Work in Stages

If you tackle a garden in sections, the improvements will seem much more achievable, be easier on the purse or wallet, and take less effort to attain. This is true even for a small garden. By all means have an overall scheme in mind and roughed out on paper if the garden is large, but work in detail on just one section of the garden at a time. Tackle the front garden, or the back garden, or perhaps just the patio, and construct that before moving on to the next task, which, perhaps, will wait for next year. In this way you see the improvements quickly without the garden construction becoming a chore.

The illustrations on these two pages show how one small garden was improved in stages and how the various parts have been treated with different styles, each tackled as a separate project in different years.

1 To reduce the maintenance involved in a narrow flowerbed, it was transformed into a "stream" and bog garden, using a long and narrow liner (you will have to order a non-standard size like this). This took a couple of weekends to finish, but added variety and attracted lots of wildlife.

2 The original paving slab path on a concrete base was left *in situ* to save the considerable effort of breaking it up. Instead, pieces of slate were simply mortared over the top of the old path, a job done in a day, so the transformation was almost instant. A pond was introduced to offset the potentially harsh outline of the conifers and gravel.

3 The back garden was tackled the following year. Despite its size, it was divided into two sections, to introduce variety and to make the garden seem larger. This also had the added benefit of having one attractive area in the garden, while construction of the other half followed at a later date. The trellis acts as a partition without shutting out too much light.

4 This half of the back garden was constructed later, using a different type of paving and with more extensive use of compact shrubs planted directly into the soil, creating a different atmosphere from the rest of the garden.

5 It makes sense to start with the front garden as this is what passers-by and visitors see first. This front garden was originally lawn with a narrow flowerbed on the other side of a plain path of rectangular paving slabs. It was transformed into an attractive low-maintenance garden in a couple of weekends by digging up the grass and planting slow-growing conifers with contrasting shapes and colours. The area between them was covered with gravel to suppress weeds.

Deciding on Priorities

It makes sense to begin any garden design by making a wish-list. It is most unlikely to be fulfiled completely, but setting down those things that are a priority to you should ensure that the most important features are included.

MAKING YOUR LIST

Everyone has different preferences, so make a list like the one shown here (photocopy it if you don't want to write your own or mark the book). Decide which features you regard as essential (this may be something as mundane as a clothes-line or as interesting as a water feature), those that are important but less essential for your ideal garden, and those elements that you regard simply as desirable. While designing your garden, keep in mind those features listed as essential. Try to incorporate as many of them as possible, but don't cram in so many that the strong sense of design is sacrificed.

It will immediately become apparent if the list of the most desirable features is not feasible within the limited space available, but you will probably be able to introduce some of the more important ones. However, only attempt to include those features ticked as desirable if you have space.

Working from a check-list will not directly aid the design, but it will act as a reminder of what is important to you. A garden that fulfils the functions that are important may be more satisfying than one that is well designed and smart but omits features that you care about.

GARDEN PRIORITIES

	Essential	Important	Desirable
Flowerbeds	[ ]	[ ]	[ ]
Herbaceous border	[ ]	[ ]	[ ]
Shrub border	[ ]	[ ]	[ ]
Trees	[ ]	[ ]	[ ]
Lawn	[ ]	[ ]	[ ]
Gravelled area	[ ]	[ ]	[ ]
Paved area/patio	[ ]	[ ]	[ ]
Built-in barbecue	[ ]	[ ]	[ ]
Garden seats/furniture	[ ]	[ ]	[ ]
Rock garden	[ ]	[ ]	[ ]
Pond	[ ]	[ ]	[ ]
Other water feature	[ ]	[ ]	[ ]
Wildlife area	[ ]	[ ]	[ ]
Greenhouse/conservatory	[ ]	[ ]	[ ]
Summerhouse	[ ]	[ ]	[ ]
Tool shed	[ ]	[ ]	[ ]
Fruit garden	[ ]	[ ]	[ ]
Herb garden	[ ]	[ ]	[ ]
Vegetable garden	[ ]	[ ]	[ ]
Trellis/pergola/arch	[ ]	[ ]	[ ]
Sand pit/play area	[ ]	[ ]	[ ]
Clothes-line	[ ]	[ ]	[ ]
Dustbin (trashcan) hide	[ ]	[ ]	[ ]
....	[ ]	[ ]	[ ]
....	[ ]	[ ]	[ ]
....	[ ]	[ ]	[ ]
....	[ ]	[ ]	[ ]
....	[ ]	[ ]	[ ]

Be flexible in your approach to features. If a pond is on your list but there does not seem to be sufficient space or an appropriate place to build it, consider a small patio pond like this one.

The tool shed is always difficult to accommodate, as it should not be obtrusive. With clever planting, however, it can usually be screened well enough to be acceptable.

A permanent barbecue may look impressive when entertaining, but bear in mind that it can also look bleak in winter. You may prefer a portable one that can be removed when it is not required.

Opposite: *If you want a pergola but there is not space for a free-standing one, an alternative is a structure that stands on the patio and joins the house. Linking house and garden visually is vital to good garden design.*

Surveying and Measuring

It is much better – and less expensive – to make your mistakes on paper first, so the starting point for any garden improvement plan should be to prepare a sketch and plan of the garden as it is. This can then be worked up into any number of imaginative designs, and if things do not work out as you expected, just rub it out or put it in the bin, and start again.

WHAT YOU WILL NEED

- A 30m (100ft) tape measure – preferably plasticized fabric as this is easy to work with, but does not stretch.
- A 1.8m (6ft) steel ruler for short measurements.
- Pegs to mark out positions, and to hold one end of the tape in position (meat skewers can be used with the tape).
- Pencils, sharpener and eraser.
- Clipboard with pad or graph paper.

POSITIONING FEATURES

With a small rectangular garden, like the one shown here, most measurements are easily determined by measuring key points from a known straight line such as the house or a fence. If the shape is more complicated, it is usually possible to determine a position by laying a piece of string at right angles from the known straight edge, then measuring at right angles from this at a point marked on your sketch.

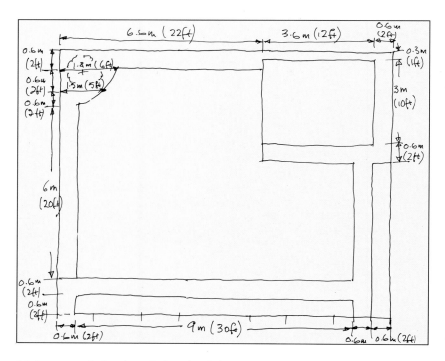

Make a rough freehand sketch of the garden. If it is very large, divide it into sections that can be pieced together later, but for a small garden, the whole area will go onto a single sheet of paper.

If necessary, join several sheets of paper together rather than cramp the sketch, and leave plenty of space around the edge on which you can write the dimensions.

Write down the measurements of all the main features, like paths, sheds and greenhouses, and important flowerbeds and large trees. Do not include anything that you are already sure you will not retain, otherwise include as many measurements as possible.

COPING WITH SLOPES

- Professional landscape architects surveying a large garden will use special techniques to determine the slope, which is then transferred to the plan as contour lines. However, most simple garden improvements can be achieved quite successfully without this degree of accuracy.

- If the slope is very gradual, you can ignore it, unless you want to create a deliberate change of level. More significant slopes can usually be estimated and the contours drawn in by eye. If the slope is steep, or if you want to create a series of terraces, you will have to measure the slope accurately and incorporate it into your scale drawing. Usually, however, it is possible to improve your garden simply by using the methods suggested in this book.

Gentle slopes over a short distance seldom present a problem. A couple of very shallow terraces that do not need strong retaining walls are usually sufficient to create plenty of level ground for a lawn, for example, and then the final steeper bank can be clothed with rock plants. These will look attractive, tolerate the dry conditions found on sloping ground and, once established, will help to stabilize the soil.

Putting the Plan on Paper

The exciting part of replanning your garden starts when you have an outline of the existing garden and permanent fixtures on which you can start to create your dream garden. It has all the excitement and promise of reading seed catalogues, where the imagination transforms the existing garden into an area full of beauty and promise. Making an accurate scale drawing of your existing garden is an essential starting point if you want to simplify the design work that follows.

QUICK ON THE DRAW

• Draw the outline of the garden first, together with the position of the house and any other features, and make sure you have the correct measurements for these before filling in the other elements.

• Next, draw in those elements that are easy to position, such as rectangular flowerbeds or raised beds and the garden shed, if you are reasonably certain of exactly where they are.

• Ink in those elements of the garden that are fixed and will not change, such as boundaries and paths that you know you will not move. Draw the other parts in pencil first, as it is quite likely that you may have to make slight adjustments. Ink them in when you know everything is in its correct place.

• Use a compass if possible to draw curves and circles. Not all curves are suitable for this treatment, but you can buy flexible rules that can be bent to any reasonable curve.

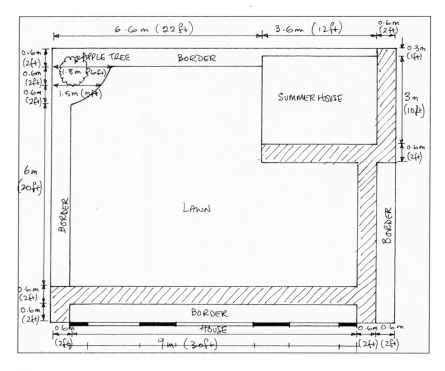

The rough sketch must be transferred to a scale drawing before any detailed plans can be sketched out. Drawing it to scale will help you to calculate the quantity of any paving required, and also enable you to make beds, borders and lawns to sizes that involve the least amount of cutting of hard materials such as paving slabs or bricks.

Use graph paper for your scale drawing. Pads are adequate for a small garden or a section of a larger one, but if your garden is big, buy a large sheet (available from good stationers and art shops).

Use a scale that enables you to fit the plan onto your sheet of graph paper (or several taped together). For most small gardens, a scale of 1:50 (2cm to 1m or ¼in to 1ft) is about right. For a large garden, however, 1:100 (1cm to 1m or ⅛in to 1ft) might be more appropriate.

Draw the basic outline and the position of the house first, including the position of doors and windows if relevant. Then add all the major features that you are likely to retain. You should have all the necessary measurements on the freehand sketch that you made in the garden.

Omit any features that you are sure will be eliminated from the new design, to keep it as uncluttered as possible. In this example, the summerhouse has been drawn in because it was considered to be in a good position and would be difficult to move. The corner tree was removed in the final design, but was included at this stage as a design might have been chosen that made use of it.

USING YOUR PLAN

1 Even expert designers make a number of rough sketches of possible designs before finalizing the chosen one, so devise a way of using your master outline again and again without having to keep redrawing it. One way is to make a number of photocopies.

2 If you have a drawing board, simply use tracing paper overlays for your roughs while experimenting with ideas. If you do not have a drawing board and the garden is small, you may be able to use a clipboard instead.

3 Film and pens of the type used for overhead projection sheets are effective if you prefer to use colours that can easily be wiped off for correction.

4 Some people prefer visual aids to move around when designing. If you find this helpful, try drawing and cutting out scale features that you want to include in your finished design, such as a raised pond, patio furniture, or raised beds. These can be moved around until they look right, but they should only be used as aids once the overall design has been formulated in your mind. If you try to design your garden around the few key symbols that you have placed, it will lack coherence.

DESIGNING BY COMPUTER

- If you feel happier with a computer keyboard and mouse than with paper and pencil, you can use one of the several computer programs that are available to help you design your garden.

- These vary enormously in capability and ease of use. The cheaper ones are likely to be fairly basic, and you may find them more frustrating to use than you imagine. The more sophisticated programs are both versatile and effective, but unless you intend to design gardens on a regular basis, they are probably not worth the money and time needed to learn how to use them properly.

- You will find pencil and paper just as effective for a one-off design for your own garden, with minimal financial outlay and the decided advantage of being able to move around your garden while modifying the plan.

TRIANGULATION MADE EASY

- Sometimes it may be difficult to measure a position simply by using right angles: perhaps there is an obstruction such as a pond or low hedge, for example, or there may be no available right angles because of the shape of the garden. Triangulation is a way of fixing a position, and is much easier than it sounds.

- Using known points, the corners of the house in this example, simply measure the distance to the position to be fixed, and note the two distances on your sketch.

- When you make your scale drawing, set a compass to each of the scale distances in turn, then strike an arc in the approximate position. The point you measured in the garden is where the arcs intersect on the plan.

To fix the position of the tree, measure to A, then B. Strike arcs on a scale drawing with compasses set at these measurements. The point where the arcs cross indicates the position of the tree in relation to the house.

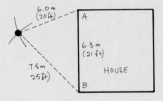

Creating your Design

The difficult part of redesigning or improving your garden is making a start. After you start drawing, the ideas are sure to flow, especially if you have other gardens in mind that you like and can use as a starting point. The many inspirational pictures in this book will provide a wealth of ideas that you can adapt for your own garden, but take elements from various gardens that you like rather than try to recreate someone else's design exactly. Designs seldom transfer easily unless your garden is very similar in shape and size, and your garden will be much more satisfying if it reflects your own personality and preferences.

CIRCULAR THEME

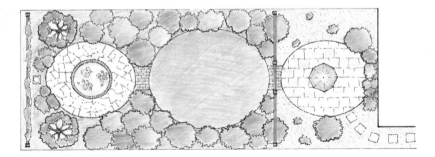

DIAGONAL THEME

RECTANGULAR THEME

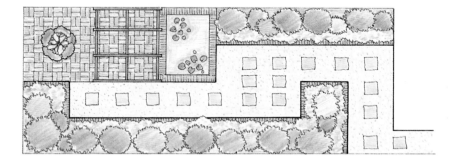

PLANNING THE SHAPE OF THE GARDEN

If you decide on a garden with strong lines, rather than irregular flowing borders, wildlife corners and semi-woodland areas, it is worth deciding on whether you are going to plan a rectangular or diagonal theme, or use a design based on circles. Any of these can be adapted to suit the size of your garden, and in the case of the circular pattern, you might want to include overlapping circles. Where circles join, try to make any transitional curves gradual rather than abrupt.

Whichever you choose, draw a grid on top of your plan to aid design (see opposite page). In a small garden surrounded by fencing, it can be useful to base the rectangular and diagonal grids on the spacing of fence posts (usually about 1.8m (6ft) apart).

A rectangular grid has been used for the example opposite, but as part of the trial-and-error phase, it is usually worth trying different grids. A diagonal grid is often particularly effective where the house is set in a large garden with plenty of space at the sides. The patio can often be positioned at a 45-degree angle at the corner of the house, for example.

The size and shape of the garden will usually dictate the most appropriate grid, but if in doubt, try more than one to see which one emerges with more possibilities than the others after a few attempts at quick designs.

Bear in mind that many excellent, prize-winning gardens are created without such a grid, and sometimes these have, to some extent, evolved in a more flowing manner, developing feature by feature. Grids like these may help you, but do not hesitate to adopt a more freestyle approach if this comes more naturally.

BEGINNING THE DESIGN

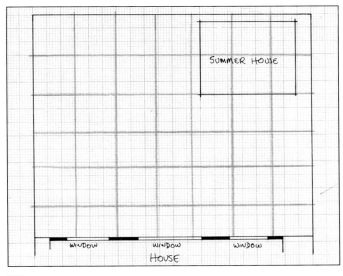

1 Draw in any features to be retained (in this example the summerhouse), and the chosen grid (unless you want an informal style where a grid may be inappropriate). Use a different colour for the grid lines, in order to prevent the plan becoming cluttered and confused.

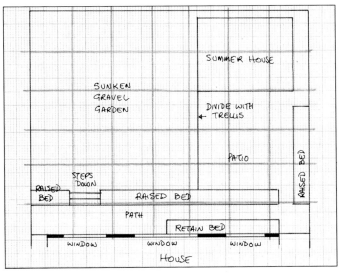

2 Use overlays (or photocopies) to experiment with a range of designs. Even if the first attempt looks satisfactory, try a number of variations. You can always come back to your first idea later if it turns out to be the best one.

At this stage, do not include details such as patio furniture or individual plants (except for key focal point plants and important trees or shrubs). When you have a design that you like, pencil in things like patio furniture (or use the cut-out features if you prepared them earlier).

TEN TIPS TO TRY

Don't despair if inspiration does not come easily, or initial attempts seem disappointing. If you try these ten tips, you will almost certainly produce workable plans that you will be pleased with:

- Look through books and magazines to decide which style of garden you like: formal or informal; the emphasis on plants or on hard landscaping; mainly foliage, texture and ground cover or lots of colourful flowers; straight edges or curved and flowing lines.

- With the style decided, look at as many garden pictures as possible – make a start in this book – and look for design ideas that appeal. Do not be influenced by individual plants, as these can be changed.

- Choose a grid, if applicable, and draw this onto your plan. This will help to carry your thoughts through on logical lines.

- Start sketching lots of designs but do not attempt to perfect them at this stage. Just explore ideas.

- Do not concern yourself with planning plants or attempt to choose individual plants at this stage – concentrate on patterns and lines.

- Do not spend time drawing in paving patterns or choosing materials yet.

- Make a shortlist of those overall outlines that you like best. Then forget it for a day. It always pays to take a fresh look at things after a short break.

- If you still like one of your original roughs, begin to work on that, filling in details like paving, surface textures such as gravel and the position of focal point plants. Leave out planting plans at this stage.

- If your original roughs lack appeal when you look at them again, repeat the process with another batch of ideas. You will probably see ways of improving some of your earlier efforts, so things will be easier this time round.

- If you find it difficult to visualize sizes, peg the design out on the ground with string and modify your plan if necessary.

Finishing Touches

When the outline plan is ready, it's time to fill in the detail and to make sure it will work on the ground. Designs can look very different in actual size and when viewed three-dimensionally rather than as a flat plan on paper. This is the time for fine-tuning, for selecting paving materials, adjusting the plan to minimize the number of cut bricks or slabs, and for visualizing the changes on the ground.

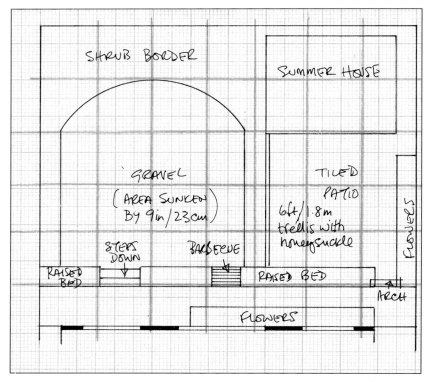

If your design includes irregularly-shaped beds, use a length of garden hose or thick rope to mark out the shape. If you have to cut the beds into an existing lawn, you will need to do this anyway when it's time to start construction.

When the main features and their position have been decided, draw up a detailed plan, such as the one above. It will almost certainly be necessary to make some adjustments to the rough plan to take into account problems on the ground.

In this example, a complicated tile design was chosen for the patio, so the width of the boundary border had to be adjusted so that only half-tiles had to be cut, which would significantly reduce breakages and wastage. This kind of detailed planning can save time, trouble and expense at the construction stage.

Pegging the plan out on the ground also revealed that by keeping to the rectangular pattern, insufficient space would have been left for shrubs at the corners, so these were rounded to provide extra planting space.

Many potential problems can be overcome by critical appraisal and minor adjustments at this stage.

MARKING OUT THE LAYOUT

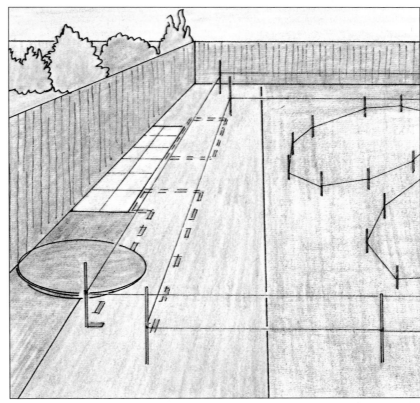

Curved borders can be marked out with a garden hose or thick rope, and the curves adjusted so that they look natural and not too acute. Adjustments are easily made by moving the hose or rope until it looks right (see above).

If you plan to plant a tree or large shrub, especially where you want it to mask a view or to be seen as a focal point from various parts of the garden, insert a pole or tall cane in the planned position. This will help you to visualize its effect, and you should be able to judge whether shadows cast over other areas are likely to be a problem.

Once the design has been marked out on the ground, look at it from as many different angles as possible, and at different times of the day. Provided you choose a sunny day, you will see where shadows fall and where shade could be a problem, but bear in mind that the time of year will affect the angle and length of the shadows. So if you are doing this in the winter, do not be too despondent.

Also, always look at your pegged-out plan from each room that overlooks it. The view from an upstairs room can be particularly useful in helping to visualize the overall plan.

Whenever possible, mark out the layout on the ground – this is the closest you can get to visualizing the finished garden.

Straight lines can be marked out with string stretched between pegs or canes (stakes), and an impression of a curve can be achieved by using plenty of pegs or canes close together. Alternatively, use a garden hose or rope, as described for marking out curved beds. Loose bricks are useful for indicating the outline of raised beds.

The Final Design Plan

No garden design is perfect and you will probably modify it slightly during construction, but it is worth drawing a final scale plan in detail before you order materials and make a physical start. This will enable you to calculate accurately the number of bricks or paving slabs and the amount of other materials you need (always allow a little extra for wastage).

This is the stage at which you can draw in your planting plans if you prefer. If time and money is limited, it may be better to concentrate on the main construction at this stage, and do the planting later. Much depends on the time of year. If you finish the construction in spring, for example, and want to restrict expenditure on major items like trees and shrubs until the autumn or following spring, you can always fill the spaces with cheerful annuals for the first summer at minimal cost. On the other hand, the sooner these long-term plants are put in, the more quickly your garden will have that sought-after mature and established look.

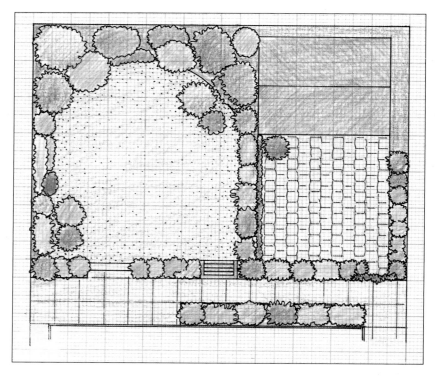

The final plan is the one you will use for construction. Depending on the scale of the plan and size of the garden, you can either mark measurements on the plan or calculate them as necessary from the squared graph paper.

You need not follow your design slavishly – be prepared to modify dimensions and features as appropriate during construction.

Low raised beds can be used to create the effect of enclosed outdoor "rooms" without keeping out light, but in a small space they need to be softened so that they don't dominate the area. Here herbs in containers have been used to add interest and soften the effect of the new walling. Containers like this need not be considered at the planning stage but can be added afterwards.

It will take several seasons for shrubs, climbers and slow-growing perennials to become established, so fill the gaps with plenty of quick-growing plants for fast results.

Right: If choosing gravel as a surface, select a type that produces the effect you like. Small pea-sized gravel looks very different from the large, angular gravel used in this picture. The actual effect will also depend on whether the gravel is wet or dry, as well as on the light. Some gravels can look very harsh when dry and viewed in bright sunlight.

A large expanse of gravel can look bleak, so it's a good idea to plant through it if you think the effect needs softening. This can always be done later, and is best improvised rather than planned like a border. Choose plants that grow well in dry conditions.

Preparing a Planting Plan

The hard landscaping acts like a skeleton and gives a garden its structure, but it is the choice of plants that gives it shape and character. Because plants become too large or straggly, or simply die from disease, the weather, or age, planting is a continuous process. But it is always worth starting with a paper plan rather than be influenced by impulse purchase and then wonder where to put the plants.

1 Start with an outline of the area to be planted, with distances marked on the graph paper to make positioning easier, and some good plant books that include pictures and likely heights and spreads for the plants. Treat likely heights and spreads with caution, as much will depend on soil, seasons and where you live.

2 If your plant knowledge is good you may be able to draw directly onto your plan, but if you find it easier to move around pieces of paper, cut out shapes to represent the plants that you are planning to include. Write on their height, spread and flowering period if this helps, and mark their name on the back or front.

It will help to colour them – evergreen in green, variegated in say green and gold stripes, golden plants in yellow, and so on. Coloured spots can indicate the colour of any flowers. Visual aids like this will help, but bear in mind that flat shapes on paper give no indication of the shapes of the plants (spiky, rounded or feathery).

Shrubs can be represented as single specimens, but border plants should be planted in groups of threes or fives whenever possible, so that they grow into each other as a drift of colour.

3 Position tall or key plants first. You may have to adjust them when the other plants are added, but it is important to get these plants correctly positioned first as they will probably dominate the finished border.

Add mid-height plants next. Make sure some of these appear to drift towards the back of the border between the taller ones, to avoid a rigid, tiered effect.

Finally, fill in with low-growing plants. The larger the drift of these, the more effective they will be. Individual small plants lack impact, and can be swamped by vigorous neighbours.

4 The initial plans can be fairly crude as they merely explore the possibilities of various plant combinations and associations. So, to visualize the final effect more easily, draw your final planting plan in more detail.

1 CREATING THE OUTLINE

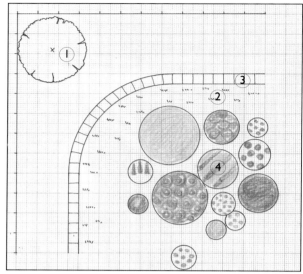

1	Existing flagpole cherry	3	Mowing edge
	(*Prunus* 'Amanogawa')	4	Cut out plants to fill in
2	Lawn		the border

2 ADDING IN THE PLANTS

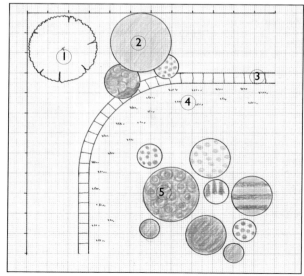

1	Existing flagpole cherry	4	Lawn
	(*Prunus* 'Amanogawa')	5	Plants still to be positioned
2	Plants in position		
3	Mowing edge		

3 FILLING OUT THE DESIGN

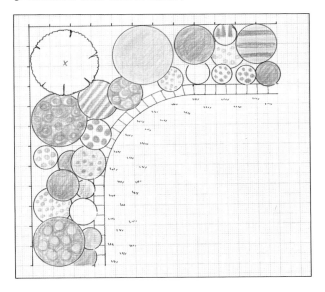

4 COMPLETING THE DETAIL

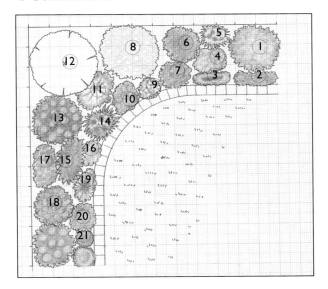

1	Houttuynia cordata 'Chameleon' 30cm (1ft)	11	Cornus alba 'Sibirica' 1.2m (4ft)
		12	Existing flagpole cherry (Prunus 'Amanogawa')
2	Bergenia 30cm (1ft)	13	Camellia 'Donation' (evergreen) 1.8m (6ft)
3	Diascia barberiae 8cm (3in)	14	Agapanthus 60cm (2ft)
4	Perovskia atriplicifolia 1.2m (4ft)	15	Hosta 45cm (1½ft)
5	Kniphofia 90cm (3ft)	16	Bergenia 30cm (1ft)
6	Rosemary 20cm (4ft)	17	Anemone x hybrida 75cm (2½ft)
7	Artemisia 'Powis Castle' 90cm (3ft)	18	Potentilla 'Princess' 75cm (2½ft)
8	Choisya ternata 90cm (3ft)	19	Lavender 30cm (1ft)
9	Dwarf Michaelmas daisy 60cm (2ft)	20	Stachys byzantina 30cm (1ft)
10	Cistus 45cm (1½ft)	21	Mahonia 'Charity' (evergreen) 2.4m (8ft)

GREEN-FINGERED RULES OF THUMB

• Be careful to ensure that tall plants are not placed in front of smaller ones. Heights given in books and catalogues can only be a guide, however, so be prepared for surprises.

• Place tall plants at the back of the border whenever possible (or in the centre of an island bed viewed from both sides), but avoid regimented tiers. A few plants that stand above the others in the middle or towards the front of the border often look good.

• Plant herbaceous plants in groups of at least three plants whenever possible. Even in a small area, a group of the same kind of plant will probably have more impact than the same number of plants of different kinds.

• Use plenty of foliage plants – they will remain attractive for much longer than most flowering kinds.

• Do not be afraid to mix shrubs and herbaceous plants – your borders will almost certainly look more interesting throughout the year. Do not overlook the role of bulbs too, especially bold ones like crown imperials (*Fritillaria imperialis*) and lilies.

• Use plenty of carpeters along the edge and to fill in gaps between large plants. It is better to cover the ground with these than to allow weeds to grow.

COLOUR SCHEMES

• Single-colour theme borders (or combinations of sympathetic colours, such as blue and mauve with grey or silver) are popular in large gardens, but difficult to achieve where space is limited and as much variety as possible has to be crammed in.

• If space is limited, it is worth concentrating light-coloured plants with golden leaves or foliage that is variegated with a pale colour in those parts of the garden that are rather shady and dull.

• If colour schemes are important to you, try creating clusters of interesting colour combinations or harmonies in parts of the border. A group of three, four or five plants that look good together can have a similar effect to a colour-theme border.

Designing the Garden

No matter how awkward its shape, or how unpromising its aspect, almost any garden can be radically improved by good design. Gardening is about more than a collection of plants in beds and borders – it is about achieving an overall effect that reflects your own tastes, lifestyle and needs. Adapt the ideas in this chapter to suit your own preferences, budget and available time, to create an outdoor "room" that combines visual interest, easy access and privacy.

Left: *A well-planned garden will reward you with year-round interest.*

Above: *The white garden furniture provides a visual link with the trellis arch, directing attention outwards to the boundary.*

Coping with Slopes

Sloping sites are particularly difficult to plan on paper, and they are much more challenging to design in general. It is also more difficult to adapt other people's designs as sloping gardens vary so much in the degree of slope – even whether it is up or down – as well as size and aspect. Sloping gardens really do have to be tailor-made to the site as well as to your preferences. You can, however, turn the drawbacks into advantages, as changes of level can add interest and provide an excellent setting for rock gardens and cascading "streams".

PLANNING A DOWNWARD-SLOPING GARDEN

A downward-sloping garden with an attractive view is much easier to design successfully. The view from the house can be the panorama beyond the garden or the garden itself as it falls away below. If the outlook is unattractive, however, it may be advisable to use the lowest part of the garden, well-screened by shrubs and small trees, as the main sitting area.

The plan on the right demonstrates several important principles when designing a sloping garden, and unusually combines terraces with a natural slope. Terracing is expensive and time-consuming: considerable earth-moving is involved and retaining walls on strong foundations have to be constructed. Likewise, simply moving the topsoil from one area to deposit lower down the slope is unsatisfactory as part of the garden will then be left with subsoil at the surface for planting – a recipe for disappointment. Topsoil should be set aside, the underlying ground levelled, and then the topsoil can be returned.

Terracing provides flat areas on which to walk and relax, and this design includes suitable flat areas along the length of the garden, and as these have been used for hard surfaces, the problem of topsoil movement does not arise. By retaining the natural slope for a large part of the garden, cost and structural work has been reduced.

Although there are some retaining walls, the two walls that zigzag down the garden are stepped so that they remain just above the surrounding ground.

Retaining a large area of naturally sloping ground also provides an ideal setting for rock outcrops and an artificial stream with a series of cascades.

Taking a path across the garden at an angle makes it seem less steep. A path that runs in a straight line down the slope only serves to emphasize the drop.

A DOWNWARD-SLOPING GARDEN

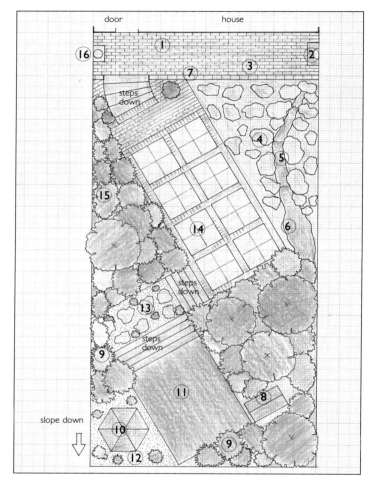

1	Bricks or clay pavers	9	Shrubs
2	Wall fountain with small pool	10	Summerhouse with views across garden and to attractive view below garden
3	Patio		
4	Rock garden bank sloping downhill and towards flat paved area	11	Lawn
		12	Gravel with alpines
5	"Stream" with cascades	13	Gravel area with natural paving
6	Pond, disappearing behind shrubs	14	Bricks or clay pavers mixed with paving slabs
7	Small retaining wall		
8	Shed for tools and lawnmower	15	Trees and shrubs
		16	Ornament (on plinth)

AN UPWARD-SLOPING GARDEN

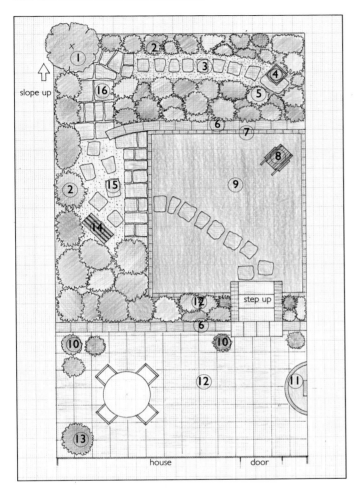

1	Small tree	9	Thyme or chamomile lawn
2	Shrubs	10	Plants in containers
3	Natural stone paving slabs set in gravel	11	Wall fountain with small pool beneath
4	Ornament on plinth as focal point	12	Patio
5	Dwarf shrubs on bank	13	Shrub or small tree in large tub
6	Retaining wall	14	Seat
7	Brick edge	15	Natural stone paving slabs set in gravel
8	Sunlounger or deckchair	16	Natural stone path

PLANNING AN UPWARD-SLOPING GARDEN

An upward slope is more challenging. Distant views are not a possibility and even upper floors may look out onto the bank. Terracing can look oppressive, but a "secret" garden full of meandering paths flanked by shrubs is an effective way to deal with the slope. Some retaining walls are usually necessary, but if planted with shrubs, the effect will be masked and the plants on the lower terraces will hide the upper walls and banks.

With this kind of garden it is important to use focal points to give the paths a purpose; just as a maze has a focal point (its centre).

Lawns are difficult to accommodate on a steeply sloping site, and difficult to mow too, as lawnmowers are awkward to carry up steps and steep ramps for access. It is generally best to avoid them, but in the example shown left a grass alternative has been used to provide a "lawn" in a small levelled area. The chamomile or thyme only requires an occasional trim with shears, which is not an onerous job for a small area.

Steep slopes are ideal for a rock garden. Construction can be difficult, however, and manhandling and positioning rocks safely on a steep slope requires considerable expertise.

A few rocks will go further if presented as outcrops on a grassy bank, and the effect is more natural and less costly. The drawback is the grass that has to be mown between the rock outcrops; it needs a suitable lawnmower and considerable care taken when cutting.

Long and Narrow

Long, narrow gardens offer great scope for imaginative design. There are opportunities to divide the garden up into a series of smaller gardens or areas with different themes or styles. Instead of a long, narrow lawn with ribbon beds on either side, break it up into a series of areas to be explored and discovered.

Long, narrow gardens are often laid out with a design that emphasizes their narrowness. Beds that run the length of the garden and long, narrow lawns make the garden predictable and usually uninteresting. Breaking it up into a series of smaller areas ensures the garden cannot be taken in at a single glance, and it makes it seem cosy and intimate rather than narrow.

The very simple design featured below divides the garden into a series of "rooms", with a trellis and screen-block wall preventing the eye seeing what lies within each section without the oppressiveness of a solid screen.

By including many fragrant shrubs, border plants and annuals in the mixed borders, especially near the garden seats, a fragrant garden can be created, with the scents tending to linger in the enclosed area. The basic design is formal in style, with a long vista leading the eye along to the end of the garden, giving it an impression of size. A simple variation, if you prefer more plants, would be to replace the lawn with border perennials, perhaps mixed with evergreen shrubs.

However you deal with a long, narrow plot, try to break up the garden so that the eye does not go straight down to the end. Make sure there are beds or features that interrupt the straight lines. In this design, two rectangular areas – one paved, the other gravel – have been used to hold interest.

1	Ornament (on plinth)
2	Herb garden
3	Shed
4	Trellis
5	Climbers (e.g. ivy, parthenocissus and clematis against trellis)
6	Sundial or birdbath
7	Mixed border
8	Large pot with shrub/shaped clipped box
9	Garden bench
10	Pool with fountain
11	Arch
12	Group of large shrubs (in tubs/large pots)
13	Screen-block wall
14	Patio furniture
15	Vegetable garden
16	Trellis arch
17	Path

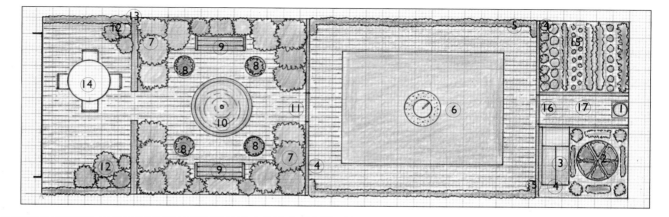

A focal point towards the centre of the garden also helps to distract the eye from the limiting shape of the garden. The role of this attractive planted urn as a focal point is plain to see.

Left: *Not everyone likes a formal style with lots of straight edges, but you can achieve a similar effect with flowing informal borders and seemingly rambling paths.*

In this garden, the borders along the long sides have been extended into broad, curved sweeps, and island beds with conifers have been used to provide visual "blocks".

This kind of design can be achieved quite easily by modifying an existing long, narrow lawn. The beds can be widened with broad sweeps and island beds cut into the grass. Simple paving and planting does the rest. You don't have to spend a lot of money on hard landscaping to create a more interesting garden.

Dealing with Difficult Shapes

Owners of rectangular gardens often wish for a more interesting shape with which to work, but gardens with an irregular shape can be particularly difficult to design. Corner sites are common but surprisingly difficult to use imaginatively, while L-shaped gardens are a special challenge if the two "legs" are to be well-integrated. There are as many solutions as there are gardens with these problems, and the two examples here explore just a few design ideas that you could consider.

The pergola effectively "turns" the garden in this design, and manages to look right even though it links two different design styles: the formal rectangular style of house, patio, rectangular lawn and straight-edged flower borders; and the flowing curves of that part of the garden not visible from the house.

Instead of this contrast of styles, you could bring the flower borders that link house with pergola out into the lawn in some gentle curves, or the straight lines of the first section could be carried on into the second. Which option you find most appropriate will be a matter of personal preference.

Instead of a pergola, you could use a summerhouse in the corner, perhaps an octagonal so that it does not appear to have just one "front", set in the corner. This would make a strong focal point, from which you could enjoy both views of your garden.

AN L-SHAPED GARDEN

If your garden is large, you may prefer to treat the two "legs" separately, perhaps keeping the one visible from the house as an ornamental area, and using the other section as a screened-off kitchen garden, or maybe a more informal wild area planted to attract wildlife. This approach can give you the best of both worlds.

If your garden is relatively small, you will probably want to combine the two areas visually to make the most of available space and to make your garden seem as large as possible. The design shown here uses techniques to make the garden seem as large as possible.

It is important to have a strong design element at the point where the two parts of the garden come together. There must be a reason for walking to the end of the garden so that the remaining part unfolds and entices you to explore.

A seat or an interesting water feature are ideal focal points, but in this example a pergola and a seat have been used, as a pivot around which the two parts of the garden have been centred.

The pergola makes an attractive focal point viewed from any position in the garden, and its rectangular shape helps to "turn" the axis of the garden in a natural and unobtrusive way.

It is desirable to have another focal point at the far end of the garden to make the most of the whole garden.

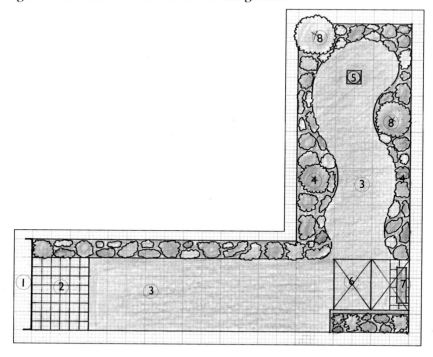

1	House	5	Sundial set on gravel planted with alpines
2	Patio	6	Decorative pergola
3	Lawn	7	Garden seat
4	Flower borders	8	Tree

A CORNER SITE

Corner sites offer lots of scope, but they can be rather "public" unless screened in some way with a fence or hedge. Always check whether this is permissible, however, as there may be restrictions in the deeds of the property or laid down by the highways department concerning the height of hedges, etc., if they are likely to obstruct the view for traffic. Usually, however, you can create a sense of privacy and still keep within any restrictions there may be.

If you want something more intensively designed than, say, a lawn that sweeps around the house, it is worth trying to create a design that integrates the two sides. In this example, a design based on a grid diagonal to the house has been used to take full advantage of the long dimension across the garden, while at the same time using shrubs to mask the curved boundary, which also gives privacy.

If this highly structured design does not appeal to you, a more informal style with lawn and sweeping beds could be used.

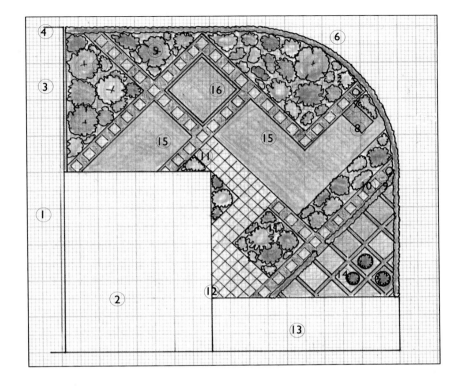

1	Back garden	9	Dwarf hedge
2	House	10	Shrubs and border plants
3	Screen-block wall	11	Plants
4	Gate	12	Front door
5	Shrubs	13	Driveway
6	Hedge	14	Coloured slabs and plants in containers
7	Ornament	15	Lawn
8	Garden seat	16	Pond

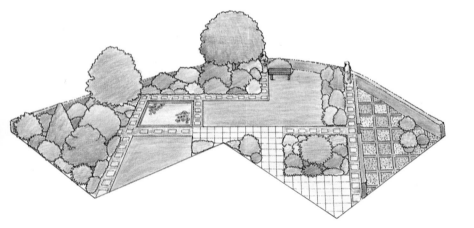

In this design it is the paths that lay the foundation for the diagonal pattern, so they have been given strong visual impact. As continuous paving slabs would look uninspiring, they have been spaced and set into a wider area of gravel. By using fine or coarse gravel, or even small beach pebbles, the character of the paths can be changed to suit individual preference.

The extra depth given to the planting areas by their angular shape provides scope for planting small trees or large specimen shrubs to add height and a greater sense of structure.

Creating Interest

Your garden will be much more interesting if it cannot all be seen at once. Whether you have an entirely different style in each area (for example, a wild border or a romantic, secluded corner) or variations on the basic theme, the more it has to be explored, like the rooms of a house, the more fascinating it becomes.

This principle applies to any size garden, where it can be used as a valuable design technique. A small garden, such as the one shown here, will hold more surprises and interest if you have to go around a few screens and negotiate a few bends or obstacles.

Right: *As the photograph shows, this garden is narrow, but sometimes even a narrow garden can be divided in both directions. This avoids the banded effect that would result if all the divisions were horizontal across the garden with no vertical divisions to balance them out.*

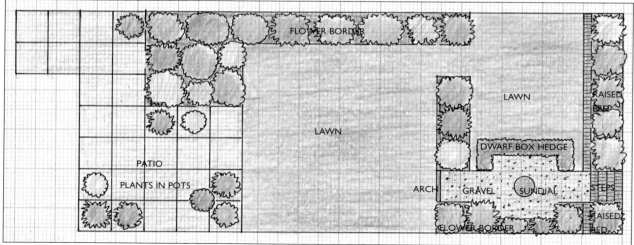

FLOWER BORDER

LAWN

LAWN

DWARF BOX HEDGE

PATIO

PLANTS IN POTS

ARCH   GRAVEL   SUNDIAL   STEPS

FLOWER BORDER

RAISED BED

RAISED BED

Left: *In plan the simplicity of this design is obvious, yet the slight changes of level and height provided by shrubs and the low hedge all help to give the impression of moving from room to room, with a series of gardens within the garden.*

Left: *By placing the arch and the steps at the end of the garden off-centre, a vista has been produced that runs along the whole length of the garden, as seen from the patio. This gives the garden a sense of depth and size, even though areas have been partitioned off for individual exploration.*

Above: *Raised beds and a gravelled area add more variety and a sense of enclosure, and provide a good point from which to view the garden, as the picture shows. The small gravelled area would have been impractical as grass, but the gravel is an ideal surface for this situation. Different surface textures are important in creating the sense of walking into different areas.*

Changing the View

The French call it *trompe-l'oeil*, and deceiving the eye is an illusion a garden designer often has to adopt to make the most of an unpromising site. The few simple forms of visual deception described here should enable you to make your garden look larger than it really is or help to distract the eye from the unattractive features by making the most of the positive ones.

Straight lines can be uncompromising, and a dominant feature at the end of a straight path will foreshorten the visual appearance. By curving the path slightly, and perhaps tapering it slightly towards the end, there will be the illusion of greater depth. If the focal point is also diminished in height or stature, the optical illusion will be increased.

If the boundary is clearly visible, and especially if plain and man-made, a small garden will seem box-like and the boundary will dominate. Simply adding a narrow border with masking shrubs will not help because the boundary, although better clothed, will still be obvious.

By bringing the border into the garden in broad sweeps, with a hint of the lawn disappearing behind a sweep towards the end of the garden, the boundaries will be blurred and there will be the illusion of more garden beyond.

A long, straight path will take the eye to the boundary unless the garden is very large, so try to introduce a feature that will arrest the eye part way along the path. A curve around an ornament, a large shrub or small tree, will keep the eye within the garden. If you do not want to move an existing path, try erecting an arch over it, with an attractive climber to soften the outline and perhaps extended along a length of trellis on either side.

Right: *Apart from their obvious role, some colours have the visual effect of making things seem nearer or more distant, dominant or receding. This yellow* Acer japonicum *'Aureum' brings the eye to rest within the garden rather than at the garden wall or beyond. In turn, it takes the eye to the attractive stone table that might otherwise go unnoticed from a distance as its tones blend so well with the background.*

Above: *If your garden is small, and your neighbour's is attractive, leave a space between the borders and bridge the gap with an inconspicuous type of fence. The eye will then go beyond the fence, especially if there is a bold plant or tree in the distance, and create the illusion that your own garden extends much further than it actually does.*

Above: *Mirrors can be used to create great illusions, and can be invaluable in making a small area look larger than it really is. A mirror placed in the frame of a disused gate – or in a false frame – will give the illusion that there is more garden beyond the door or gateway.*

The combination of mirror and water, one reflected in the other, can have a dramatic effect, as this photograph shows.

Consult a mirror supplier before installing one in your garden, and explain what it is required for. You should be able to have one made to the required size if you measure up carefully first.

The illusion is soon shattered if you allow the glass to become dirty, so be prepared to keep the mirror really clean.

Deceiving the Eye

No garden is ever the exact shape the owner wants, but if you use the principles of *trompe-l'oeil*, you can effectively change the perception of shape and distance. If the garden is long and thin, or wide but shallow, it may be desirable to use a little trickery.

OPTICAL ILLUSIONS

Although there are limits to how much you can change the site physically, you can take advantage of some optical tricks to adjust its appearance visually.

A long, straight view will be foreshortened by a tall object or bright colours at the far end of it. If, on the other hand, the distant end has a scaled-down ornament and misty, pale colours, the ornament will appear to be further away.

A straight lawn can be narrowed towards the further end to make it seem longer, and the effect can be enhanced by using a bright splash of colour near the beginning. If your garden is wide but not very deep, you can give an impression of enhanced depth by positioning a mirror almost opposite the entrance, surrounded by plants.

If the area is surrounded by walls, they can be painted white (for extra light), green (to blend in), or with a floral mural where the planting is sparse. Shaped trellises can be added to give the impression of a distant perspective rather than a flat wall, and a false doorway with a *trompe-l'oeil* vista disappearing away behind it can be wonderfully effective at

enlarging a confined space. The key is not to overdo either the effects or the planting. Mix the elements, making sure that the vertical aspect of the garden is catered for as well as the horizontal. Even a small plot can usually support a few climbers and tall containers or ornaments, as well as a tree, as long as it is in proportion with the rest of the garden scheme.

Above: *A cleverly positioned mirror will reflect the plants back into the garden, suggesting it is larger than it actually is.*

Left: *Features such as this arched trellis will create the illusion of distance in a small garden.*

Opposite: *Statuary placed at the bottom of the garden will draw the eye down the garden's length.*

Planning Good Access

Keeping the routes clear to certain points around the garden will reduce the risk of damage to the plants, but this does not have to mean having a straight concrete path down the middle.

PRACTICAL PLANNING

The back garden can have such a multitude of uses that the points for access are many and varied, and are seldom as simple as just in-and-out. There may be a back gate, for reaching a rubbish (trash) storage area or garage; a shed, compost heap or greenhouse; a clothes-line; or a children's play area, all of which will need a direct line of access. Not providing this direct route will result in "desire lines" being worn across the lawn or through the plants as short-cuts are inevitably taken. Watching these develop is often the easiest way of working out exactly where the paths ought to go, but by then, the damage may be done.

There are many different surfaces to choose from for paths, from bark to stone, brick to gravel, and the choice is entirely personal. Aim to keep the surface material in context with the house wherever possible. Use bricks that look similar to those used on the house or select a complement-ary shade of gravel.

If the path runs across, or next to, a lawn, it is important to remember that loose gravel will seriously damage the blades of a lawnmower. Unless the gravel can be resin-bonded to keep it in place, it is probably better to go for slabs or bricks, which can be set lower than the grass, or bark, which is softer and will not cause so much damage.

Right: *When planning seating areas, consider where the access routes will lead across the garden.*

Below: *A winding path leads the visitor through the garden past points of interest.*

Above: *Paving stones surrounded by ground-cover plants form a practical and decorative surface for a garden path.*

Opposite: *Steps leading from the house and patio area to the rest of the garden are softened with pots and containers.*

Front Gardens

If you make sufficient allowances for the need to get to key places within the design, then there should be no need for anyone ever to walk on a border to get to your front door.

HOME FRONT

Front gardens have special problems – especially if they have to accommodate a driveway. Perhaps, for this reason, they frequently lack interest and yet it's the front garden visitors see first, so it's worth making a special effort to create a good impression.

Even enthusiastic gardeners with delightful back gardens are often let down by an uninspired front garden. However, with a little imagination and forethought, you can create visual interest without compromising on practicalities.

PRACTICAL PLANNING

At the front of any building, there is always a question of access. While a straight line from the gate to the door may be relatively uninspiring, any attempt to deviate from it may cause less interested visitors to continue to walk on the same line as usual and trample the planting. If there is room, a straight path can be broken up simply by placing a large object,

such as a sundial or birdbath, in the middle, and running the path in a circular pattern around each side of it, so that the deviation from the original line is minimal and the option is open to pass on either side of the ornament.

It is usually more practical to accept the need for a straight path, and work around it; such a path can soon be given added interest, by softening the edges with low-growing, spreading plants which will tolerate being stepped on.

Above: *This garden makes the most of a small square area by combining plants with paving.*

Left: *Although you may spend less time in the area at the front of the house, plants growing by the door, positioned up stairs and under windows, will create a welcoming impression.*

Opposite: *A path leading to the front steps is softened by a colourful border.*

In Cottage-garden Style

English cottage gardens are difficult to define, yet a garden with the attributes of a cottage garden is instantly recognizable. The emphasis is on dense planting, with a bias towards perennial border plants, and the "design" lies more in the planting than the structure of the garden. They look uninspiring in plan view – frequently two wide borders with a path down the middle between gate and door. If your interest lies more in the plants than the hard landscaping, a cottage-garden style could be the solution.

A typical English cottage garden is very simple in design – often straight, but wide borders and little else. If your garden is squat, square, and small, you can create a similar effect by treating the whole area like a large border, with a path running around the edge.

To create the appropriate period atmosphere, keep to species or early hybrids rather than highly-bred plants that look too modern. Delphiniums, oriental poppies and achilleas, along with plants such as border pinks and lady's mantle (*Alchemilla*) were commonplace in country gardens and will help to create the style and "atmosphere" that you are seeking.

An old building and roses around the door clearly help, but you can create cottage garden borders in a modern setting if you use another part of the garden, rather than the house, as a backdrop.

In the garden shown here, the plants are all border perennials – in effect large herbaceous borders – but traditionally there would be lots of annuals such as calendulas and love-in-a-mist (nigella) *too.*

PLANTING SUGGESTIONS

Use the two schemes opposite as a guide for your own cottage garden border. Do not follow them slavishly, but add plants that you prefer (provided they are appropriate), and drop those that you do not like. Each of these borders is approximately 3.6m x 1.8m (12ft x 6ft), so you may have to drop some plants if your border is smaller. The borders are shown as mature, with clumps of border perennials that have been established for some years – you may be able to accommodate the same number of plants in a smaller space if you lift and divide more frequently.

In many cases, more than one plant is represented by the areas shown in the borders opposite (border plants are generally best planted in groups of three to five of each kind if there is space). The lupins, for example, represent the bold drift of a number of plants.

These are just some of the cottage garden plants that you could use: there are many more. Remember to keep to types that would

have been around, say, 50 years ago or more: do not use modern hybrid lilies in place of the *Lilium regale* shown here, for example.

Hardy perennials shown in the borders include aquilegia, bear's breeches (*Acanthus mollis*), bergamot (*Monarda didyma*), bleeding heart (*Dicentra spectabilis*), catmint (*Nepeta*), coral bells (*Heuchera sanguinea*), delphinium, flag iris, gaillardia, geum, globe thistle (*Echinops ritro*), hollyhock, lady's mantle (*Alchemilla*), lupin, Michaelmas daisy, oriental poppy (*Papaver orientale*), herbaceous peony, perennial gypsophila, pinks, pyrethrum, red hot poker (*kniphofia*), regal lily (*Lilium regale*), sea holly (*Eryngium bourgatii*), shasta daisy (*Chrysanthemum maximum*), sneezewort (*Achillea ptarmica*), viola and yarrow (*Achillea filipendulina*).

Biennials used are Canterbury-bells and foxgloves. Annuals are cornflowers, pot marigolds (*Calendula*), sunflowers (*Helianthus*), and Virginia stocks (*Malcolmia maritima*).

COTTAGE BORDER PLAN A

1	Delphinium
2	Shasta daisy (Chrysanthemum maximum)
3	Gypsophila
4	Gaillardia
5	Pyrethrum
6	Pinks or border carnations (Dianthus)
7	Flag iris
8	Red hot poker (Kniphofia)
9	Aquilegia
10	Pot marigolds (Calendula)
11	Coral bells
12	Regal lily
13	Hollyhock
14	Michaelmas daisy (Aster)
15	Crocosmia
16	Canterbury-bells (Campanula)
17	Virginia stocks (Malcomia)
18	Viola cornuta
19	Sneezewort (Achillea ptarmica)

COTTAGE BORDER PLAN B

1a	Delphinium
2a	Foxglove (Digitalis)
3a	Yarrow (Achillea filipendulina)
4a	Geum
5a	Catmint (Nepeta)
6a	Lupin
7a	Globe thistle (Echinops)
8a	Oriental poppy (Papaver)
9a	Peony
10a	Sea holly (Eryngium)
11a	Cornflower (Centaurea)
12a	Lavender (Lavandula)
13a	Bleeding heart (Dicentra spectabilis)
14a	Lady's mantle (Alchemilla)
15a	Bergamot (Monarda didyma)
16a	Flag iris
17a	Bear's breeches (Acanthus)
18a	Sunflowers (Helianthus)

In Courtyard Style

Privacy and seclusion is something most of us appreciate at some time, and it can be even more precious when we are relaxing in the garden. Even in a garden without overlooking neighbours, it is nice to have a cosy and secluded corner that feels snug and enclosed, but in a town or city it may be the whole garden that needs to be encapsulated in its own "cocoon", a private green oasis among the surrounding buildings.

There are two fundamental approaches to a courtyard or tiny town garden: the formal one that depends on structures such as walls for privacy, like the one shown on the opposite page (*top*), or an informal approach that depends on the lush growth of trees and shrubs. The picture opposite (*below*) is a good example of a garden designed with this approach: the sitting area in the centre is like a clearing in woodland.

This type of dense planting with tall-growing shrubs and small trees can become very shady in summer, but on a hot day this can be a welcome attribute. It is also a super way to enjoy a lot of plants in a small area – provided you are willing to cut back and prune fairly ruthlessly on a regular basis, you can pack in a surprising number of plants in a small area, but concentrate on shade-lovers.

Often, however, it's impossible to pretend that your garden is anywhere other than in a town or city, surrounded by other buildings, in which case a formal style that makes a bold and challenging statement despite its surroundings is a pleasing solution.

Tall walls are an asset. They have a sense of age and permanence that a fence never gives, and they can be taller. If well constructed and wide, you can even stand pots and finials on top, especially where there are supporting columns. Walls also provide an ideal support for climbers and for trained fruit or ornamental wall shrubs.

Whether you want to draw attention to the tops of the walls with ornaments or plants will depend on the background. If it is particularly unattractive, it is advisable to draw the eye down into the garden and not upwards to its perimeter.

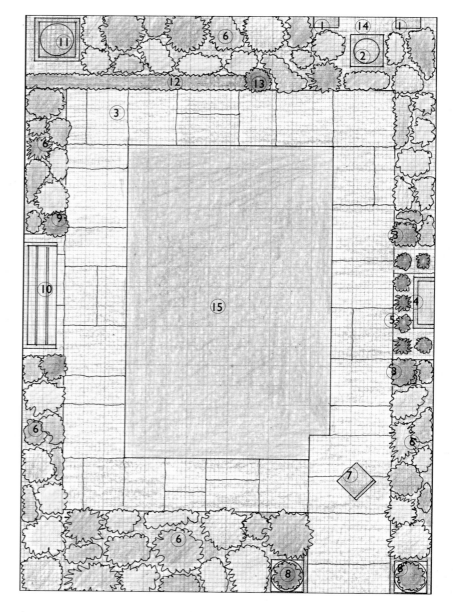

1	Pillars covered with ivy and topped with finials	8	Clipped box in pots on plinths
		9	Box spiral
2	Urn on pedestal	10	White garden seat
3	Natural paving stones	11	Large urn on pedestal
4	Wall fountain	12	Dwarf box hedge
5	Box balls in pots	13	Clipped and shaped box
6	Border plants	14	Decorative trellis covering old gate
7	Garden chair	15	Lawn

Left: *If you decide on a classical or period style like this, it is advisable to use materials that do it justice. There is not a lot of hard landscaping, so be prepared to pay for natural stone paving, and invest in a few ornaments that complement the garden. Trained and clipped box like these specimens can be expensive, but you will not have to spend much on shrubs for the rest of the garden. And because there are few areas for which you will have to buy seasonal plants, the ongoing costs will be minimal.*

Right: *The designer here has chosen a strong rectangular theme for the paved area, to contrast with the luxuriant and overhanging plants that soften the straight lines. The choice of plain square slabs, arranged in unstaggered rows, gives the design a simple uncluttered appearance.*

Opposite: *The essentials of this design plan are simplicity and restraint, with the emphasis on shape and form provided by the urns and shaped box plants. Add touches of seasonal colour in small containers that can be moved around the garden to suit the season.*

The Herb Garden

No garden is complete without its complement of herbs, and finding a suitable place for them should be considered at the planning stage. A special herb garden is ideal, and can be a highly decorative feature, but many herbs make good container plants, and many are pretty enough to be grown in borders along with the ornamentals. You can simply grow herbs in the kitchen garden together with the vegetables, but why not make more of a feature of them?

A formal herb garden divided into "compartments", like the one featured on the right, is practical and a powerful focal point. Separating the various herbs makes cultivation much easier, as some are annuals, some perennials, some self-seed prolifically and, if surrounded by soil, can become weeds, and others have spreading roots or stems that benefit from containment.

The suggested planting in this plan should be treated only as a starting point for your own choice. There is little point in growing herbs that you do not use unless they are particularly decorative. If you use a lot of one kind of herb, allocate more than one area. There is space for 24 different herbs in this design, but you may prefer to grow only the dozen that you use most often and create a mirror image in the two halves of the herb garden.

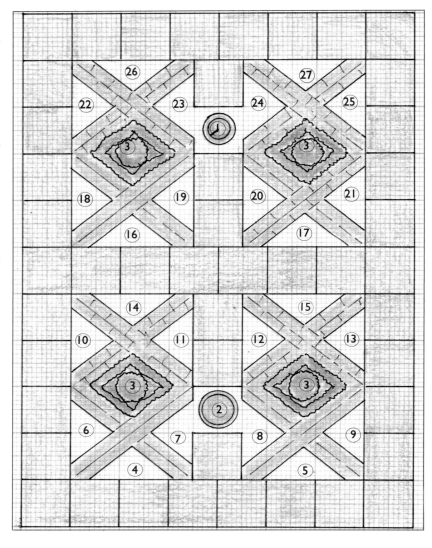

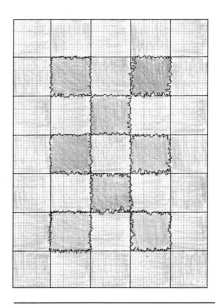

Left: *A chequerboard herb garden can be very effective for a paved area. It has a strong visual impact, and you can easily keep each herb contained within its own small plot while still being able to walk among them.*

1	Sundial	14	Winter savory
2	Birdbath	15	Lavender
3	Dwarf box hedge with bay in centre	16	Thyme
	Suggested planting	17	Borage
4	Summer savory	18	Chives
5	Variegated lemon balm	19	Golden marjoram
6	Variegated apple mint	20	Rosemary
7	Purple sage	21	Mint
8	Cotton lavender	22	Caraway
9	Parsley	23	Bergamot
10	Hyssop	24	Sweet basil
11	French tarragon	25	Chervil
12	Sorrel	26	Garlic
13	Oregano	27	Pot marigold (Calendula)

Left: *The herb garden can become a decorative part of the overall garden design. Bear in mind that herb gardens can be a dull in winter, as most of the plants will have died down. They are best used to create interest in a part of the garden that you suddenly discover. Most herbs prefer to be in full sun, so try to choose a position that is in good light for most of the day.*

Below: *There's always space for a few herbs, even if you have to put them in containers. This group of pots contains chives, French tarragon and winter savory.*

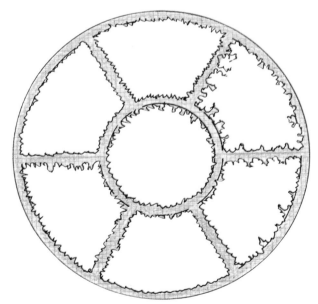

Where space is limited, a herb wheel is a popular choice and can be achieved with the use of bricks. Plant a different herb in each space created by the spokes of the circle.

The Kitchen Garden

The traditional kitchen garden demands little design but lots of planning for crop positioning and rotation. Usually an area out of sight of the main ornamental part of the garden is set aside and the crops are grown in straight rows. This simplifies crop rotation and makes cultivation easier – you can weed more easily between straight rows, and it is easier to give each specific crop the appropriate fertilizer and supplementary water when it is required. If you want to make vegetable growing a more high-profile part of your garden, however, you may have to be bold.

Dedicated areas set aside for traditional rows of vegetables make cultivation relatively simple, but integrating flowers and vegetables can be an interesting experiment. It also may help reduce the level of pest and disease infestation that often comes with large areas devoted to a small range of plants.

The term *jardin potager* is French for "kitchen garden", but the word "potager" has come to mean primarily a kitchen garden that usually contains both vegetables and fruit, laid out ornamentally and often with the beds edged with low hedges like a parterre.

A potager is a striking way to combine vegetables and flowers, and though expensive to construct and time-intensive to maintain (lots of dwarf box hedging to plant and clip, for instance), it can be justified if it forms a main feature. In a large garden you can enclose the area with hedges, but in a small garden you may want to make this the whole of your design. This is most likely to appeal if your interest lies as much in cooking and a love of fresh vegetables as in ornamental gardening.

On the other hand, the traditional vegetable plot can be improved simply by giving it a structure with paths. The design on the right is ideal if you want to practise the 1.2m (4ft) bed "no-dig" system, where cultivation is done by reaching across from the paths so that the soil is not compacted.

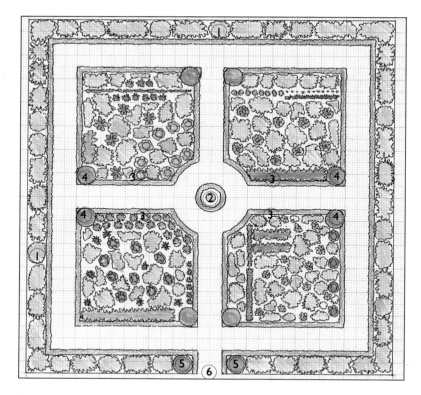

1	Flower border around edge	4	Topiary shapes
2	Ornament	5	Large clipped box
3	Dwarf box hedge	6	Gate/entrance

This design is a more decorative vegetable plot. The use of an ornament such as a birdbath or sundial in the centre emphasizes the formality of this type of vegetable garden.

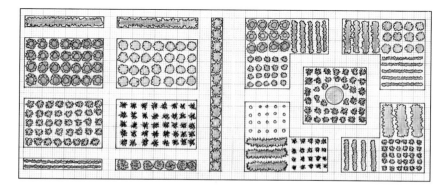

In a potager like this, you can devote the main beds purely to vegetables, and even grow them in straight rows in the conventional manner, but if you want to be bold, try growing flowers and vegetables together.

Many vegetables are ornamental enough to be used in flower borders, among bedding plants, and even in containers – like this rhubarb chard planted alongside lobelia.

Mixing vegetables, herbs and flowers, will make your vegetable plot full of surprises, and interesting too.

This method of growing vegetables, some in rows, others interplanted more randomly with flowers, may not appeal, but breaking up the usual solid blocks may actually assist with pest control.

ORNAMENTAL VEGETABLES

- Where space is really restricted, and there is insufficient room for a vegetable garden, or it is inadequate for the amount that you wish to grow, try growing some of the more decorative vegetables among the flowers.

- This has drawbacks of course – there may be gaps once harvesting time arrives. This may not be a problem if you use the vegetables as gap fillers though, and the surrounding plants grow to fill the space left after harvesting.

- Beetroot, carrots and rhubarb chard are all decorative foliage plants. Use them to help to fill in gaps in beds and borders, but don't forget that you still have to thin them, even though they are grown in clusters or groups rather than rows.

- Lettuces can be attractive until they run to seed, especially red varieties. The best ones to use are the "cut-and-come again", oak-leaf types because you can harvest the leaves without destroying the whole plant and leaving a gap.

In Japanese Style

True Japanese gardens, designed according to strict rules, should only be tackled after much research and study of the subject, as the placing of stones and positioning of particular lanterns have special meanings. And if you want to avoid high maintenance, give raked sand a miss too. It is perfectly possible to create a garden that simply has a strong Japanese influence, however, and it does not matter if you break a few "rules", provided it looks good and has that distinctive Japanese character.

Seasonal variations in a Japanese garden are subtle rather than dramatic. Water, rocks and ornaments can vary in appearance according to the light, but the emphasis is on shape, form and texture, rather than bright colours from flowers. Adding too many 'alien' flowers spoils the effect.

In a large garden the Japanese influence can be achieved by the use of bridges, lanterns and features like deer-scarers within a landscaped area that includes plenty of plants such as Japanese acers, bamboos, and suitably placed rocks. It is much more difficult to create that kind of garden in a small space, but a formal shape can be very successful in creating an oriental style modified to suit a small Western back garden.

Choose plants that fit the image, like small acers, small pines, azaleas, camellias, small ornamental grasses and dwarf bamboos, and Japanese irises (*I. ensata*). Moss adds to the effect, but thrives best in moist conditions out of direct sun. If mosses cannot be encouraged to grow, try moss-like plants such as *Sagina subulata* (syn. *S. glabra*) and *S. procumbens*. The ground-hugging carpeter *Soleirolia soleirolii* (syn. *Helxine soleirolii*) will produce a similar affect, but tends to become rampant where winters are mild and conditions suit, and is prone to winter losses in very cold areas.

The addition of bonsai trees in pots helps to reinforce the strong Japanese theme.

Always try to choose individual rocks for a Japanese garden, as they form an integral part of the Japanese style. If you just leave it to a supplier to select and deliver, the rocks may lack the necessary shape and form to make useful focal points.

A JAPANESE-STYLE GARDEN PLAN

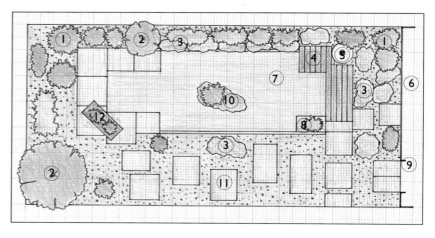

1	Dwarf shrubs and plants	7	Water
2	Japanese acer	8	Bonsai in pot
3	Rocks	9	Door
4	Timber flat bridge	10	Rock with bonsai
5	Lantern	11	Large paving slabs set in gravel
6	House	12	Low display table, in style of timber

IN SEARCH OF AUTHENTICITY

- If you want to make your oriental garden as authentic as possible, buy or borrow several books on Japanese gardening. Do not be put off by the Japanese words that you will find sprinkled throughout the text, all you want from them is the meaning and the philosophy that lies behind this form of gardening. It may become a fascinating hobby, and you will start to position the rocks with more care as you realize the symbolic significance of the various aspects of this kind of garden.

- Your garden is unlikely to be judged by an expert, or even a native Japanese, so it does not really matter if the symbolic significance passes you by. The only real test is whether it pleases you.

- Send for the catalogues and brochures produced by specialists in Japanese features such as lanterns, deer-scarers, and bamboo and rock ornaments. These will provide you with plenty of inspiration.

Above: *Use plants with restraint, but make the most of their shape and outline. The juxtaposition of the reed-like leaves of the water plant, rounded lantern, and angular rock is what gives this grouping so much impact. Surface textures are also important, with the strong lines of the red timber bridge contrasting with the fine gravel.*

Below: *This stand for displaying bonsai trees reflects the material and style of the bridge at the other end of the pond. Keep the style simple and uncluttered, and do not over-plant if you want to retain the typical Japanese style of gardening.*

Above: *Fine gravel is an ideal ground covering, much more Japanese in style than the same garden set in a grass lawn. It also helps to make this kind of garden a good choice for low maintenance.*

A Sense of Fun

Gardens tend to reflect the personality of their owners, and if you have a fun personality or a sense of humour, you will probably want to express that in the way your garden is planned.

Eccentric gardens are not to everyone's taste, but subtle humour can be achieved in odd corners or through tasteful focal points that hint at that sense of mischief.

If the structure of a garden has a bold, even eccentric, appearance, it will make a bold statement regardless of the plants. It needs confidence, however, because done half-heartedly it may not work.

The garden on the opposite page could look rather green and dull with an ordinary arch, path, traditional raised bed and container, especially in winter. The choice of colours and materials, however, ensures that this garden looks spectacular, whatever the season.

The garden does not readily conform to the design principles commonly suggested, but its charm lies in its defiance of tradition, and any suggestion of straight lines or even symmetry of curves would be out of place. Even the path has been laid in a way that challenges orthodoxy. It is a straight path with bricks that follow a curving, snake-like pattern. The arch, too, demands attention. A normal arch would be attractive with a clematis in flower, but this one cries out to be noticed at all times.

Ornaments can be used among the plants in borders too, where their unexpectedness adds an extra dimension. Moving them around periodically also adds to their unpredictability. Use them to add drama to an area of the garden that lacks impact: the berberis in this picture are unexciting, but the boy crawling out from between the bushes immediately makes this a magical part of the garden.

Small ornaments offer enormous scope because they are easily moved around until they look right. You can even reposition them on a regular basis to add variety to your garden.

These two birds change a fairly ordinary garden scene into something special. They act as a focal point, but their positioning as a pair also gives them a light-hearted look.

These flowers would look attractive in a group of ordinary pots, but their fun containers will almost certainly bring a smile to the face. Gardening has its lighter moments, so do not waste the opportunity to bring a breath of fresh air to potentially gloomy corners.

Above: *Even in a conventional or traditional garden there is scope for the unexpected, especially if it brings a smile or creates a focal point in an otherwise dull spot. These "sunflowers" are in a shady position at the end of a path that leads to an uninteresting fence. If you imagine the picture without the focal point, this is immediately seen as a dull part of the garden.*

Flowers like this can be cut from marine plywood, or other weatherproof material, and painted before being fixed in position.

A feature like this will almost certainly generate comment, some favourable some unfavourable, it depends on an individual's sense of humour. If you have a sense of fun, however, you won't be deterred from trying something a little different.

Not everyone could live with this kind of garden, but if it works for you it's right. Challenging the senses is a good idea, but you need confidence to do it on this scale.

With Children in Mind

Gardens are seldom designed for children, but they should sometimes be designed with children in mind. Small children pose special problems of safety if you are planning water features. Young children require safe play areas, and older children can be tough on a garden if they do not have an area where the grass and the plants are not easily damaged.

If you are planning to stay in your home for many years, however, it pays to plan with the long term in mind too. Features that are suitable for children can often be converted into a more ornamental part of the garden when your offspring have grown up.

A play house is always popular with children, but positioned in a conspicuous part of the garden, it can dominate the scene and detract from the design and the plants. If you paint it attractively, in a light colour, it can be used as a focal point in a less obvious corner of the garden.

Bear in mind, however, that you may prefer to have it within easy sight and earshot of the house.

Trampolines and large activity toys like swings are always difficult to accommodate, and they will mar the most well-designed garden if placed in a prominent position.

If you have a large lawn with borders along the side, try bringing the border out in a couple of grand sweeps, so that a large bay of lawn is hidden.

Children like a sense of adventure, and older children will appreciate a tree house as much as younger ones. An old tree that forks close to ground level is ideal, as the house will then be easier to construct and safer to play in. A tree house is something that a responsible adult should construct, not a child.

TOUGH LAWNS, TOUGH PLANTS

- Play lawns require tough grasses – avoid seed mixtures or turf of the type used for immaculately kept lawns. You can still enjoy a quality lawn that will look green and lush (provided you water it in dry weather), and the modern strains of hard-wearing grasses are much finer and more attractive than the older ones, which were often rather coarse.

- Shrubs are a better choice than bedding plants until children are old enough to respect the boundaries of play, but avoid those with thorns and beware of any that can cause severe allergies if they come into contact with exposed skin – such as rue (**Ruta graveolens**).

Small children love a sandpit, and if the children are of that age, a pond is not a good idea (you can make a pond secure with metal protection, but this kills its natural beauty). If you intend to build a pond when the children are a little older, it makes sense to construct a sandpit that can be converted into a pond later. The sandpit illustrated could easily be visualized as a pond when its present function is redundant.

Always make sure there is free drainage at the bottom while being used as a sandpit, otherwise it will become waterlogged after heavy rain. And make a lid to fit over it when not in use, otherwise animals such as cats will foul it.

Patio Pleasures

Patios are popular because they bridge the gap between house and garden, and even though they are sometimes located remotely from the house, they provide an opportunity to "live" in the garden. They are great for entertaining, and are a perfect place to sit, relax and admire the rest of your garden. Patios are for people, but they should be places for plants too. Be prepared to spend time planning a patio that will look beautiful. The more "room-like" you make it, the more effective it will be as a place to relax or entertain in.

Situating a patio next to the house, with adjoining patio doors or French windows, integrates house and garden and makes it an extension of the living area. Choosing a surface such as timber decking or glazed tiles also helps to tie it more closely as an extension of the house in a way that is difficult to achieve with paving slabs or clay pavers.

If a room opens onto the patio, it is more practical to use stylish and upholstered chairs as they can easily be moved indoors at the end of the day.

Sometimes, however, simplicity is appropriate, especially if the patio is located away from the house. An area paved with bricks or clay pavers often blends more sympathetically with the surrounding garden than concrete blocks or slabs, and if any pillars for a patio overhead are made from bricks, the design will look well-integrated and carefully planned.

In a large garden, setting the patio at a 45-degree angle to the house can be very effective. It helps to join two sides of the garden, while at the same time linking house and garden over a broad angle. In this example, the angle has been emphasized by the use of rows of bricks that take the eye across the patio.

Mixing materials, such as bricks and paving slabs, creates a more interesting surface texture than using just one kind of paving. Do not use more than three different kinds of paving, however, otherwise the effect may look fussy and confused.

The more "room-like" you can make a patio, the cosier and more intimate it will appear as a place to sit and relax or to entertain friends. Useful techniques to use are a wall to give a sense of enclosure and a change of level or a "gateway" to the rest of the garden. Paving that simply joins onto the lawn at the same level tends to lack impact because it has no clear-cut boundary.

When not actually used for entertaining, this kind of paved area is often best furnished with just a few simple, but elegant, chairs. The use of space can bring its own sense of tranquillity.

An abundant use of containers helps to make a patio look furnished and welcoming, but they add considerably to the maintenance required. Patio plants should always look in tip-top condition, which demands regular watering, feeding and dead-heading.

TIPS FOR A TIP-TOP PATIO

• Make sure it is large enough to be able to move around freely, even when you have a few guests. If it is heavily planted and has a lot of furniture, you may need to allow a little extra space.

• Choose a sunny position, away from overhanging trees (insects, leaves and drips after a shower can all be problems).

• Provide shelter from wind. If on an exposed site, or near a wind tunnel – perhaps between houses – provide a windbreak. A screen block wall, with shrubs in front, can be decorative and will filter the wind. Solid brick walls can look oppressive if tall, but a low wall can be effective, as you are often less exposed when sitting.

• Give your patio clear bound- aries – a low wall or a raised bed, even an ornamental hedge or dwarf shrubs can be used. If the patio is large, a balustrade can look impress- ive. A simple change of level, with a step up or down to the rest of the garden, is a good way to create the illu- sion of a boundary while maintaining a seamless link with the rest of the garden.

• Consider having a pergola overhead, especially if the patio adjoins the house. This can provide shade in summer if it is covered with a vine or climber (nothing with spines or long, cascading shoots however).

Ways with Water

Water has a fascination for most of us, and there is almost always a way to introduce it into your design. If you have small children, it might be best to confine water to wall-spouts and self-contained wall fountains, or to bubble fountains where the water runs into a hidden reservoir. If you do not have young children to consider, however, there are plenty of imaginative ways to use water.

A conventional garden pond is the first choice for anyone who wants to grow aquatic plants and encourage wildlife. A pond is more than just a water feature; it is a living community of plants, fish, insects and amphibians. By placing it in the foreground of the garden, it is also a dominant element in its design.

The sound of running water is an added attraction, but in a small pond a fountain or cascade can cause water turbulence that is to the detriment of plants such as water lilies, and probably some of the insect and amphibian visitors too. A simple trickle of water will be enough to create the magical sound of running water, yet by the time it has trickled around the sphere, disturbance within the pond will be minimal.

Water can be used as an "architectural" feature. Plants will not thrive in a small pond like this with constant turbulence from the fountain, and the scope for introducing fish is limited. None of this matters, however, when it is being used as a focal point as part of the hard landscaping.

It is the sight and sound of the water that gives this corner so much impact, and the planting acts as a frame that softens the background and helps to make a corner by the house one of the focal points of the garden.

When positioning moving water like this close to the house, make sure the sound does not become an irritation. Some sounds that are pleasant for a short time can be annoying over a long period.

Water used in a very formal setting, with the simple sound of a gentle trickle rather than the rush of a geyser, adds a sense of tranquillity.

In this situation, the water is a texture, and is best left unplanted. The open surface plays a similar role to the surrounding Pachysandra terminalis *ground cover, and the neatly clipped hedges. In this kind of garden, light and shade, symmetry and texture are all part of its beauty, and it is appropriate either for a corner of a large garden or as the centrepiece of a small town or city garden.*

Still water also has its charm, especially in a formal setting or where there is a definite "architectural" design, where shape, form and texture are strong elements.

This small area shows many good design principles: the excitement of a change of level, contrasting textures for the garden floor (brick and timber, with black mortar to enhance the bricks), water used as a texture and to act like a mirror, and the use of lush green plants and white-painted walls to compensate for the lack of colourful flowers.

Floors and Boundaries

Important though an overall design is, it is individual features that make a garden special. Deciding whether to have a patio, path, lawn or hedge and if so, of what sort, will have a significant impact on the feel of the garden as a whole. Thinking about the details too, such as planting to create privacy, can make a real difference, so it is worth taking time to devise the best combination of structural features.

Left: *This quiet corner has been transformed by a white-painted trellis and seat.*

Above: *Attractive effects can be achieved simply – these bricks give a formal air to the flowerbed.*

The Garden Floor

The chances are that beds and borders form only a small part of your garden. The major part is probably devoted to flat surfaces such as lawns, paths, and paved areas. Lawns are labour-intensive, especially if they cover large areas and can be expensive to maintain. Plain paving needs added interest in the form of foliage or container-filled plants, but there are many imaginative options that combine different floor surfaces and that are neither hard work nor dull to look at.

In addition to paving and gravel, there are other living alternatives to grass.

Giving some thought to structure is well worth the effort, as the end result will be very pleasing to the eye. Here are just some ideas that could be adapted for your own garden with a little imagination.

You can reduce the work involved in beds and borders simply by choosing suitable plants and keeping them weed-free with chemical controls or by mulching, perhaps with a decorative product such as chipped bark. But the garden floor – lawns and paving – may need a radical rethink.

Many people weary of cutting the grass think of paving as the obvious option. However, for many garden lovers the idea of a large expanse of unexciting paving sits uneasily with the soft lines and lush growth that is the traditional image of a beautiful garden. When paving fails, however, it is usually because it is used unimaginatively, or in a monotonous way.

If you use paving of different sizes and avoid rigid outlines, perhaps mixing it with other hard landscaping materials such as gravel, the effect can be dramatic and very pleasing. Gravel is a particularly useful material as it will conform to irregular outlines, but it can also be effective even in a small area that most people would

Top: *Gravel is an ideal, easy-care background for plants.*

Above: *Curves present no problem for gravel.*

Right: *Paving is not dull if offset by attractive plants.*

Above: *Moss is a possibility for a shady problem area, but not suitable for a hot, dry site.*

Right: *If the design is strong and the garden well planted, a lawn will not be missed.*

pave. Gravel only needs the occasional five minutes' work to keep it looking really smart.

There are living alternatives to grass, of course, and some of those, such as thyme and camomile, are described later in this chapter. The shady Japanese garden illustrated above, however, shows that if you can't keep the moss out of your lawn there's something to be said for a moss "lawn" instead!

The Lush Green Lawn

The lawn is often the centrepiece of a garden, the canvas against which the rest of the garden is painted. For many gardeners this makes it worth all the mowing, feeding and grooming that a good lawn needs. If your lawn has to serve as a play area as well, be realistic and sow tough grasses – these may not give you a showpiece lawn, but will be hard-wearing and will still look green and lush. Lay your lawn – from seed or from turf – in the spring.

USING RECTANGLES
Rectangular lawns can look monotonous, but sometimes they can be made more interesting by extending another garden feature – such as a patio or flower bed – into them to produce an L-shaped lawn.

AN ANGLED LAWN
A rectangle of lawn becomes much more interesting when set at an angle of about 45 degrees. By lifting and patching the lawn, you may be able to achieve this without having to start from scratch.

CREATING CURVES
A sweeping lawn with bays and curves where the flower borders ebb and flow is very attractive. It can be difficult to achieve in a small garden. However, you can bring out a border in a large curve so the grass disappears around the back. You may be able to do this by extending the border into an existing rectangular lawn.

Above: *Stepping stones set into the lawn help link the planted area of the garden to the paved areas.*

Left: *A small pocket of grass set in tall, dense foliage helps to create the impression of a private outdoor room.*

LAY A LAWN FROM TURF

Turf provides the best method of creating a lawn quickly and instantly and soil preparation is less demanding than when sowing a lawn from seed. You will usually find it a more expensive option than seed, but many gardeners are happy to pay a premium for the convenience.

Lay your lawn in the spring, to allow it sufficient time to become established before the onset of colder winter weather. Avoid laying turf in very wet or cold weather.

MAINTAINING THE LAWN

Once established, a lawn needs regular feeding and grooming if it is to become the lush green centrepiece of the garden.

Select a fertilizer appropriate for the time of year – some have higher quantities of nitrogen which promotes growth, making them more suited to the spring and summer months. Always follow the instructions carefully, since overfeeding can scorch and ruin the grass.

Regular mowing is essential to keep grass in peak condition and to maintain a tidy appearance. Avoid cutting grass in wet and very dry weather.

Autumn is a good time to prepare the lawn for the year ahead. Tasks such as raking out lawn debris, eradicating moss, feeding and aerating, will improve the quality of the lawn if carried out on a yearly basis.

1 Dig the ground thoroughly, and make every effort to eliminate difficult or deep-rooted perennial weeds. Then rake the soil level. Use pegs marked with lines drawn 5cm (2in) down from the top as a guide, having checked with a spirit-level on a straight-edge that the pegs are level.

2 Allow the soil to settle for about a week, then consolidate it further by treading it evenly to remove large air pockets. Do this by shuffling your feet over the area, first in one direction, then at right angles. Rake the soil to produce a fine crumbly structure.

3 Start laying the turf along a straight edge. Use a plank to stand on while you lay the next row, as this will help to distribute your weight. Stagger the joints between rows to create a bond like brickwork. If using turf as a long roll there will be fewer joints. Make sure these do not align.

4 Tamp down each row of turf (you can use the head of a rake as shown), then roll the plank forwards to lay the next row.

5 Brush sieved sandy soil, or a mixture of peat and sand, into the joints. This will help bind the turfs together.

6 Shape the edges when the lawn is laid. Lay a hose or rope to form the shape for a curved edge, or use a straight-edged piece of wood for a straight edge, and trim with a half-moon edger.

A Natural Lawn

A lawn is time- and energy-consuming but there are legitimate – and attractive – ways to reduce the frequency with which you have to mow.

Simply mowing different areas of the lawn to different lengths, to create a textured effect can be significantly time-saving but needs a fairly large lawn for the best effect. Naturalizing spring-flowering bulbs in a lawn of any size gives you the justification for leaving the grass uncut until late spring or early summer, when the leaves have died down.

A wild-flower lawn will bring many insect, animal and bird visitors to your garden, and regular mowing will be unnecessary. This kind of lawn can look untidy at times, so it's more suitable for the back garden than the front.

NATURALIZING BULBS IN GRASS

Choose bulbs that will multiply and flower freely, such as crocuses, daffodils, snowdrops, small fritillaries and winter aconites. There are many different kinds of crocuses and daffodils, so you'll have plenty of choice even if you limit yourself to these particularly reliable bulbs and corms.

Above right: *Hyacinth bulbs will make bold drifts if left undisturbed for several years, and there is the bonus of the flowers' fragrance.*

1 For large bulbs, such as daffodils, scatter the bulbs randomly then make individual holes with a bulb planter (or use a trowel). Most bulb planters are designed so that the core of soil is easily released.

2 Place the bulb into the hole, making sure there isn't a large air pocket beneath it, then return the core of grass. You may need to remove a little soil from the bottom of the core for a snug fit. Firm the grass gently back into place.

3 For small bulbs or corms such as crocuses, you can lift an area of grass instead. Make an H-shaped cut with a spade blade or edging tool, and fold back the turf. Then fork in a little slow-release fertilizer.

4 Scatter the bulbs or corms randomly and leave very small ones where they fall. Larger ones may need planting with a trowel. Level and firm the soil, then return the grass. Firm it in carefully to ensure the ground remains level.

A WILDLIFE HAVEN

You can encourage birds, butterflies and other creatures by having a wild-flower lawn instead of a conventional lawn. You may still want to retain a grass lawn for practical purposes, but some of the area can be allowed to "go wild", especially if the area is not on public view.

1 The most satisfactory way to make a wild-flower lawn is to sow a special wild-flower mixture instead of lawn seed. Be sure to remove problem perennial weeds first.

2 To bury the seeds, simply rake first in one direction and then in the other. It does not matter if some seeds remain on the surface. Keep the area well watered until the seeds germinate.

3 For a very small area, you may prefer to buy wild-flower plants from your garden centre (garden supply store), or to raise your own plants, starting them off in seed trays or pots.

4 You can plant into bare ground or put them in an area of lawn left to grow long. Don't forget to keep them well watered until established.

Above: *An area like this, full of wild flowers, can look drab at certain times of the year, but is enchanting when the plants are in bloom.*

THE ANNUAL HAIRCUT

A wild-flower lawn cannot be left uncut, or it will become an untidy wilderness. Cut the area down to within a few centimetres (inches) of the ground in the autumn when most of the flowers have bloomed and shed their seeds. This will make it look tidier for the winter, and new growth next spring will not become entangled with old growth.

Cutting the Mowing Time Down to Size

For those with a minimalist approach to gardening, there's a lot you can do to keep mowing time to a minimum. Just cutting out curved edges might simplify and speed things up by allowing you to mow up and down in straight lines. Or you can take a sideways look at the problem and cut different parts of the lawn at different intervals, leaving some areas longer.

KEEP A STRAIGHT LINE

Beds cut into the lawn will increase mowing time. Although they reduce the area of lawn, the inability to mow up and down in straight lines will probably slow you down. Creating a striped finish is particularly difficult and beds also create more edges to trim. Consider filling them in with grass or at least making them into rectangles.

KEEP A STRAIGHT EDGE

Untrimmed edges can make a garden look untidy, but trimming with long-handled shears – or especially with ordinary shears – is tedious and time-consuming.

If you have a lot of lawn edges to trim, buy a powered lawn edger, or choose a nylon line trimmer with a swivel head that can be used for this job as well as scything down weeds.

Curved beds add to the mowing time, as you will not be able to mow in a straight line.

A nylon line trimmer will enable you to trim edges with considerable speed.

MULTI-LEVEL MOWING

Another way to cut down on the mowing for a large lawn is to create a "sculptured" effect. Keep the broad "pathways" cut regularly, cut other areas with the blade set higher, and mow only every second or third time. Leave some uncut except for a couple of times a season. Remember that very long grass can't easily be cut with a lawnmower; you need to get out your nylon line trimmer.

If the lawn is large, try leaving the grass in part of it to grow long. Wild flowers will start to thrive, and you will only need to cut it once a year.

MAKE A MOWING EDGE

If you have a mowing edge like this, edge-trimming will be required much less often. If the edging is set level with the grass, the lawnmower, which is run onto the edging, will trim off the long grass at the edge. You may still have to trim any spreading grass stems that grow over the paving, but this will only be necessary occasionally.

1 Lay the paving slabs on the grass for positioning, and use a half-moon edger (edging iron) to cut a new edge.

2 Slice off the grass with a spade, and remove enough soil for a couple of centimetres (inches) of sand and gravel mix, mortar and the slabs. Consolidate the sub-base.

3 Use five blobs of mortar on which to bed the slab, and tap the paving level, using a mallet or the handle of a club hammer.

4 Make sure the slabs are flush with the lawn, and use a spirit level (carpenter's level) to check that the slabs are laid evenly. Mortar the joints for a neat finish and to prevent weeds.

Bricks can be used instead of paving slabs, and in a formal setting these can give an attractive crisp finish to the bed.

CUT WIDE, SAVE TIME

Next time you buy a lawnmower, think about the cutting width. Wider lawnmowers cost more but will save time. However, if your lawn is small the saving may not be significant and the extra manoeuvrability of a smaller lawnmower can be important if there are long straight runs.

Alternatives to Grass

For many gardeners, a lawn is the centrepiece of the garden; for others it represents a chore and can become a source of resentment. A grass lawn is still the only practical option for a large area, but in a small garden there are plenty of alternatives to consider. Some of the living alternatives are less practical as areas to walk on, but gravel will stand any amount of wear, and needs practically no maintenance.

Chamomile, sometimes used in Great Britain and other parts of Europe, is less popular in America as the climate is not so conducive to this use of the plant. It may, however, be successful in moist regions.

Gravel is the most practical option for a small area if you are looking for a minimum-maintenance alternative to grass. Gravels come in many different colours as well as sizes, so choose one that suits the rest of your garden design.

Living substitutes to grass can also be very attractive, but do not expect them to be as hard-wearing and trouble-free as grasses. For a start, you probably will not be able to use selective hormone weedkillers on them, so weeding will be a hand operation, and although they will tolerate some foot traffic, they will not put up with the hard punishment that most grass lawns have to take. For those reasons, these living alternatives to grass are best confined to a small area that is decorative rather than a place for the kids to play football.

Plants to try include chamomile and creeping thymes such as *Thymus serpyllum*, and *Cotula squalida* (this dies back in a cold winter but forms a fresh thick carpet in spring).

The small, rounded gravel used in this garden produces a very smooth finish and is easy to walk on after it is well-compacted. This example shows gravel as a straight alternative to grass, because the area covered used to be a lawn before it was lifted and replaced. The edging that is necessary to retain the gravel and keep it off the flowerbeds emphasizes the gravelled area as a strong design feature in its own right.

Gravel can also be used in a less formal way, so that it flows between the plants and there is no clear-cut edge between a walking area and plant area. This means there are no edges to trim and weeding is kept to a minimum.

Some people find gravel disconcerting to walk on, but if you find it uncomfortable, try including paving slabs, rather like stepping-stones, across the area that you walk on most frequently.

If you use gravel as an alternative to grass, it's a good idea to make a positive feature of it. If the area is large, like this, there is a risk that it can look flat, especially if viewed in harsh sunlight, but strong planting around the edge will help to offset this effect, and the use of a focal point plant within the gravel, like this Cordyline australis, will ensure that your alternative to grass is always an attractive feature.

If you find that trying to control the clover in your grass lawn is a battle that is difficult to win, why not try a small lawn of clover instead of grass? As you will know, it tolerates walking on, and can look quite attractive in summer, *and is probably greener than grass in dry weather. White clover (Trifolium repens) is a good one to use for lawns, but you will probably have to buy it from a company specializing in wild flower or agricultural seeds.*

Planting a Grassless Garden

If you like a green lawn, but don't enjoy the regular grass cutting, why not try a grass substitute? None of those suggested here will stand up to the hard wear of a children's play area like grass, but just for occasional foot traffic and as a feature that is for admiration only, there are some practical alternatives that don't need regular mowing.

THYME

Thyme is aromatic when crushed, and makes a good substitute, but don't use the culinary thyme (*Thymus vulgaris*), which is too tall. Choose a carpeter like *T. pseudolanuginosus* or *T. serpyllum*.

CHAMOMILE

Chamomile (*Chamaemelum nobile*, syn. *Anthemis nobilis*) is also aromatic and looks good too. Look for the variety 'Treneague', which is compact and does not normally flower.

CLOVER

If clover is a problem in your lawn, it may make a good grass substitute. Once established it will keep green for most of the year, and will tolerate dry soils. You'll only have to mow a couple of times a year, after the flowers appear, to keep it looking smart. You will need to order clover seed from a seed company that sells wild or agricultural seeds.

PLANTING A THYME LAWN

Prepare the ground and eliminate as many weeds as possible.

1 Prepare the ground thoroughly by digging over the area and levelling it at least a month before planting. This will allow the soil to settle and weed seedlings to germinate.

2 Dig out any deep-rooted perennial weeds that appear. Hoe out seedlings. Rake level again.

3 Water all the plants in their pots first, then set them out about 20cm (8in) apart, in staggered rows as shown (a little close for quicker cover, a little further apart for economy but slower cover).

4 Knock the plant from its pot and carefully tease out a few of the roots if they are running tightly around the edge of the pot.

5 Plant at their original depth, and firm the soil around the roots before planting the next one.

CHEAP PLANTS

Pot-grown plants from a garden centre (supply store) can be expensive if you need a great number. You can cut the cost by buying some plants and using these for cuttings. Grow them on for a year before planting. Some thymes are easily raised from seed.

BEWARE THE PITFALLS

Grass substitutes have drawbacks as well as advantages. You won't be able to use selective lawn weedkillers on them, so weeds will have to be removed by hand. Once a new lawn is established and the plants have knitted together this will not be a problem, but weeding will be a chore for the first season or two.

Beware of common stonecrop (*Sedum acre*), an attractive yellow-flowered carpeter sometimes sold as a grass-substitute. It looks great, but it will probably become a serious weed in your garden. You will almost certainly regret its introduction.

6 Water the ground thoroughly and keep well watered for the first season.

Right: *Thymus makes an attractive alternative to grass if the area is small and is unlikely to take much wear.*

Gravel Gardens

Gravel is great if you want an easy-to-lay, trouble-free surface that looks good and harmonizes well with plants. It's worth getting to know your gravels, especially if you're looking for practical alternatives to a lawn.

Right: *Many garden centres (garden supply stores) and stone merchants sell, or can obtain, a wide range of gravels in different sizes and colours. You will find the appearance changes according to the light and whether the stones are wet or dry.*

MAKING A GRAVEL GARDEN
Gravel is an easy and inexpensive material to work with, and a small gravel garden can be created in a weekend.

Below: *Gravel gardens can be a formal or informal shape, but an edging of some kind is required otherwise the gravel will become scattered into surrounding beds.*

1 Clear the area to a depth of about 10cm (4in), with a slight slope to avoid waterlogging after heavy rain. If the gravel garden is low-lying, provide a sump for excess water to drain into.

2 Make sure the surface is reasonably smooth, then lay thick plastic sheeting over the area (to suppress weed growth). Overlap the joints.

3 Tip the gravel over the plastic sheet, and rake it level. It is difficult to judge how deeply or evenly the gravel is being spread once the plastic sheet has been covered, so if necessary scrape back the gravel occasionally to check progress.

4 If you want to plant through the gravel, scoop back the gravel to expose the plastic sheet. Then make cross-slits through the plastic with a knife.

5 Make a planting hole, enrich the soil with garden compost and fertilizer and plant normally. Fold back the sheet, and replace the gravel without covering the crown if it's a small plant.

Surface Options

Changing the material covering the "floor" of the garden can completely alter its appearance, by changing the perception of length or width, or by giving a definite flow of design, leading the eye onwards into the garden.

PRACTICAL CONSIDERATIONS

The "floor" surface in the garden fulfils the same function, in design terms, as a fitted carpet inside the house, providing a unifying link . It is the foil against which the planting can be arranged and, for every group of planting, there should be a balancing amount of open space.

The surface should also be practical. For instance, wooden decking positioned under overhanging trees will quickly become covered with slippery algae. Paving can be natural stone, brick, or concrete, and it can be laid in lines to lengthen the appearance of the garden, or in patterns to shorten it. Decking and timber are both softer than paving, and are very flexible materials to work with, both in terms of actual installation, and in how they are treated (stained or painted)

afterwards. Timber can be mixed with other surfaces, such as paving and gravel, to give interesting textural variations, and laying it across, rather than along, the run of the path will make the distance look shorter. Railway sleepers (ties) are extremely useful in the garden, and can be used for edging borders and making raised beds as well as edging paths.

Small changes in contour and direction will alter the appearance of the garden, and can be used to give an interesting shape and pleasing sense of proportion. Steps should be wide enough to be functional, especially where food is carried, and shallow enough to be safe for both the very young and elderly.

Left: *A patio is broken up by areas of planting. The plants offer a degree of privacy by screening the dining area from the rest of the garden.*

Opposite: *A small paved patio area teeming with plant life and pots of different heights.*

LAYING PAVERS

1 Clay pavers look like bricks but are thinner and are designed to fit together without mortar joints. Prepare a sub-base of 5–10cm (2–4in) of compacted hardcore. Mortar into position a firm edge to work from. Lay a 5cm (2in) bed of sand, making sure the pavers are level with the edging. Adjust the depth of the sand if necessary. Use battens (laths) as a height gauge to enable the sand to be levelled with a piece of wood.

2 Lay the pavers in the required pattern, making sure that they butt up to each other and the edging.

3 Tamp the pavers in place using a club hammer over a length of timber. Brush more sand over the pavers to fill the joints, then tamp down again to lock in position.

Paving

Paving can look interesting if you choose attractive slabs. You could use clay pavers that match the house or surrounding raised beds, and soften them with suitable plants.

A paved area needs practically no maintenance – just an occasional brush and clean with a high-pressure sprayer every three or four years to bring back the fresh look. Paving should always be balanced with low-maintenance plants to avoid it looking bleak and harsh. It is also important to choose materials that blend in with the rest of the garden, so that they add to the sense of design.

1 Always lay paving on a firm base. Excavate the area to a depth that allows for hardcore, mortar and paving. Firm the ground, then add 5–10cm (2–4in) of hardcore for foot traffic, about 15cm (6in) if vehicles will use it. Compact the ground thoroughly.

2 Bed the slabs on five blobs of mortar, using five parts of sharp sand to one part cement.

3 Alternatively, you can lay the slabs with a solid bed of mortar, although this will make it more difficult to adjust them.

4 Start at a known straight edge, then position each slab in turn. The best way is to lower the slab down from one side, then slide it if adjustments are necessary.

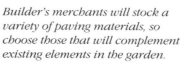

Builder's merchants will stock a variety of paving materials, so choose those that will complement existing elements in the garden.

5 Tap the slab level with a mallet or the handle of a club hammer, using a long spirit level (carpenter's level) that spans adjoining slabs. If a large area of paving is being laid, you may need to lay it on a slight slope to drain rainwater, in which case you must allow for this.

6 Unless the slabs are designed to be butt-joined, use spacers to ensure a gap of consistent width. You can make these from scraps of wood. A few days after the slabs have been laid, point with mortar.

This paved area is softened by the addition of container-grown plants.

Patio Surfaces

As with the rest of the garden, the surface sets the mood in the courtyard or on the patio. It should suit the surroundings and also be practical.

PAVING

There are many different types of paving available, in a range of materials, shapes and sizes. Traditional Yorkstone paving is attractive and hard-wearing, but is expensive. There are many concrete imitations that are equally attractive, widely available and much cheaper. Larger paving slabs can be smooth or textured ("riven"), and their use will depend on the purpose of the patio. Young children might find some of the textured slabs difficult to walk or ride a small bicycle across, and furniture placed on them may be slightly unsteady. In order to create a variety of patterns, the slabs can be square, rectangular or hexagonal, and they are designed to be easily laid on to a level, well-prepared base. Small paving blocks (paviors) and ordinary bricks are equally easy to lay, although this does take a little longer because you have to lay so many more of them. They can be laid in a number of decorative patterns, such as basketweave and herringbone; or used to change the apparent perspective of the area. By laying them crossways you will shorten the view, whereas lengthways they will extend it.

A small seating area with chair positioned to catch the sun.

WOODEN DECKING

Using wood as a surface has always been popular in countries with a plentiful supply of timber, but it is becoming ever more popular elsewhere as a result of its sheer flexibility. Decking can be used in the smallest of areas, is light to handle, easy to lay, and can be cut to fit even the most awkward shape with ease. It will cope with uneven surfaces that would be difficult and expensive to level and, unlike hard surfaces such as concrete, it can be laid around an established plant or tree without causing any damage. The open nature of the decking means that the plant will still receive rainfall around its roots and continue to grow undisturbed, although some allowance for the expansion of the plant or tree trunk must be made when the timber is measured to fit.

The colour of the wood for the decking can be chosen to complement the surroundings, either by staining or painting. Soft greys, greens and blues all make a perfect foil for nearby plants. This effect can be enhanced by using the same colours to stain nearby trellis, wooden furniture or containers.

Timber can be of hard- or softwood, but it must be properly treated to ensure its durability. Hardwood should need only periodic brushing with a stiff brush and some fungicide; softwoods will need an annual treatment with a wood preservative.

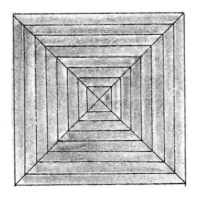

Above: *Decking provides a durable, practical and easy-to-care-for floor surface for the patio or courtyard.*

Left: *Wooden decking can be laid in a number of decorative patterns.*

Paths and Paving

Paths and areas of paving such as patios give the garden its backbone and shape. While seasonal plants are momentarily spectacular, they come and go, but the hard surfacing remains as a year-round reminder of the basic garden design, and will show up its strengths and weaknesses. It is worth spending time, thought and money on getting the framework of paths and paving right.

Concrete paving blocks remain a popular choice because they are readily available in a wide range of finishes and are much cheaper than natural stone alternatives. The formal and regular shape needs to be offset by lavish planting that spills over the edges to create a soft, well-clothed look. A neutral colour is often more successful than a mixture of bright colours (which soon become uniformly dull with age). Small sizes usually look best in a small area, and are easier to handle and lay.

LAYING BRICKS

1 If a path will have to take heavy use, bed bricks on mortar, but for paths only subject to occasional foot traffic you can bed them on sand, like clay pavers. In either case, prepare a stable sub-base.

2 Lay several rows of bricks, then tap them flat using a mallet or the handle of a club hammer over a straight-edged piece of wood. On a narrow path you will not need to build in a slight fall, but on a large area such as for a patio, this will be necessary to ensure water drains away freely.

3 The easiest way to mortar the joints between bricks is to brush in a dry mix, pressing it down between the bricks with a small piece of wood to eliminate large air pockets.

4 Finally, spray with water from a compression (high-pressure) sprayer or a watering-can fitted with a fine rose. Apply just enough water to clean the surface of the bricks and moisten between the joints. If necessary, clean off any mortar stains with a damp cloth before they dry.

In parts of the garden where the path is not subject to regular heavy use, a more random appearance can be effective. Allowing a few suitable plants to meander between and around the paving can be very pleasing.

Even in a small area, mixing materials and providing strong lines will create a positive impression of imaginative design. In this garden, the main surfacing materials are concrete paving slabs and gravel, but they have been separated by old railway sleepers (ties) that add a contrast of texture and colour. A garden area like this will remain attractive even when the summer plants have died down.

Even small paths leading to odd corners of the garden deserve careful thought. This short path that leads from the main garden to a wooden seat has been made into a feature as strong as the borders that flank it or the seat that it leads to. If only rectangular paving slabs had been used it would have been unremarkable and uninteresting, but the addition of a few patterned pavers and pebbles has managed to transform it into something special – a distinctive path packed with interest.

Planting the Paving

Make your paved areas more interesting by mixing materials, and leaving plenty of space for plants. That way it will always remain high on impact and still low on maintenance.

PLANTING IN PAVING

A large expanse of paving needs some plants to soften the effect. Keep containers to a minimum unless you have an automatic watering system. Instead, try lifting a few paving slabs and plant straight into these prepared areas. The effect will be similar but with much less commitment than containers demand.

MIX AND MATCH MATERIALS

Paving often looks a more integrated part of the garden if you combine it with raised beds or low walls made from the same or matching materials – but always check that bricks used for walls are suitable for paths as well.

Using the same or matching paving for paths and patios is another way of giving your garden a more integrated look.

If the area is large, try mixing materials. Using two or three different materials usually works well, but more than three is likely to look confused. Try bricks or clay pavings with timber, or railway sleepers (ties), or natural or man-made paving slabs. You could perhaps leave out some areas of paving and fill them with gravel or pebbles.

Above right: *This paved area is combined with a raised bed made from contrasting materials.*

1 Lift one or two slabs, using a cold chisel or bolster with a club hammer to break the mortar and lift the paving slabs.

2 Remove the mortar and any hardcore, then fork in several buckets of garden compost (soil mix) or a proprietary planting mix, together with a handful of slow-release fertilizer.

3 Plant the shrub normally, firming the soil around the roots and watering thoroughly. Keep well watered in dry weather for the first season.

4 Beach pebbles or gravel may be used to cover the soil and make it look more attractive. This also reduces the chance of soil splashing onto the paving.

ADDING PEBBLE TEXTURE

1 Beach pebbles – you can buy these from builder's merchants, garden centres (garden supply stores) and stone merchants – are a good way to create an area of different texture. Leave out as many slabs as appropriate and fill the area with a dryish mortar mix. Then lay the stones close together.

2 If the area is likely to be walked over, make sure the stones are flush with the surrounding paving. Use a stout piece of wood laid across adjoining slabs to ensure they are flush and reasonably level. Press them further into the mortar if necessary. Spray lightly with water if the mix is too dry, and clean any mortar off the stones.

Mixing materials breaks up a large area of the garden and prevents it from looking dull.

Boundaries

Hedges, fences and walls are often overlooked at the garden-planning stage. It is tempting to see them simply as boundary markers within which the garden proper is arranged. Often it is only when the garden is complete and the boundary lowers the standard of the whole garden that its importance is realized. A tatty fence or an ugly and overgrown hedge will mar the garden it borders. It is much easier to consider the boundary at the design stage than it is to modify it when construction is complete.

Low walls are very practical as boundaries, and generally require much less maintenance than fences and hedges, but they are usually too low to support most climbers and wall shrubs. Walls with a planting cavity at the top offer scope for colour and interest, but the picture on the opposite page (below) shows how planting can be taken a step further by providing a planting trough towards the base.

If you don't want to go to the trouble and expense of making a tiered wall, a similar effect can be achieved by planting slightly taller plants directly into the ground. Bear in mind, however, that plants used within the wall or at the base must receive regular watering. The soil at the base of a wall is often much drier than it is some distance away because of the rain shadow effect.

Fences, too, make good boundaries but some are more elegant than others. If well maintained, white-painted picket is one of the most attractive. This is not the first choice if privacy and security is required – when a more practical but less attractive solid panel fence might be a better option – but in a setting with plenty of greenery and the protection of shrubs beyond the garden, it can be ideal.

Traditionally, picket fences are made from wood, but there are plastic versions if you prefer a wipe-down finish.

Right: *Many flowering shrubs can be clipped into hedges, though pruning must be done with care to avoid cutting away next year's flowers. They are also best left informal rather than clipped too rigidly. This is* Spiraea x arguta.

If you have a functional but unattractive boundary fence or wall, you can hide it with shrubs, which then become the effective boundary from the visual viewpoint. In a small garden like this one, the skill lies in choosing shrubs that will grow to the height of the true boundary to mask it, without growing much larger – otherwise they can appear oppressive. Most shrubs tolerate regular pruning to keep them within bounds, however, so height and spread can usually be controlled by regular use of the secateurs (pruners).

In this town garden, the boundary has, in effect, become the garden – and what lies within it is cosily protected as well as stylish in appearance.

Left: *A planting trough has been added to this low wall on the road side so that passers-by derive most of the pleasure, but the same technique can be used on the garden side, too.*

Above: *The use of white-painted garden furniture with a white picket fence helps to make a garden look more serene, designed and co-ordinated.*

Hedges

Few gardens are without a hedge of some sort. They are used as a defensive barrier around the garden as well as having a more decorative purpose within. The defensive role is to maintain privacy both from intruders and prying eyes (and, increasingly, against noise pollution). This type of hedge is thick and impenetrable, often armed with thorns to discourage animals and humans pushing through. Hedges also have less sinister functions, more directly related to gardening. One is the important role of acting as a windbreak to help protect plants. Another is to act as a foil for what is planted in front of it. Yew hedges, for example, act as a perfect backdrop to herbaceous and other types of border.

Above: *A formal beech hedge (*Fagus sylvatica*) makes a neat and tidy boundary to any garden. Beech, yew (*Taxus baccata*) and hornbeam (*Carpinus betulus*) also make good formal hedges as long as they are kept neat. They are all slow growing and need less attention than many others.*

USING HEDGES

Hedges are widely used within the garden, where they are perhaps better described as screens or frames. Screens are used to divide up the garden, hiding one area from view until you enter it. In some cases, the hedges are kept so low that they can hardly be called hedges; they are more like decorative edging to a border. Box reigns supreme for this kind of hedge. Others are informal hedges, in which the plants are allowed to grow in a less restricted way, unclipped, so they are able to flower, adding to their attraction. Roses and lavender are two popular plants for using like this.

We all want hedges that grow up as quickly as possible and usually end up buying one of the fastest growers. However, bear in mind that once grown to the intended height, these fast growers do not stop, they just keep growing at the same pace. This means that they need constant clipping to keep them under control. A slower growing hedge may take longer to mature, but once it does, its stately pace means that it needs far less attention. In spite of its slow-growing reputation, in properly prepared ground, yew will produce a good hedge, 1.5–1.8m (5–6ft) high in about five to six years from planting.

Right: *Although often much maligned, leyland cypress (x Cupressocyparis leylandii) makes a good hedge. The secret is to keep it under control and to clip it regularly. Here, although soon due for a trim, it still looks attractive, as the new growth makes a swirling movement across the face of the hedge.*

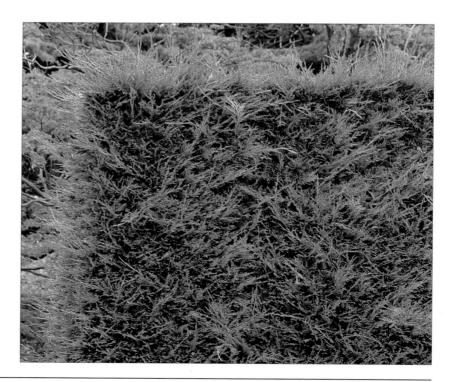

This tapestry hedge is made up of alternate stripes of blue and gold conifers. Here, the bands have been kept distinct but, if deciduous shrubs are used, the edges often blend together, which gives a softer appearance.

A country hedge makes an attractive screen around the garden. This one is a mixture of shrubs: there is box (Buxus sempervirens), hawthorn (Crataegus monogyna), hazel (Corylus avellana) and holly (Ilex aquifolium). The only problem with this type of hedge is that the growth rates are all different so it can become ragged looking, but then country hedges always are!

Informal hedges of lavender border a narrow path. The joy of such hedges is not only the sight of them but the fact that, as you brush along them, they give off the most delicious scent. Such hedges fit into a wide variety of different situations within a garden.

An informal flowering hedge is formed by this firethorn (Pyracantha). The flowers make it a most attractive feature while the powerful thorns give it a practical value as an impenetrable barrier and effective deterrent to unwanted visitors. Flowering hedges should not be clipped as frequently as more formal varieties and trimming should be left until flowering is over and in the case of berried shrubs, it should be left until after fruiting.

Screens and Disguises

Unless you are extremely fortunate, there will be a view or objects within the garden that you want to hide. Focal points can be used to take the eye away from some of them, but others will require some form of screening or disguise.

Many common hedging plants can be allowed to grow taller than normal to form a shrubby screen. Space the plants further apart than for a hedge, so that they retain a shrubby shape, and clip or prune only when it is necessary to keep within bounds. Avoid a formal, clipped shape unless you are screening within a very formal garden. Most hedging plants will grow to twice their normal hedge height if you give them more space and do not restrict them by frequent clipping and pruning.

Choose plants appropriate to the setting. In a Japanese-style garden, many of the tall bamboos will make an excellent screen for, say, a garage wall or oil storage tank. Use shrubby plants in a garden where there are lots of shrubs, and especially if the shrub border can be taken up to the screening point. On a patio, a climber-covered trellis may look more appropriate.

In town gardens, and especially in the case of balcony and roof gardens, the problem is to minimize the impact of surrounding homes, offices or factories. These usually require impracticably huge walls to mask the view, which would also make the garden excessively dark. In a very small garden, trees may not be a practical solution for this type of screening either, although in a large one they will probably provide the answer.

A sensible compromise is to extend the wall or fence with a trellis, or similar framework, along which you can grow climbers. This will not block out the view completely, but it will soften the harsh impact of buildings and help to concentrate the eye within the garden by minimizing the distractions beyond. The boundary itself will be given extra height and interest.

A combination of plants and hard landscaping is often the most pleasing way to screen a view beyond a boundary. Trees are a particularly pleasing solution. Even if they lose their leaves in winter, the network of branches is often sufficient to break up the harsh outline of buildings beyond, and in summer – when you are in the garden and require more privacy – the canopy of foliage will usually block out most of the view beyond. Trees are a particularly good solution if the aspect is such that most of the shadow falls away from your garden rather than over it.

A painted trellis makes an attractive and easily erected screen, and if you make it tall enough and use it to form an L-shaped corner where you can create a cosy sitting area, the screen can become an attractive feature in its own right. The secret of stylish screening is to turn it into a positive feature whenever possible. If you give it a purpose, it will be less obviously a screen intended to hide something and become a positive part of your garden.

Left: *Using bright flowers or interesting focal points within a garden concentrates the eye on the positive points and not the negative surrounding ones.*

Above: *In this garden, an arbour has been created that provides height and privacy, with climbers over the top adding even more screening.*

The strong formal design, with a circle at its centre, also uses a design technique that takes the eye inwards rather than outwards to what lies beyond the boundary. This clever use of clay pavers shows a circular centrepiece laid to an angled herringbone pattern, with basket-weave used for the rectangular areas of paving.

Screening for Privacy

Privacy is important in the garden, particularly around the area intended for eating or relaxation. Plants, used either as a living screen or to clothe an artificial one, are the ideal solution.

REAL SOLUTIONS

It is difficult to relax completely in the garden if there is no sense of privacy and protection from outside interference. The problem can be physical, visual or psychological, but if it is essential to the enjoyment of the garden, it should be addressed.

You can increase the height of too-low walls and fences by adding a trellis to the top. This will create a barrier to deter nearby animals from trying to enter, without preventing contact with people on the other side or blocking the view completely. Painting the trellis will add interest until the plants have grown to cover it and will help harmonize it with the surroundings.

If the item to be hidden is within the garden and is not too large, such as a garden compost container or tool shed, a single evergreen shrub or conifer should suffice to hide it from view. If there is one intrusive eyesore beyond the boundary of the garden that is spoiling the view, a strategically placed upright tree or conifer may be

the answer, so that the offending object is hidden but the rest of the scene can still be appreciated.

If taller protection is required, trees such as birch (*Betula pendula*) are excellent for screening from nearby houses. Because the leaf canopy is light and airy it will not block out too much light.

Privacy is particularly desirable around an eating area, and again, a trellis is useful, as it provides screening without blocking out the light, is

Top right: *A trellis can blend in well with the surroundings. It should act as a deterrent to animals without blocking out light or the view beyond.*

Right: *Tall hedges provide a dense and very effective screen.*

durable, supports plants easily and can be painted or stained to suit the area. Its main disadvantage is that it allows in cold winds. Wattle fences, bamboo and reed screens are also extremely attractive, although they are not as long-lasting as trellises. More flexibly, shrubs, tall grasses and small trees in containers can all act as screens, and can be moved to different positions according to need at the time.

For a more solid barrier, especially where a wall cannot be built, a fence of closely spaced boards will provide good shelter. Close-board, interlock and interwoven fencing is usually available in 1.8m (6ft) wide panels of varying heights.

PLANTS FOR SCREENING

Arundinaria nitida
Buxus sempervirens
Carpinus betulus
Chamaecyparis lawsoniana
    'Green Hedger'
Crataegus monogyna
Elaeagnus x *ebbingei*
Escallonia 'Iveyi'
Fagus sylvatica
Griselinia littoralis
Ilex aquifolium
Ligustrum ovalifolium
Osmanthus delaveyi
Prunus cerasifera
Prunus laurocerasus
Pyracantha 'Mohave'
Taxus baccata
Thuja orientalis
Viburnum rhytidophyllum

A combination of trees and plants of different heights has been used to shield one part of the garden from the next.

Trellis and Fences

One of the simplest, yet most decorative ways of displaying climbers is to grow them over free-standing trellises or fences. This is an impressive way of bringing planting right in to the garden's fundamental structure.

BOUNDARIES AND SCREENS

Fences tend to be functional, in that they create a boundary; this is usually between the garden and the outside world but a fence is sometimes used as an internal divider. Many existing fences are ugly and covering them with climbers is a good way of hiding this fact. Those erected by the gardener need not be ugly but they still provide an opportunity for climbers. Trellises are usually much more decorative than fences. They are not so solid and allow glimpses of what lies on the other side. They are either used as internal dividers within the garden, as screens, or simply as a means of supporting climbers. Used in this way, trellis can make a tremendous contribution to a garden design, as they can provide horizontal as well as vertical emphasis. As screens, they are useful for disguising eyesores such as fuel tanks, garages or utility areas.

ERECTING TRELLIS

The key to erecting a good trellis is to make certain that it is firmly planted in the ground. Once covered with climbers, it will come under enormous pressure from the wind and will work loose unless firmly embedded in concrete. Do not try to take a short cut by simply back-filling the post-hole with earth; unless

the trellis is in a very protected position, it will eventually fall over. Panel fences are erected in a similar way.

Virtually any climber can be grown over trellis. But unless it is in a sheltered position, trellis will not offer the same protection as a wall to tender climbers.

1 Dig a hole at least 60cm (2ft) deep, deeper in light soils. Put the post in the prepared hole and partly fill the hole with a dry-mix concrete. Check that the post is upright and not sloping, using a spirit level (carpenter's level). Adjust the position of the post, if necessary, and then continue filling the hole, tamping down firmly as you go to hold the pole still.

2 Continue filling the hole with concrete, ramming it down firmly; frequently check that the post is still upright. The post should now be firm enough in the ground to work on and, once the concrete has "cured", it will be permanently secure. Lay the panel on the ground, to work out where the next hole should be. Dig the hole, again to at least 60cm (2ft) deep.

3 Nail the panel on to the first post, while a helper supports the free end.

4 Place the second post in its hole and nail it to the panel, checking that the tops of the posts are level and the panel is horizontal. Fill the second hole with dry-mix concrete, tamping it down as you proceed. Check that the post is upright and adjust, if necessary.

5 Repeat the steps by digging the third post-hole, nailing on the second panel, positioning and nailing the third post and so on, until the length of trellising is complete. This is more accurate than putting in all the posts and then fixing the panels, when, inevitably, some gaps will be too large and some too small.

Planting for Height

Planting for the "third dimension", height, allows the space within a patio or courtyard to be used to the full. Heat retained by a south- or west-facing wall will protect tender and exotic plants.

PLANTING IDEAS

Having a wall to plant against adds an extra dimension to your possibilities, especially if it faces south or west, because the heat from the sun is absorbed during the day and given off overnight. Nearby plants will be kept several degrees warmer than those beyond the wall's influence.

Most shrubs can be grown near a wall. Wall-shrubs are specifically those that can be pruned back to form a covering for the wall, supported against it using wires and ties, and through which other plants such as climbers can be grown. Climbers support themselves in a number of ways: by twining their stems around a support; by twisting tendrils or leaf-stalks around a support; by using thorns to climb; or by the use of aerial roots or sucker pads to attach themselves.

Whether the plant is intended for a wall or a pergola, it should be of a size chosen to be in context with its surroundings, otherwise it will need regular pruning to keep it under control, and this may be at the expense of the flowers. Do bear in mind that, after rainfall, the plant will drip for some time, and this may result in the surface underneath becoming slippery. If this is also a well-used route through the garden, it may be advisable to replace a smooth surface, such as decking, with a non-slip one, such as gravel. This can be edged with brick or bonded with resin to keep it from interfering with mowing the lawn.

1 Take the trellis to the wall and mark its position. Drill holes for fixing spacers and insert plastic or wooden plugs.

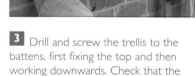

2 Drill the equivalent holes in the wooden batten (lath) and secure it to the wall, checking with a spirit level that it is horizontal. Use a piece of wood that holds the trellis at least 2.5cm (1in) from the wall. Fix a similar batten at the base and one half-way up for a trellis above 1.2m (4ft) high.

3 Drill and screw the trellis to the battens, first fixing the top and then working downwards. Check that the trellis is not crooked.

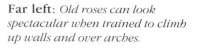

4 The finished trellis should be fixed tightly to the wall so that the weight of the climber or any wind that blows on it will not pull it away from its fixings.

Far left: *Old roses can look spectacular when trained to climb up walls and over arches.*

PLANTS FOR PERGOLAS

*Akebia quinata**
Aristolochia macrophylla
*Campsis radicans**
Clematis montana
Humulus lupulus 'Aureus'
Jasminum officinale
Jasminum x *stephanense*
Lonicera x *brownii*
    'Dropmore Scarlet'
Parthenocissus henryana
Rosa 'Dorothy Perkins'
    'Saunder's White Rambler'
    'Wedding Day'
    'Zéphirine Drouhin'
Vitis coignettiae
Vitis vinifera
Vitis vinifera 'Purpurea'
Wisteria floribunda
Wisteria sinensis

* Unsuitable for very cold or exposed gardens

GROWING CLIMBERS ON WIRES

1 For walls, wedge-shaped vine eyes can be hammered in place. Those with screw-fixings can be used on walls or wooden fences or posts, first drilling and plugging holes.

2 Thread galvanized wire through the hole in the vine eye and wrap it round itself. Thread through the intermediate eyes (at no more than 1.8m (6ft) intervals). Fasten off the wire firmly.

3 Curve long stems over the wires, using either plastic ties or string. Tie at several points if necessary. Tie the stems in a series of arches, rather than straight up, to encourage flowering buds.

Growing climbers will allow you to make the most of the space in your garden.

Garden Features

In a large garden most ornaments, furniture and fixtures – like garden lights– are a static part of the design. In a small garden, a slight rearrangement of the furniture, the changed position of a light, or the simple exchange of one ornament for another according to mood and season, means that the garden need never be predictable despite limitations of size. Use features such as water, arches, pergolas, ponds and walkways to set the tone for your garden.

Left: *The addition of a gently-flowing fountain to a pond helps create a mood of peace and tranquillity.*

Above: *This permanent garden feature can change with the seasons.*

Focal Points

Focal points are an essential part of good garden design, relevant whatever the size of garden. They help to take the eye to a favourable part and away from the less favourable, and can act as signposts to lead the eye around the garden.

Even a well-kept lawn will look bare if it is large and all the interest is in beds and borders around the edges. It can be useful to create a focal point within the lawn, but this often works better if it is offset to one side or towards the end of the lawn, rather than in the centre. Position it where you want to take the eye to an attractive view, or use it to fill an area that lacks interest. Try to avoid placing the focal point against a background that is already interesting or colourful; otherwise one will fight with the other for attention.

A sundial is a popular choice, but should be placed in a sunny position if it is to look in the least credible. A birdbath is another popular choice, especially if it is close to the house where the birds can be seen and enjoyed.

Above: *Gateways and arches make excellent focal points, and if used to divide a large garden can add a sense of mystery and promise from whichever side you view. This device works best if the areas at each side are in contrasting styles or are visually very different. The garden on one side of this wall is heavily planted and enclosed, whereas the view beyond suggests open lawns and spaciousness.*

In a long, narrow garden, you could produce a series of arches or gates, each taking the eye further on into a journey of exploration.

Left: *Focal points can be plants as well as inanimate objects. When the two are used together, the effect can be particularly striking.*

In this garden, the mature hedges produce a predominantly green effect: restful but visually uninspiring. A statue has transformed an unexciting view into an arresting scene that demands attention. But foreground plants are important too and, if large, can help to put the rest of the garden into more reasonable proportions. These bold red hot pokers (Kniphofia) have the height to counterbalance the statue, and their strong colour accentuates the effect.

In a small garden it can be a good idea to have the sitting area away from the house so that there appears to be a larger area of interest between home and boundary. In this attractive scene, the white chairs provide the necessary contrast and height to act as a focal point. This only works well, however, if the background is attractive.

A tall, narrow object such as a birdbath or sundial on a plinth needs visual impact from a distance, and setting it on a bold base like this gravelled area edged with bricks is one way to achieve this.

In a small garden, a spectacular focal point can be used to dominate a corner of the garden so that the limitations of scale and size become irrelevant for the moment. A well-placed ornament or figure will serve as a simple focal point. In this garden, the white trellis that frames the statue helps to fill this particular corner, and immediately creates the impression of style and elegance.

Archways

Arches are very versatile and are well suited for growing a variety of climbers. Archways can be incorporated into a dividing feature, such as a wall, hedge or fence, or can be free-standing along a path, to support climbers.

USING ARCHES

Archways exert a magnetic effect on visitors to your garden. No matter how interesting the area you are in, an archway draws the eye to what lies beyond. It creates mystery with tantalizing glimpses of other things.

Those forming entrances are important features. They are often the first thing that a visitor is aware of on entering a garden. Arches frame the scene beyond and create atmosphere. A cottage garden, for example, looks particularly fine when seen through a rose arch, while a formal town garden may be better suited to a simple arch of foliage, such as ivy.

The possibilities of creating an arch are almost endless. They can be purchased in kit form, made to order or made by the gardener. They can be made from metal, wood, brick or stone work. Plastic ones are also available, but are neither very attractive nor long lasting. Wooden ones present the biggest range. They can be formal ones created from panels of trellis, or informal ones made from rustic poles. The choice is normally limited by cost and the appearance that is required – climbers themselves will generally climb over anything. Always choose or make one that is big enough for people to walk through when it is fully clad with climbers – which may stick out as far as 60cm (2ft) or more from the supports. Make certain that the supports are well sunk into the ground, preferably concreted in. When covered with a voluminous climber, an arch may be under great pressure from the wind and a storm may push over a badly constructed one, destroying your display.

Virtually any climbers can be used with archways, although over-vigorous ones can become a nuisance – they seem to be constantly growing across the entrance itself. Other types of climbers to avoid, unless there is plenty of room, are thorned roses which may cause injury, or coarse-stemmed plants such as hops. These can be dangerous to the unwary. If you want a rose, use something like 'Zéphirine Drouhin', which is thornless.

CLIMBERS FOR ARCHWAYS

Akebia
Campsis radicans
Clematis
Humulus Impulus 'Aureus' (golden hop)
Lonicera (honeysuckle)
Rosa (roses)
Vitis (vines)

A simple arch, constructed from rustic poles and covered with a variegated ivy. The simplicity of the foliage allows the eye to pass through to the garden beyond, without distraction.

Wisteria makes a good covering for an arch because, once it has finished flowering, its foliage still retains interest. It is accompanied here by Vitis coignetiae, *whose foliage turns a magnificent crimson and scarlet colour in autumn. Together, these climbers provide interest from spring to autumn.*

Above: *A golden hop,* Humulus lupulus *'Aureus', and a honeysuckle,* Lonicera periclymenum, *combine to decorate this archway. Again, interest should be provided from spring to autumn.*

Above left: *This wonderfully romantic arch seems to come from the middle of nowhere. The roses and long grass create a soft image that provides nothing but delight.*

Left: *Roses make excellent subjects for archways. Repeat-flowering ones provide the longest interest; once-flowering roses can be combined with late-flowering clematis, to extend the season.*

Arbours

An arbour is a framework over which climbers are trained to create a shady outdoor room. Best of all is an arbour large enough to accommodate a table and several chairs, where you can sit and linger over *alfresco* meals.

CLIMBERS FOR ARBOURS

Clematis (some slightly fragrant)
Fallopia baldschuanica (Russian vine – very vigorous)
Hedera (ivy – evergreen)
Humulus (hop – dies back in winter)
Lonicera (honeysuckle – many fragrant)
Rosa (roses – many fragrant)
Vitis (vines – some fruiting)

DESIGNING AN ARBOUR

The structure can be of metal or wood or the arbour can have brick or stone piers with a wooden roof. The design can be any shape that takes the fancy or fits the site. It may be triangular, semi-circular, rectangular or octagonal, to suggest but a few. The climbers can be any that you like. If you do not like bees, stick to climbers grown for their foliage. In areas designed for relaxation, fragrant climbers are most welcome. Honeysuckle provides a delicious scent, particularly in the evening. Jasmine is another good evening plant. For daytime enjoyment, fragrant roses are ideal.

An arbour may have to remain in place for many years, so make sure you build it well. Take trouble to use timbers treated with preservative (not creosote, which may kill many climbers) and make certain that it is a strong design, well supported in the ground. As with similar structures covered in heavy climbers, the wind can wreak havoc on weak construction.

Here, the overhanging fig, Ficus carica, *and the surrounding rose, clematis and other climbers create an intimate area for sitting and relaxing, which fulfils all the functions of an arbour, even though there is no supporting structure.*

This arbour is dappled with shade from a number of roses. It is big enough for small dinner parties as well as simply sitting in the evening with a drink.

A large arbour, built for entertaining, this example is covered in a variety of climbers, including a purple grapevine. This provides a wonderfully dappled shade, as well as colourful foliage and grapes at the end of the autumn. Clematis montana *supplies the colour in the spring and early summer.*

A dual-purpose arbour: the newly planted beans will provide shade during the hotter part of the year, as well as a constant supply of runner beans for the kitchen. As a bonus, the flowers provide an added attraction.

Walkways and Pergolas

Extending the use of arches and trellis brings the possibility of pergolas and walkways. On the whole, these are not suitable for the smaller garden, although it is surprising what can be achieved with a bit of imagination.

USING WALKWAYS AND PERGOLAS

Walkways are open pergolas, with no roof. They can be double-sided, that is, down both sides of a path, or you can use a single piece of trellis down one side. The simplest way is to build them out of either trellis or rustic poles. For a romantic version, use a series of pillars linked with swags of ropes. Both can become massive structures that have to support a great deal of weight, especially when there is a strong wind blowing, so it is important to make certain that, whatever the material, the walkway or pergola is well constructed.

A wide range of climbing plants can be used to clothe the pergola or walkway; fragrant plants are especially pleasing. Roses are ideal, as long as they are either thornless or well tied in so that they do not catch passers-by with their thorns. Evergreen climbers, such as ivy, make a dark, intriguing tunnel and may even help to keep passers-by dry in wet weather.

Right: *An arch leads through into another part of the garden. The poles are covered with* Rosa *'American Pillar' and R. 'Albertine'. On the side of the arch is* Clematis *'Alba Luxurians'.*

Clematis tumbling over the corner of a pergola. Here, C. 'Etoile Violette' combines with some late flowers of C. montana *to create an attractive picture.*

Colourful foliage makes a long-lasting covering for a pergola. Here Vitis vinifera *'Purpurea' creates an attractive screen up a wooden pillar. As the year proceeds, the colour of the foliage will deepen, so there is a change of appearance, even without flowers.*

A romantic walkway created from a series of arches, passing along a clipped path through long grass. The arches provide a delightful tunnel effect, while the statue at the end draws the eye and adds to the romantic image.

Creating Storage Space

Storing less attractive bits and pieces – such as a clothes line – is a fact of life, but the clutter does not have to be on show. With a little imagination, it can be hidden behind a living screen.

MEANS OF DISGUISE

In an ideal world, rubbish bins and recycling containers would be beautiful in themselves, but, unfortunately, in reality they are seldom an attractive sight. They are necessary, however, and they do need to be accessible.

You can simply ignore your rubbish bins or spend a little time and effort blending them in, by painting them to co-ordinate with the overall scheme (if this is feasible), using a screen of plants to hide them or camouflaging them with a trellis with plants growing up it.

You will need to consider external factors, such as the amount of room available and how the area is to be accessed. Plant screens, in particular, tend to take up quite a lot of space widthways and they need regular attention to prevent them from becoming straggly. The advantages of using a trellis are that it is compact, long-lasting, and attractive in its own right. Even without a lot of plants, with a coat of paint or varnish, a trellis can harmonize with the surroundings. If you then train plants against or over it, you will introduce an extra dimension that will bring colour and interest throughout the year.

Above: *Here, a trellis grown with climbers was erected to obscure the view of the garden shed. The shed was painted to match the trellis to allow it to blend as much as possible into its surroundings.*

Left: *In a small garden, screen areas with attractive fencing which can be made into a feature.*

Opposite: *Clever use has been made of the area below the verandah, allowing access to tools without taking up space that could be used for plants.*

Water Features

Water plays an important part in most good garden design, and if you look at the work of many professional garden designers you will find water somewhere. Not everyone wants a pond, of course, especially if safety is a concern where there are young children, but there are lots of water features where the risk is minimal while still creating maximum impact as a focal point. Whether or not you include a pond, try to find space for a simple water feature such as a wall or pebble fountain.

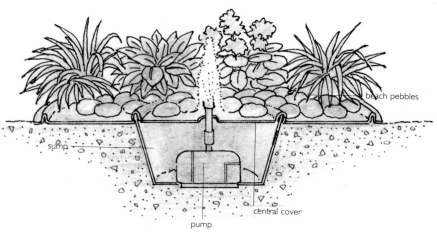

Simple fountains like this can be bought complete with reservoir and pump. Making this pebble fountain can take just one day.

Wall fountains are a good choice for a formal garden or a patio, although they can also be used with great effect in an informal setting too. Lion faces and gargoyles look perfectly in place in a period garden.

You can buy suitable wall masks complete as a kit with pump. If you don't want a small pool at the bottom like the one in the photograph on the opposite page, buy an integrated wall fountain that includes a shallow dish that fixes to the wall along with the spout. This can be positioned beyond the reach of small children, and in any case the basins contain very little water.

Only a small pump is required, and many can be powered by a simple low-voltage system. The mains power is reduced by a transformer indoors so that only a low-voltage cable is required outdoors.

A wall fountain is usually fitted by drilling and plugging the wall so that it can be screwed into position. The difficult part is disguising the pipe between the submerged pump and the wall spout. The pipe is best hidden within the brickwork when the wall is constructed, but often this is not possible. You may be able to remove a channel in the brickwork, but the pipework will still be visible unless you camouflage it. The simplest way to fix the pipe to an existing wall is to clamp it to the face of the brick and then plant ivy or some other evergreen climber to cover it. After a year or two, the pipe probably won't be visible from a distance.

MAKING A PEBBLE POOL

1 For any bubble fountain or pebble pool you will need a reservoir, or sump, to house the pump and hold a generous reserve of water. Proprietary products are by far the easiest to install as they are designed with a wide rim to catch water that has drifted, with a centrepiece to support the pebbles over the reservoir. Some garden centres (garden supply stores) stock these, or you can order them from water garden specialists.

   Make sure the reservoir is well supported, removing or adding more soil as necessary. If the soil is very stony, bed on a layer of sand. Make sure it is level with the rim at or just below the surrounding paving or soil. If surrounded by soil, positioning the lip slightly above bed level will reduce the amount of soil contaminating the fountain.

2 Insert the pump and take the wire out at a side where it can be hidden easily as it emerges from the wide rim. If there is paving on one side and a flowerbed on the other, take it out on the flowerbed side so that it can easily be camouflaged.

3 Insert the central cover, then add the beach pebbles. You can buy these from some garden centres, otherwise obtain them from a stone merchant or builder's merchant.

4 Fill with water and turn on the pump. Installing a spectacular water feature like this is that simple.

Above: *It is always a good idea to have plenty of plants growing around a wall fountain, otherwise attention will be drawn to what could be an expanse of plain brickwork.*

Right: *Rock gardens and streams with cascades are a natural choice for a sloping site, and they can often be combined. If the slope is gentle, the design could be mainly lawn with rock and water features as the main theme of the garden.*

Left: *Simple but effective water features can be built for little cost. This one has been made from an old dustbin (trash can) lid! The lid is supported over a reservoir that also contains a small low-voltage pump, and beach pebbles have been used to give the feature more interest and character. The water simply flows over the rim and into the reservoir to be recirculated.*

The reservoir can be made from the base of a cut-down dustbin, or a waterproof container (you can even just use an excavation in the ground and line it with a waterproof pond liner). Some water is lost regularly through evaporation and splashes that drift in the wind. So if you cannot see the water level in the reservoir, make a point of topping it up every few days (simply pour more water into the basin or over the stones – if the reservoir is full, it will overflow into the surrounding ground).

Creating a Pond

Overcrowded plants benefit from division and replanting in spring, and in autumn it's best to cut down dead foliage that might pollute the water, and to rake out most of the leaves that fall in. Apart from that, however, ponds are very low on maintenance. They don't require cleaning out annually, although it is worth giving them a spring clean every second year.

MAKING A LINED POOL
Make this in a weekend. The hard part is excavating the hole.

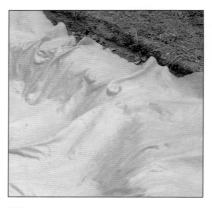

3 Remove any sharp stones or large roots, then line the pool with a 12mm (½ in) layer of sand (it will stick to the sides if damp). If the soil is very stony, use a polyester mat (sold by water garden suppliers) instead of sand.

4 Drape the liner loosely over the excavation, with an overlap all round. Hold the edges in place with a few bricks, then fill with a hosepipe.

2 Excavate the soil to the required depth, but leave a shallow ledge about 23cm (9in) down around part of the pond. This is for plants that require shallow water. If you are having a paved edge, remove enough grass for this, remembering to allow for the mortar bed as well as the thickness of the paving. It is essential to check the levels all round. Use a spirit-level (carpenter's level) in all directions.

1 Make your pool as large as possible – it will make a better feature, the fish and wildlife will be happier, and the water will probably stay clearer. Mark out the shape with a hosepipe or rope.

5 As the weight of the water takes the liner into the pool, lift the bricks periodically to allow the liner to mould easily into the excavation. Try to remove some of the worst creases as the water fills, but don't expect to be able to eliminate all of them.

6 Once the water has reached its final height, trim off the surplus liner, leaving a 15cm (6in) overlap all round. Lay the paving on a bed of mortar, trapping the edge of the liner. Make sure the paving overlaps the edge by an inch or two, so that any drop in water level is not so noticeable.

PLANTS FOR PONDS
Iris laevigata (Japanese iris)
Pontederia cordata
   (pickerel weed)
Aponogeton distachyos
   (Cape pondweed)
Acorus gramineus 'Variegatus'
   (grassy-leaved sweet flag)
Juncus effusus spiralis (Corkscrew rush)

PLANTING A POND
The best time to plant aquatics is spring and early summer.

1 Use a planting basket designed for aquatic plants, and line it with a special basket liner made for the purpose (or use a piece of horticultural fleece cut to size). Plant in garden soil or an aquatic soil. Do not use a potting soil intended for ordinary pots as this will contain too much fertilizer.

2 Cover the surface with gravel. This will reduce the chance of the water becoming muddied when placing the basket in the pond, and should also deter fish from stirring up the soil.

3 Most waterlilies should be planted in deeper water, but miniature waterlilies and all the "marginal" plants should be placed on the planting shelf at the edge.

Above: *A raised patio pool like this makes an eye-catching feature for a small garden. You can also use a liner to waterproof this kind of pool.*

The Magic of Ornaments

Ornaments should be used around the garden just as they are in the home. Use them simply to display their inherent beauty, to brighten up otherwise uninspiring areas, to make a statement about taste or style, and as punctuation points that form part of the garden decor.

Small ornaments can be moved around, so they are also a means of making subtle changes of emphasis over time. You may want to use them as a focal point in one part of the garden in winter, and in another in summer.

Shrub borders can become tired-looking when there are no flowers, but a well-placed ornament can transform the ordinary into something special. The ornament can easily be moved to different positions as different parts of the border or garden need a little uplift.

Ornaments and figures are frequently placed in a prominent position, such as on a plinth at the end of a path or vista, in an alcove, or in a conspicuous open area such as a lawn or area of paving. Sometimes, however, a more subtle approach can be particularly pleasing, and placing an ornament within a flowerbed is often very successful.

This figure is subtle rather than bold, and set in a flowerbed it does not make a strong focal point across the garden. But if you choose an ornament because of its pleasing appearance, this may be the best way to view it, as it is in harmony with its surroundings. Just as a painting in a gallery is not necessarily positioned as a focal point but in a way that shows it to advantage, so the placing of an interesting ornament can be done in a similar way.

Right: *Ornaments often come into their own in winter, when much of the garden is drab and lacks colour or impact.*

Japanese gardeners use ornaments symbolically, and lanterns like this one have particular purposes and meanings, but they can be used anywhere that pleases you, whether or not the garden is in a Japanese style. This lantern has been used to add interest to a conifer bed, which is mulched with a layer of gravel.

Left: *A good garden designer always keeps an eye open for suitable materials with which to create statements. A natural material, like a piece of rock, can be as beautiful and attention-grabbing as any abstract man-made ornament. These four stones look almost casual in their positioning, but they have been selected and positioned with great care. In fact, they are more likely to be the subject of admiring glances than the striking plants that surround them.*

Improving Dull Spots and Corners

One of the skills of good garden design is not to waste any available space. Even those unpromising, problem positions between houses, awkwardly shaped spots and corners that do not seem to fit easily into the main design; dry and shady areas beneath trees and shrubs where nothing seems to thrive, and anywhere that looks bare or uninteresting should be exploited, and planted whenever possible.

Bare ground – or steps – in a dull spot can often be transformed by the simple addition of an ornament or a group of containers. But try to make it a little special; choose different shapes and sizes of containers, and a range of flowering and foliage plants. If the dull corner is in a flowerbed, try using a broken urn or pot set on its side with soil covering the rim, then plant a widening and winding "flow" of low-growing and long-flowering bedding plants such as pansies, so that it appears as if the plants are pouring out from the tilted container.

Ornaments and statues can be used in a similar way, but they should be light in colour to contrast with a dark background.

Statues can look incongruous in the wrong setting, but superb in a style of garden that is appropriate. They look best in traditional country-garden styles with lots of shrubs and flower borders. If you can set them with plants around the base they will look less pretentious and appear to be a more integrated part of the overall garden design.

In a very unpromising corner, be content with an attractive statue, and a tough climber like ivy planted against the wall (choose a gold-variegated variety to lighten the area). Interesting paving also helps, so try mixing paving materials, or perhaps create pebbled areas on which to stand the containers.

Corners where fences meet can be particularly difficult to brighten up, especially if they are in a shady position. This corner previously had grass almost to the edge of the fence with just a narrow ribbon border. It has been transformed by taking a large sweep out of the lawn and filling the area with a coloured gravel on which to frame a collection of plants in containers. This simple device can be used in most gardens to transform an otherwise dull and uninteresting corner into an eye-catching feature.

The shady side of a hedge can be a particular problem, as few flowering plants will thrive in dry shade. An attractive container at the end of a path or in a corner of the lawn or flowerbeds where nothing much grows will act as a focal point; and bring a touch of much-needed lightness if pale flowers and foliage are used.

A container raised on a plinth will generally be more successful in design terms than one at ground level. It will make more of a feature and the additional height may bring the plants into better light. White or pale-coloured flowers and pale foliage plants can look particularly stunning against a dark background such as a conifer hedge.

Focus on Containers

If a plant is spectacular or a container interesting or eye-catching, it is best to display it in isolation rather than in a group of plants or pots. Use it as a focal point to take the eye to a particular part of the garden. Or use them formally to flank a front door or guard a flight of steps.

Do not cover a spectacular container with trailing plants. Use upright plants that make the most of the container itself.

Garden objects from watering-cans to wheelbarrows make interesting containers. In a modern garden you can use modern objects, but in a country garden or one created in a rural or old-fashioned style, an old container will be more appropriate.

This old wooden wheelbarrow has long since been replaced by a lighter modern version, but with a coat of bright paint and a few drainage holes made in the base it will see many more years of eye-catching service.

Everyday objects such as old paint tins (though nowadays they are usually plastic) can be pressed into use with a little imagination. They will give your patio or garden that individual touch that bought containers simply cannot achieve. These two old paint containers have been painted white first, then had coloured "drips" added to match the colour of the gerberas.

Always make drainage holes in the base of containers that do not already have them before you plant them up.

There are some places where flowers will fail to thrive, but if the container is striking enough, you will not need them. The shrub border in this picture was uninspiring before the addition of this large empty jar, which has transformed the area into one of great interest.

Above: *If both plant and container are big and bold, they do not have to be colourful or spectacular. This* Fatsia japonica *brings instant appeal to a shady part of the garden that would otherwise lack any points of interest.*

Left: *If the container is striking enough, the flowers can be almost incidental. In fact, a very bold floral display may actually detract from a spectacular or unusual container.*

The container illustrated is eye-catching in both shape and colour, and in its own way challenges the flowers to compete. This kind of container commands attention and takes the eye to that part of the garden. Avoid too many containers like this in close proximity, however, as they will vie for attention and the impact will be lessened.

Using Furniture

A garden without furniture implies a garden that is all work and no play. Furniture creates the impression of a garden designed to be used for relaxation, a place to rest and enjoy the fruit of earlier labours. It has to be used with care, however, as the choice of material and the style of furniture can look incongruous if it does not reflect the mood of the rest of the garden. Some furniture is purely functional, while other pieces can be as important a focal point as a well-chosen ornament.

Furniture can become the feature of a paved area, especially if it lacks a natural focal point. Although the garden featured on the right immediately generates a pleasant atmosphere, any clear-cut lines that relate to an overall plan are obscured by the difficult site. In an area heavily shaded by trees, the paving gives the illusion of an area in a forest clearing, with dappled light filtering through. Without the containers and the furniture, this kind of area could lack visual stimulation and look rather barren. The lavish use of plants in containers gives it colour and texture, but it is the furniture that draws the eye and holds the area together.

Tree seats have a special charm, and are often useful as a focal point in a part of the garden otherwise lacking interest, such as areas of grass with large trees and little else. If painted white, a tree seat will stand out across the garden, and is sure to add a touch of elegance. Tree seats are more use as a focal point and garden ornament than as practical seats, however, and drips, insects and falling leaves are always a risk if you sit beneath the overhanging branches of a tree.

In this setting, white plastic or resin furniture would sit uneasily, but wood blends with the paving and the woodland effect of the setting. Cushions – which must be taken inside when not in use – add another dash of restrained colour, and will help to offset the rather austere appearance that some wooden furniture often has.

Use an attractive garden seat to liven up an otherwise dull area of the garden, perhaps where mainly green shrubs or a dark hedge forms a backdrop to the lawn. As these pictures show, a scene that is rather mundane and uninteresting can be transformed by the simple addition of a garden seat. It also invites you to walk over to it, and to use a part of the garden that may not otherwise hold special appeal.

BUILT-IN FURNITURE

Built-in furniture is a sensible option for a patio where space is limited. If you have plenty of space, free-standing furniture is much more adaptable, and by rearranging it you can add variety. In a small area, however, built-in seats and a barbecue can give your patio a very "designed" appearance. You will still require supplementary free-standing furniture of course, but less of it.

Barbecues and wooden seats are commonly integrated into the walls created as part of the patio boundary, but if you have a raised bed around the edge, a simple sitting area like the one illustrated below will give that special feeling that you get when surrounded by plants. Bear in mind, of course, that when certain plants are in flower, like this geranium, bees and wasps may be a problem.

Above: *Tree seats almost always have to be made to measure and adapted to suit the diameter of the tree – or in this case the area occupied by multiple trunks – which gives great scope for that touch of individuality in design.*

Left: *Built-in seats can be very straightforward to create, like this concrete "seat".*

The Seating Area

Create a relaxed area in which to sit and enjoy a mild spring day or a warm summer evening. When thinking of the garden in terms of a "room outside", it is vital to include a seating area. There is no need to think in grand terms: a simple rustic chair is sufficient in a small garden, and will provide an excuse to rest and unwind amid the sights and sounds of nature.

DESIGN PRACTICALITIES

The scale of the area allocated to seating should reflect its intended use, and may be much larger in a warm area than a cold one where conditions do not favour lingering outdoors. Ideally, the furniture should be situated in a position to enjoy sunshine at the time of day it will be used, even if this is not an area adjacent to the house. It can always be linked to the house for the purposes of carrying food and drinks safely, by means of a specially created and planted walkway.

The planting around the seating area should provide privacy and shelter, shielding it from intrusions by the outside world. It can also be used to give shade if the area is a hot one. Climbers such as jasmine, honeysuckle, wisteria and rose will provide shade, and their flowers will fill the air with perfume on warm evenings.

Introduce additional plants, either permanently or on a seasonal basis, by using

containers. Place them at the entrance to the area, or use them to brighten a dark corner. Containers can be colour-coordinated with the furniture, chosen to look like part of the garden in natural, earthy shades or hidden altogether under a mass of lush, trailing foliage.

Extend the use of the seating area and install lighting, from simple oil lamps or candles to a more complex electrical system. Your enjoyment of the garden will not then be restricted to daylight hours, and the lighting will endow the plants with a completely new look.

Left: *Here, a trellis frames the seating area. Lanterns provide candlelight in the evenings while the structure itself is painted to complement adjacent plants.*

Above: *This tiny patio area adjacent to the house catches plenty of sun. Tubs, planters and a window box soften the bricks and paving.*

Caring for Furniture

There is an enormous choice of furniture available for the garden, from convenient folding plastic chairs to whole suites of hardwood dining furniture.

CARING FOR FURNITURE AND ACCESSORIES

For seating that is to be left outside all year, choose a durable material such as teak or painted metal, which will need only annual maintenance. Softer woods should always be well seasoned and treated with preservative, and this should be renewed annually. Plastic needs little maintenance, but has a limited life outdoors and will eventually become brittle. To harmonize the accessories with the garden, a number of acrylic paints are available that can be applied to wood, metal and terracotta. A shiny galvanized bucket can be given the verdigris effect of ageing copper by applying a coat of primer, a base coat of dark grey-green, and then shades of green.

The walls surrounding the garden or seating area can also be transformed by painting them in complementary colours. A dark garden can be lightened by reflecting the available light off white- or (less glaringly) cream-painted walls. Using a muted, soft green will blur the wall into the planting, making the boundary less distinct and the garden seem bigger. On a more bold note, bright sunshine yellows and rich blues will liven up a dull area or a small courtyard and provide a splash of colour behind lush foliage.

DISTRESSING WOODEN FOLDING CHAIRS

Folding chairs are readily available and will weather with age. They can be enhanced with this simple effect.

Give a new, plain wooden chair a distressed look.

1 Rub down the surface of the chair with sandpaper to provide a better surface for the paint to adhere to. Rub over the surface randomly with a household candle, applying the wax thickly on the corners and the edges.

2 Paint the chair with white emulsion (latex) paint using random brush strokes and leave to dry completely. Rub down the paintwork with wire (steel) wool to remove the paint from the waxed areas.

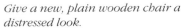

Far left: *Metal furniture is robust enough to need very little maintenance over the winter.*

Lighting

There is no reason why you can't enjoy your garden even after dark. Lighting can give a completely different appearance to plants and features such as water or statuary. Using lighting in the garden at night expands the usable living area and creates a mood, as well as discouraging intruders, or showing up changes of level and other hazards. It allows the best features to be highlighted while leaving others hidden, and brings the garden to life in a totally different way.

USING ELECTRICITY
Electric lighting can be used among the plants in different directions. "Up-lighting" entails positioning light fixtures so the object is lit from below. It is extremely effective for highlighting coloured leaves in the autumn, a tree with

interesting bark, or a statue. When "down-lighting", the object or area is lit from above, for safety or security reasons, or to give a softer, more diffuse overall light. Done well, it can imitate natural light – moonlight gently passing through trees, for instance.

Above: *A lantern is suspended from the same bracket as a hanging basket. The soft light will enhance the flowers after sunset.*

Left: *A candle display cleverly designed to emphasize garden paraphernalia: candles in vegetable shapes share storage space with terracotta pots.*

If you have more than one circuit installed you will have more flexibility. Lights can be switched on and off at different times to create different effects.

CANDLES AND LANTERNS

Candles may not provide much light but they are wonderful for atmosphere, and outdoor ones often deter insects, too. Flares resemble large candles, burn for 6–8 hours, and cast a warm, romantic glow. Lanterns, either candle or oil, can be hung or stood around the garden to cast a gentle, golden light.

Whatever system of lighting you choose, use it to enhance the garden and seating area subtly, rather than flooding them with a great glare of light. Garden lighting will need to be totally waterproof if it is to be left outside permanently and, if it is to be used in water, it will need to be approved waterproof underwater lighting. Candles, flares and lanterns should never be left unattended, and should be kept out of the reach of children and animals.

Right: *This light hidden among ivy draws attention to the lush greenery as well as lighting the boundaries of the garden path.*

Installing Lighting

Enjoyment of your garden should not cease at sundown. Garden lighting will enable you to sit outside on warm evenings when you can see your garden in a new light, and in the cold dark days of winter you can enjoy spectacular effects from indoors.

Do not be afraid to try garden lighting just because electricity is potentially dangerous. There are lots of excellent low-voltage systems that should remove the worry, and for mains voltage consult your local qualified electrician for assistance.

In small town gardens, roof gardens and on balconies, floodlights and spotlights of the kind that can be so effective in a large garden may be inappropriate. Glaring lights may annoy neighbours, so subtle lighting is usually more suitable. Small lanterns, and low-voltage lights that cast their beam downwards or over just a small area, are unlikely to offend anyone. The use of some stronger patio lighting will be necessary, however, for an area that you are going to use in the evening. Just make sure most of the beam is focused towards the ground, which is where it is needed for safety.

For lighting to be a permanent feature, electric lighting is the practical option, but candles and flares can be used for the odd occasion when you want to invite your friends around for an evening out with a difference, a true candlelight dinner perhaps. Patio flares burn quite brightly, and lanterns are available that will protect candles from the wind and cast a reasonably localized light. Candles are for "atmospheric" light, however, and are really only practical where there is some supplementary light from a nearby electric lamp, from the house for instance.

Garden lighting can also be used to create focal points after dark, but the spotlights for this are best installed during construction to avoid the problem of laying cables across or around paved and heavily planted areas. Ideally, several lighting points should be wired in at this stage, giving you plenty of flexibility later so that the lights can be moved around to make the most of seasonal variations.

Spotlights should be unobtrusive by day – preferably well hidden among some plants. Upward-pointing beams can be very striking and effective, but it is best to avoid them if the beams are likely to be thrown into your neighbours' windows.

INSTALLING LOW-VOLTAGE LIGHTING

1 Low-voltage lighting is simple to install, and usually comes in a kit with everything you need. Always follow the manufacturer's instructions on the kit. If you are unsure of what to do, or if you are installing mains (high voltage) lights, always seek professional help.

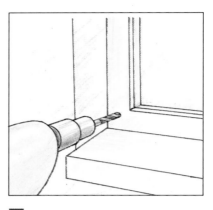

2 Drill a hole in the wall or window frame to pass the low-voltage cable through. Remember to fill the hole with mastic (caulk) to produce a waterproof seal around the cable.

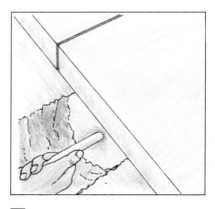

3 Whenever possible, take the cable underground. Electrically, it is not a hazard to life because of the low voltage it carries, but trailing cables are a hazard as you may trip over them. Paths are a special problem, and the cable should be passed under them whenever possible. Excavate an area on either side, undercutting the path a little, and then push through a piece of conduit. Thread the cable through the conduit.

4 You should have a choice of designs for the lights, so choose those that are appropriate to the style of the garden and their position. A kit usually includes several lights, which are easy to fix and reposition if you follow the manufacturer's instructions.

Spotlights are often used to pick out ornaments or striking structural features, but bold plants such as red hot pokers (Kniphofia) and yuccas make good focal points at night. In this picture fennel takes centre stage.

In this beautiful garden, the decorative lighting has been confined to chains of small lights draped through the tree, and to a small lantern. Light from the house, or supplementary lighting, is turned on when the area is used for sitting out in the evening during the summer.

Candlelight contribute enormously to the atmosphere when you are relaxing outside in the evening.

Beautiful Borders

The border is a traditional garden feature, for growing favourite plants and showing them off to best advantage. In ground that has been well-prepared border plantings can be maintained easily and enjoyed for their special ornamental qualities. In a border, a selection of plants becomes an entity. How they combine, how their foliage and flowers mingle, and the definition that different shapes give, are the factors that make a border so pleasing to look at.

Above: *Blue, yellow and white blooms are always a welcome and refreshing sight in spring.*

Left: *Plan borders carefully to provide year-round colour, scent and interesting foliage.*

Designs for Borders

A well-designed border brings out the most interesting and individual combinations of plants. Garden visits, photographs and sketches are the means to develop ideas, translating someone else's garden schemes into your own setting. This is an acceptable form of copying, and most gardeners, generous and open about their planting ideas, are quick to acknowledge the source of their inspirations.

PLANNING A BORDER

The main elements you should be aware of in the design and planning of a beautiful border are: season, site, soil, colour scheme and form or shape of the border.Consider plant themes, such as roses, foliage or giant plants; or where you can use plants to create a subtle effect, as in a romantic border.

SEASON

Most borders have times when there is not a full display of colour and foliage, but if you are able to plan well, it is possible to have some interest in the border at most times of the year.

In spring, bulbs and early flowering plants such as primula, pulmonaria and wallflowers provide bright splashes of colour to cheer the gardener's heart after winter. But by late spring and early summer the rush to grow and flower, or produce attractive foliage, is well under way. In late summer and autumn, colour and form come from bright and hot colours, and as the season turns into winter, seedheads, grass panicles and evergreens or evergreys offer a continuity of interest.

SHAPES

The shape of the border will determine the style and look of your planting scheme. A formal border, where the plants are repeated in a definite pattern, is one of the breathtaking wonders of gardening. It looks good in a large garden, but can be equally attractive in a small garden, if the setting invites such formality. Formal borders are straight-

This narrow border is only about 1.2m (4ft) wide, but herbaceous perennials have been allowed to tumble over at the front to provide useful colour contrasts with the yellow shrub behind. This is the evergreen Choisya ternata *'Sundance' with* Aster novi-belgii *'Audrey' (left) and 'Jenny' (right) and a pink chrysanthemum in the centre. In front is a pink-flowered rock rose that would have bloomed in late spring and early summer. This kind of combination of shrubs and herbaceous plants ensures season-long colour.*

edged and backed by evergreen hedges, which act as frames or backdrops for the border's palette of plant colours. Such a border can really only be viewed from the front, unless there are formal paths leading up to it, at right-angles to the grass and to the hedges.

Borders do not have to have straight edges, however, although it can be a plus when it comes to mowing the lawn around the border.

Less formal than a long, traditional straight border, but equally creative, is an island bed which can be seen from all round, so every part of it has to have an attractive look. Island beds usually have one or several high points that take the eye from ground level plants at the edges of the border to the middle. It is not necessary to have a formal, repeated pattern, unless the style calls for a rigid bedding-type planting.

Moving the eye upwards is a part of the design of any area of the garden, and this can be fully achieved where a border backs onto a wall or fence, and a vertical border can be created.

This very narrow bed shows how charmingly shrubs and herbaceous plants may be combined. However, if slugs are a problem in your garden, you may find the hostas are an unwise choice.

The Soil in Your Garden

The soil is probably the most important element of your borders – the plants depend on it for water and nutrition. Get the soil right at the beginning and you will have a wonderful collection of plants in your borders.

HOW GOOD IS YOUR SOIL?

The basic ingredient of any planting scheme is the soil. The best results are achieved by getting the growing site in a good condition, before you even purchase or propagate a plant. Once you have plants in the soil, it will be difficult to get at it again to dig it over or add compost in bulk. Add mulches and compost in selected areas, but never to the whole border, unless you renovate it completely.

TESTING FOR MAJOR NUTRIENTS

Plants need nutrients to survive, and these are held in solution in the soil and absorbed by the roots. They are used with carbon dioxide and water to make food for the plants. Phosphorus, potassium and nitrogen are needed in fairly large quantities for plants to thrive. Trace elements including magnesium, manganese, iron and molybdenum are also needed in smaller quantities.

You can test the soil for major nutrients with a proprietary kit. Nitrogen (keeps the plant growing well), phosphorus in the form of phosphates (encourages root growth) and potassium (gives greater impetus to flowers and fruiting) need applying regularly.

THE TYPE OF SOIL

The soil you have in your garden is the most precious basic material for beautiful borders, so you have to take care of it. Never attempt to work it when the weather is very dry or very wet, or when the soil is covered in frost or snow. In these kinds of conditions, any pressure on the soil will compact it, or in the case of dry conditions, erode it. In frost and snow, it will simply be too hard to shift at all. Border soil is traditionally prepared in the autumn or springtime, when it is easier and far more pleasant to work with.

1 Gather your soil sample, using a trowel, from 5–8cm (2–3in) below the surface. Take several samples from around the garden, and test each one separately.

2 Mix 1 part soil to 5 parts water. Shake or stir the mixture in a clean jar, then allow it to settle – it may take half an hour to a day to become reasonably clear (clay soils are the slowest).

3 Using the pipette, carefully draw off some of the clear liquid from the top few centimetres (inches) for the test.

4 Using the pipette, transfer the solution to the test and reference chambers of the plastic container.

5 Pour the powder from the capsule provided into the test chamber. Replace the cap and shake vigorously until the powder has dispersed.

6 Wait for a few minutes for the colour to develop, then read it off against the comparison chart. There will be a key that explains the reading, and instructions to tell you how to correct any problem.

TESTING FOR STRUCTURE

For newly-cut-and renovated borders, first test the type of soil you have. Begin by finding out its texture. To do this, pick up a handful of damp soil and roll it between your finger and thumb; if it feels rough and granular, but the grains don't adhere to each other, the soil is sandy. If it forms a ball when you roll it between your thumb and forefinger, it is a sandy loam. If it is rather sticky and makes a firm shape, it is a clay loam. But if you can mould it into shapes, it is a clay soil.

A clay soil presents plants with problems because the soil particles are so closely packed and moisture-retentive that the plants' delicate root hairs and root system cannot obtain water. Nor is there enough oxygen available in the soil for them to use. In effect, the root system cannot move and so becomes trapped in a waterlogged soil. During the summer, a clay soil bakes hard and dry, and great fissures or cracks appear all over the surface. To improve a clay soil, either put in a drainage channel or add grit and sand to the soil when you prepare it for planting. Adding compost or manure will also help, as both these improve the structure of the soil and aerate it.

ACID OR ALKALINE

You can determine whether a soil is acid or alkaline by measuring the soil pH. This is done on a scale which ranges from 1 to 14, and can be tested with small samples of garden soil. Use a soil tester kit to see what the pH level of your soil is. If the reading is below 7, then the soil is acid or sour. If it is at

7, the soil is neutral and if it is above 7, it is alkaline. For most plants 6.5 is ideal. The pH level is determined by the amount of calcium or lime there is in the soil. It can be boosted if you lime the soil, and this may increase the range of plants you can grow.

Below 6.5, you will be able to grow fewer plants, and only those that tolerate acid conditions, such as azaleas and rhododendrons will thrive in 6 or lower. Also, fewer plants will tolerate a soil with a high pH level (very alkaline), as vital minerals may not be available.

The best type of soil for healthy, all-round growth of a good range of plants is a loam soil with an average pH content between 6 and 7. This soil is usually very fertile as soil organisms that help to aerate the soil and break down bulky organic matter are also more prevalent in a soil with an average pH level.

FERTILIZING THE SOIL

Where a number of plants are growing and competing for space, light, water and nutrients, you will need to fertilize most soils if you want all the plants to do equally well. Fertilizing during the growing season is particularly important. You can either do this once a week, by applying a liquid feed, or you can use slow- or controlled-release pellets or granules that hold fertilizer. If you apply fertilizer in the form of concentrated mixes of blood, fish and bone, apply them during warm weather in the spring, when the activity of soil organisms helps in their slow release into the soil.

Of the inorganic chemical fertilizers, balanced general-purpose or flower fertilizer granules or powders are less expensive than slow-release or controlled-release types. The general purpose fertilizers are usually applied in spring, and

FEEDING BORDERS

1 Most established plants, but especially demanding ones such as roses, benefit from annual feeding. Apply a balanced flower fertilizer in spring or early summer, sprinkling it around the bushes. Keep it away from the stem, sprinkling it further out where most of the active root growth is.

2 Hoe it into the surface so that it penetrates the root area more quickly.

again if the plants need a boost later in the growing season. Controlled-release (which only release nutrients when the soil temperature is warm enough for growth) and slow-release fertilizers (which release nutrients steadily over three to six months) are more expensive but should ensure more sustained growth.

PLANTS FOR ACID SOIL

If your soil is acid, without altering its nature you can enjoy a range of plants including camellias, heathers, rhododendrons and pieris.

PLANTS FOR ALKALINE SOIL

Many shrubs and perennials will grow well in an alkaline soil, so the range and choice here is greater. Anchusa, bergenia, galega, hellebore, heuchera, kniphofia, verbascum and brunnera are among the perennials; box, hebe, buddleja, choisya, philadelphus and Jerusalem sage are among those shrubs which will grow particularly well in such a soil.

3 Water it in. This will make the fertilizer active more quickly.

Making Borders

After you have tested the soil and determined the soil type and the acid or alkaline character of it, you can decide which plants will do best in it. Although you can alter the nature of the soil, it is probably easier to opt for the plants that are known to do well in the conditions you have.

TYPES OF BORDER

The main principles to remember when designing a border are that it is a place to grow choice plants well and in harmonious combination with each other. You can create tranquil moods with pastel colours, or fire the imagination with brightly-coloured flowers and angular foliage.

The bones, or structure, of the border will come from evergreen and shapely deciduous shrubs. They will provide a mass and greater interest, especially if their foliage has autumn colours. The border's ultimate form then comes from the shapes of plants. Some, low-growing and small plants with delicate flowers, will

WHEN TO PLANT

Traditionally, spring and autumn are considered the best times for planting, when the soil is either just warming up or still warm enough for the plants to get established. This was also the only time that field-grown plants were available to gardeners. Now with so many herbaceous plants and shrubs available as container-grown plants, the advice to plant in these two seasons is not always necessary. Provided the soil is workable, i.e. it is not frosty, waterlogged or too dry, you can plant up at any time of the year.

Before planting, water the plants in their containers. If you are planting up a large border, set the plants out into the positions you have chosen for them, section by section, and get an idea of how they will look. Dig planting holes large enough to take the roots comfortably and deep enough to keep the plants at the same level to which they were planted in the containers. Back-fill the planting holes with the soil you have taken out. Water the plants well, swirling water and soil into the planting holes. Then firm the surface down and water regularly until the plants are well established.

PLANTING A BORDER

1 Always make sure the pots have been watered before planting, otherwise the rootball may remain dry as water runs off it when watering after planting.

2 Space the plants in their pots before you start to plant, as changes are easy at this stage. Try to visualize the plants at their final height and spread, and don't be tempted to plant them too close.

3 Knock the plant out of its pot only when you are ready to plant, so that the roots are not exposed unnecessarily to the drying air. Carefully tease out some of the roots.

4 Plant small plants with a trowel, large ones with a spade, and always work methodically from the back or from one end of the border.

5 Return the soil and make sure the plant is at its original depth or just a little deeper. Firm it with your hands or a heel to expel large pockets of air in the soil.

6 Water thoroughly unless the weather is wet. Be prepared to water regularly in dry weather for at least the first few weeks after planting.

need close inspection, while others, growing taller and flowering at a greater height, will rise out of the border and appear to float in bands of colour above it. Each plant association should work well as an individual combination, and as a whole in the rest of the border. Look at the border as a series of small cameos and as a whole sweep of interesting plant and colour combinations.

BORDER COLOURS

The colours of flowers, foliage, berries and stems are perhaps the most evocative of all elements in the border. Using pale pastel colours you can create a quiet, serene effect, whereas hot vibrant colours in late summer make the opposite statement and are challenging to create. You can also make an interesting display using a restricted colour palette, or even just one colour. It is fun to find the plants in such a scheme that will provide you with a succession of blooms or foliage through many seasons.

If your garden is small or non-existent under the paving of a patio or balcony, do not despair: you can still grow a border by creating a mobile garden in containers. Although it will need higher maintenance than one grown directly into the soil, since you will have to provide water and nutrients for the plants, it can be an exciting, ever-changing scene.

If you plan well with seasonal changes in mind, you can create a succession of interest through the year to hold the cheery spring colours, strong summer colours, golden autumnal tones and fragrant blossom to take you through the winter.

PLANTING BULBS IN A BORDER

1 Excavate a hole large enough to take a group of bulbs. If the soil is poor or impoverished, fork in garden compost or well-rotted manure.

2 Space out the bulbs, planting at a depth that will leave them covered with about twice their own depth of soil.

3 To deter slugs and encourage good drainage around the bulbs, sprinkle grit or coarse sand around them before returning the soil.

4 If planting summer-flowering bulbs in spring, position with small canes (stakes) so that you do not accidentally hoe the area before the shoots come up.

BULBS IN THE BORDER

Much of the colour and interest in a spring border comes from flowering bulbs. Daffodils, tulips, snowdrops, bluebells, crocuses, *Iris reticulata, Cyclamen coum,* aconites, dog's tooth lilies, and hyacinths can be used en masse in borders or singly under trees.

Plant spring-flowering bulbs, except tulips, from late August

Above: *Crocuses show the true versatility of bulbs. They can be used in beds and borders to bring pockets of colour when there is not much else out, and can even be naturalized in the lawn.*

through to November so that they have a long growing season in the ground and can establish well before the cold of winter sets in. Plant tulips later, from October through to November. Plant the bulbs in layers or decks, with late-flowering varieties deeper into the ground, and early-flowering bulbs nearer the surface. In this way, you achieve a simple succession of

flowering bulbs without too much disturbance of the soil. Summer-flowering bulbs such as lilies, alliums, nerines and galtonia extend the season and continue to provide interest in early and late summer.

When bulb flowers are spent, take off the flower-heads, but allow the foliage to die down naturally. In a border, this can make for unsightly, untidy

DIVIDING OVERCROWDED CLUMPS

1 If a large clump of established bulbs, such as daffodils, begins to flower poorly, overcrowding may be the cause. Lift, divide and replant. You can do this when the plants are dormant, but if you do it before the leaves die down completely it is easier to see where the clumps are.

2 Separate the clump into smaller pieces, and replant some of the large, healthy bulbs in the same place. Either discard or give away the surplus bulbs if you have too many, or replant them elsewhere.

effects, but by using raffia you can loosely tie the foliage together, but do not waste time and effort bending it over. When the foliage turns yellow, usually after about six weeks, cut it back to the ground and leave the bulbs undisturbed. If the bulbs are not hardy, such as some summer-flowering varieties, lift them and clean and dry them off before storing them for planting again next spring. Tulips should be lifted as well and stored as they are attacked by pests and disease if left in the ground during the summer.

Every two or three years it is worthwhile to lift and divide large, established clumps of bulbs. Overcrowding may reduce their flowering vigour and by dividing and replanting, you will renew their flowering capacity. You will not be able to replant all the bulbs in the same position and therefore you will need to find additional space elsewhere in the garden.

THE GARDEN AS A HABITAT
Get to know the site and soil in different parts of your garden, and plant them with the right plants for that particular habitat, as if they were outside the manipulated garden and growing where they were best suited in a natural situation. To do this well, you have to know a little about the plants you want to grow. The conditions they need are an indication of the habitats they originally came from. Epimediums, for example, with their delicate spring foliage, good autumn colour and small, but interesting flowers, suit the shadier areas of a border, a clue to their woodland edge origins.

Hostas have been planted at the front of this mixed border. The height differential gives you the benefit of two borders.

SHRUBS IN THE BORDER
Shrubs, such as *Choisya ternata* 'Sundance', deutzia and weigela, offer bursts of foliage and flower colour that are substantial for long periods during the year, unlike some herbaceous border plants. They act as a framework, as their shapes are stronger and more pronounced, and they add height, shape, foliage and floral interest, as well as providing a variation of rhythm to the whole of the border.

ROSES IN THE BORDER
Old shrub roses, including damask, centifolia, gallica, musk and alba, bourbon, hybrid perpetual and portland roses, make a romantic and soft addition to the border. Although they are often described as needing little attention, like most plants they respond well to care given at the right time to prevent problems later. You must remember to remove their dead or damaged wood in spring, and you should also mulch and fertilize them well in spring. If they are growing in a border where they have to compete with other plants, make sure they are well watered throughout the dry seasons. If they need spraying against black- or green fly (aphids), use a beneficial insect-friendly spray, and only use it on calm windless days, when the roses are in shade. Deadhead when the blooms are spent, unless the rose is also grown for its autumn hips, in which case, leave the spent flowers in place.

Modern roses, specially bred as carpet or ground-cover plants, are also highly useful in sloping borders or on banks, if you want to make a good floral effect. Often their foliage is attractive too, which extends their usefulness. They will also help to maintain the border, by suppressing weeds.

Maintaining the Border

Last, but equally important, is the maintenance of the border so that it continues to please and delight its home gardener, as well as any others that may visit. Low maintenance is the aim and dream of most gardeners, but whether the garden is large or small, there will always be something to do to make the border look better. Staking, deadheading, training plants, weeding, mulching, watering – all these are part of the seasonal and regular activities that make gardening such an enjoyable pastime.

MULCHING

Once you have got all the planting done, the new border will look bare, and it will look this way for a while, until the roots are well established and the plants begin to make some top growth. To keep annual weeds down, conserve soil moisture and raise the temperature of the soil surface, it is useful to apply a mulch that acts as a ground cover.

In your initial soil preparation you will have removed the bulk of the perennial weeds, but if there are any still in the soil, remove them before you apply the mulch. Do not apply a mulch in cold weather, as it will then act as an insulator of the cold conditions. Instead, mulch the soil in spring, when it has warmed up considerably. Bark chippings or compost are suitable and can be applied to a depth of 5cm (2in).

WATERING

Water in newly-planted shrubs and perennials well, continuing to do so during the first growing season. Water as much as you can during very dry seasons, but try to do this early morning or late in the day, when the plants are not in full sun, otherwise their leaves may get scorched. On really hot days, this might mean waiting until well after sunset to give the garden any real benefit from the watering.

PLANT SUPPORTS

Many perennials, including *Knautia macedonica, Gaura lindheimeri* and sisyrinchiums, will support their flower stems without any extra staking or supports that you can provide. Others though, like the sumptuous large-flowered peonies with their heavy buds and full flowers, will flop onto other plants, especially during a spring shower.

At that stage it is more difficult to get into the border to put in supports or stakes to keep the peony in place. Instead, when you are planting up the border, put stakes or supports in place around the plants that are going to need it, even though it may look a bit odd until they have grown enough to warrant the support. Sweet peas, although annuals, make a lovely English cottage garden effect when planted around cane (stake) wigwam supports in the centre of borders. You can use hazel twigs or pea sticks for the most natural-looking support system. Bamboo canes, metal ring stakes, as well as plastic-coated stakes also look natural, once the plants are established. All are arranged so that they either form a single support for the plant or surround it, so that the plant can grow through the support, or they form a semi-circle, simply holding it at the front so that it does not flop over other plants.

Similarly, some plants that are used as wall plants do not support themselves. Use vine eyes inserted into the masonry and linked with green plastic-coated or plain wires. Wooden trellis or plastic netting can also be used for this purpose.

WEEDING THE BORDER

Good preparation of the soil should have rid you of the deep-rooted and creeping perennial weeds, such as dock and couch grass. Once the border is planted up you will have to remove any fresh growth carefully with a hand fork so that you do not damage the border plants. As soon as the ground covering plants are growing well, they will begin to play their part in suppressing annual weeds which will compete with your expensive perennials and shrubs for water, light, nutrients and space.

If the annual weeds persist, work carefully through the border, hoeing or hand weeding them out. Although time-consuming and sometimes awkward, hand weeding is the most effective method and, in my experience, has its therapeutic value!

In a densely planted border it is not sensible, nor is it cost-effective, to use liquid systemic chemical weedkillers. The chances of spray damage on expensive plants is high and not worth the risk. If there are perennial weeds that persist too close to the root system of the border plants, wait till autumn, and then when you are lifting and dividing large clumps, sift through the roots and remove those belonging to the weeds.

WINTER PROTECTION

Some plants that are tender or borderline hardy will need winter protection. This can either be done by mulching the soil surface above the root with straw or by setting up a temporary pole-supported hessian windbreak. As a precaution, take cuttings in autumn, so that if the plant does not survive, you will have propagated new plants to take its place.

Dahlia tubers will have to be lifted, cleaned and stored in frost-free conditions. Some tender wall shrubs can be protected by making a conifer blanket of branches to keep them insulated through the winter, without digging them up and bringing them indoors. Straw layers on the soil around the crown of tender perennials will insulate them in mild winter weather, but if you live in a very cold winter area make sure that the plants you use in your border are hardy for the area.

Annual Border

Bright and cheery annual flowers provide the
quickest and easiest colour in a flower border,
and they are useful as seasonal fillers in a
perennial border.

Annual is the term used to
describe plants that are sown
every year and that grow, flower
and set seed all in the same year.
There are many annuals to
choose from to achieve a
colourful, but seasonal, display
in the garden. Some can be
sown directly into their growing
sites, while others, known as
half-hardy annuals, need
cosseting with warmth and
protection before they are
planted out into the warm soil

in spring. If you want to, you
can sow hardy annuals into trays
in a greenhouse to plant out
when the soil warms up again,
but unless you have both the
time and the resources, this is
not necessary.

Instead, rake the already
prepared soil in the border until
there is a fine tilth. Then decide
where you want different blocks
of colour, and of course, bear in
mind the varying heights and
spaces that should be allocated

to different plants. Use a cane
(stake) to mark out various
shapes in the soil. These will
then be the sites for sowing.
Within each block, mark out
parallel lines or drills along
which you will sow the seed.
Most annual seed should be
sown to a depth of 5–15mm
(1/4–1/2in) and in rows that are
evenly spaced to 20–30cm
(8–12in) apart.

Sowing into neat rows in
blocks means that in a few

weeks time, when the seed has
germinated, it will be instantly
recognizable and stand out from
any weed seeds that will have
germinated as well. It will be
easy to hand weed at this stage
and also to thin out seedlings
from overcrowded rows. Leave
space in the planting scheme to
allow for the half-hardy annuals
that you have sown in the
greenhouse, and when the
plants are large enough, plant
them out into their growing site.

Watering is necessary while
the plants become established,
particularly in dry seasons, but
beyond that, the only
maintenance is to deadhead and
tidy up the plants as they grow.
The more you deadhead the
plant, the more flowering is
encouraged. During the summer
it will give the plants an extra
boost if you give them liquid
feed when you water. At the end
of the flowering season leave
some flowers to develop seeds
and then some of your work

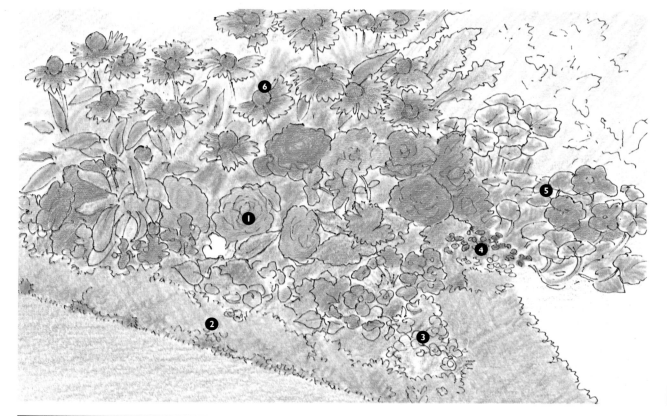

PLANT LIST

1 *Begonia* 'Non-Stop Mixed'
  hybrids
2 *Matricaria*
3 *Begonia* 'Burgundy'
4 *Lobelia erinus compacta*
5 *Tropaeolum majus* 'Alaska'
6 *Gaillardia* hybrids

next year will be done for you, when the self-sown seedlings germinate in spring.

The range of plants and colours is wide, and seed companies are always extending their lists with new and better seed strains. Some offer colour-coordinated selections with a variety of heights, so that you can achieve a harmonious effect just by sowing into different parts of the border.

Below: *In this vibrant border, hardy and half-hardy annuals are used in combination with the perennial blanket flower,* Gaillardia *hybrids. At the edge, the half-hardy annual,* Matricaria *is growing as a low frame. The half-hardy annual* Begonia *'Non-Stop Mixed' rises above the smaller-flowered, fibrous-rooted half-hardy* Begonia *'Burgundy'. Half-hardy* Lobelia erinus compacta *and hardy annual nasturtium* Tropaeolum majus *'Alaska' tumble over the paving.*

Spring Choice

Freshness and vitality are the keynotes of spring borders. Bright yellow narcissi, white and green-tipped snowdrops, soft mauve crocuses and the rainbow colours of tulips are all popular choices.

Regularity and uniformity of planting are often associated with spring schemes. Tulips or narcissi rise high on their long stems above a mass of frothy bedding plants such as forget-me-not, *Myosotis*. It is as if we are imposing a strict management on the waywardness of what are essentially garden versions of wild spring flowers, tamed through intensive breeding programmes for our borders.

Here in the garden recreated at the home of the French Impressionist painter, Monet, in Giverny, France, that regularity and single-minded planting of just two or three different plants provides a sense of infinite space, as well as infinite resources of labour and finance.

The soft-coloured gravel of the hard landscaping in the path defines the border edges clearly. The main plant choices offer a unity of colour and continue the regularity established by the path. Their varying heights and flower colours, though, relieve the monotony of this uniform look and make for a natural rhythm. Edging the long lines of the beds, and making a soft line with the path is the low-growing, mound-forming favourite of spring, *Alyssum maritimum* 'Royal Carpet'. Its curved outline spills out of the bed and softens the edge of the path, linking it with the planting.

Soft, billowy white and pale blue, tall bearded iris flowers float high above their angular, lance-like leaves in spring, imitating some exotic butterfly. Before the flowers appear, the fresh green and uniform shape of the foliage plays its own part in the border's overall look. Making a softer contrast are the more natural-looking flowers of the Siberian wallflower, *E.* x *allionii*, on the left of the path, and the scented wallflower, *Cheiranthus cheiri* on the right. Both are perennials, but in spring bedding schemes they are treated as annuals.

Above: *In contrast to the regularity of the spring border at Giverny, this more natural effect is achieved by mass planting spring-flowering bulbs and perennials. Here purple crocus and yellow aconites show their faces above the marbled leaves of* Arum italicum *'Pictum', while the mauve flowers of hellebores stand atop their leafless stems. The white bells of snowdrops provide the background.*

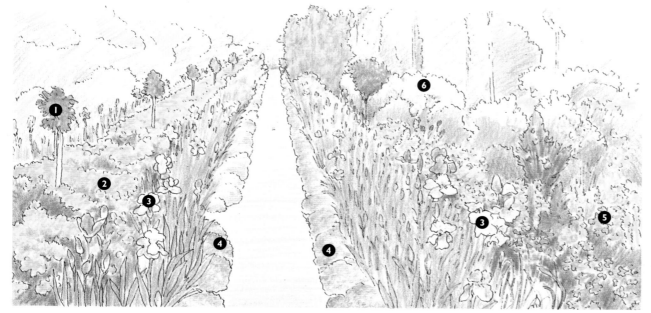

PLANT LIST

1 Standard roses
2 *Ergsimum hieracii folium*
3 Tall bearded iris
4 *Lobularia maritima* 'Royal Carpet'
5 *Cheiranthus cheiri*
6 *Hesperis matronalis*

Adding to the perfume of the wallflowers is the white-flowered form of dame's violet, *Hesperis matronalis,* with its head of massed small flowers. Once their flowers are over, they may seed, but will probably be cut back to allow the leafy rosettes to establish well for the following year's flowering.

To give the border height, there are regularly-spaced and very trimly-shaped standard hybrid tea roses that will flower on their round pom-pom-shaped heads in summer. All these plants, with their different colours and very different shapes and heights, planted out so repetitively, present a seemingly infinite perspective. Later, when the spring flush of flowering is over in this long border, the lobularia flowers will be cut off, probably in a back-breaking shearing over with secateurs, and once it has recovered, the foliage will continue to edge the path.

The iris stems and foliage will have to be cut back to a traditional fan shape. The iris root or rhizome which rests just on the soil surface, will be able to bake in the summer sun, unshaded by the foliage of other plants, building up its resources for future spring flowering. The scented wallflower in this border is treated as an annual spring bedding plant; it will later be replaced by a similar summer bedding plant.

Below: Lobularia maritima *(syn.* Alyssum maritumum *'Royal Carpet' spills across the gravel path, tall bearded blue and white iris, a fragrant mass of Siberian wallflowers, scented wallflowers and* Hesperis matronalis *provide the spring colour within the border.*

Summer Interest

Flowers that make pools of colour and shafts of sunlight over a long period are the most popular choice for pleasing effects in a stately summer border. To achieve this there is a wide choice of herbaceous perennial and annual material.

Using plants that offer either vertical or horizontal colour, you can vary the pace of the border's planting. Here the wide, flat heads of closely-packed flowers of *Achillea* 'Cloth of Gold' sway on long stalks above the felt-like, slightly aromatic leaves to make a burst of sunlight-yellow. The streak of yellow is repeated through the border, sometimes with similar plantings of achillea or with sunny-coloured but differently shaped flowers, such as *Verbascum* 'Gainsborough'. The candelabra-like flower stems of the verbascum offer a different shape, but a similar block of colour, and make a

break between the busier or more varied colours and hues of its neighbouring plants.

Lowering the height, and thus the focal level, is a swathe of salmon and rosy pink Peruvian lilies, *Alstroemeria ligtu* hybrids. Lily-like, and with their foliage playing hardly any part in the planting, they tumble forwards in the border, separating the yellows and blues. Just as you have taken in the change of height, it rises again, this time with the stately mauve-pink flowers of *Salvia turkestanica* and the deep blue of *Delphinium* 'Fenella'. Holding the line of the blue

flowers, but moving lower in height are clumps of borage and the starry blue of *Anchusa*. *Papaver* 'Mrs Perry', with shapely foliage, holds the front of the border at this point.

The continuity of colour and rhythmic alteration of height hold your attention and demand you shift your gaze, but at a measured and relaxed pace.

A herbaceous border, such as this, can never be described as low maintenance, as there is always a plant that needs deadheading, tying back or staking. Achillea and delphinium in particular should be staked, especially in exposed sites. It is

best to put the stakes or supports in place at the planting time or in spring each year, before the plants have begun to grow away. Then, when they do need the support, they will have grown into it and you will hardly see that it is there.

At its best between June and September, a summer herbaceous border is packed with more than just the plants you can see at any one moment during the season. This allows for some to come to maturity, and then when their blooms are spent, their place is taken, centre stage, by a plant that has been waiting in the wings.

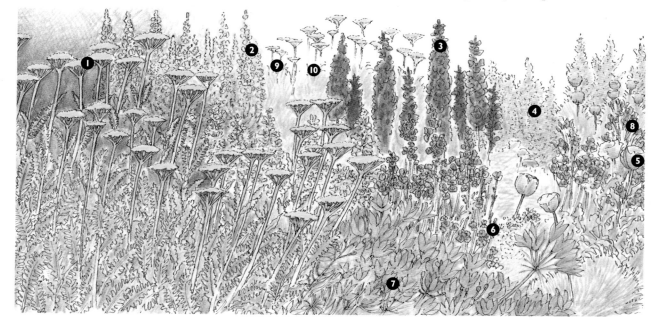

PLANT LIST

1 *Achillea* 'Cloth of Gold'
2 *Verbascum* 'Gainsborough'
3 *Delphinium* 'Fenella'
4 *Salvia turkestanica*
5 *Papaver* 'Mrs Perry'
6 *Anchusa azurea*
7 *Alstroemeria ligtu* hybrids
8 *Penstemon* 'Sour Grapes'
9 *Salvia uliginosa*
10 *Gaura lindheimeri*

In this border the dancing blue flowers of *Salvia uliginosa* and the delicate, butterfly-like flowers of *Gaura lindheimeri*, wait their turn at the base of giant cardoons, planted through the border. To hold the blues and white of the flowers, and combine them with the grey of the cardoon foliage, *Penstemon* 'Sour Grapes', sparkles to life at the front of the border.

Below: Achillea *'Cloth of Gold' and* Verbascum *'Gainsborough' provide the sunlight, while lighter shades of mauve come from* Salvia turkestanica *and* Papaver *'Mrs Perry', making softer accents. Deep blue blocks of colour are the offerings of* Delphinium *'Fenella' and anchusa, while a flame of salmon and rosy pinks light the front of the border.*

Late Summer Border

As late summer turns into mellow autumn, the colours in the border seem to imitate the tawny colours of foliage, russet fruits and orange vegetables. Even the glow of autumn sunsets and misty early mornings finds an echo in the border.

One group of flowers in particular that fills the colour gap between summer and winter comes from the daisy family – *Compositae*. Once known under such familiar names as chrysanthemum, they now belong to several genera whose names are as mellifluous and honeyed to roll off the tongue as the season itself. Dendranthema, argyranthemum and aster are among their number, with a range of bronze, yellow, mauve, white and ruddy flowers. The most important contribution this range of perennials makes to the autumn border is to maintain colour and interest for as long as possible beyond the full splendour of summer.

Mostly hardy, this group of flowers needs full sun or part-shade to grow well. Well-drained, enriched soil is best for them, but in dry summer seasons, they will need watering to prevent fungal outbreaks. With many species and cultivars growing to a considerable height and carrying flowers on every stem, they are bulky characters that need space for their tawny display to look its best. To keep them from flopping forward dramatically, they should be supported early on in their growing season.

Flowering over a long period, they need deadheading regularly, with their stems cut back to allow for new flowers on shorter spurs. Asters with their smaller, less densely packed flowerheads make a soft focus. In this planting, penstemons, the butterfly-attracting *Sedum spectabile* 'Brilliant' and the hybrid Japanese anemone, *Anemone* x *hybrida* 'Bressingham Glow', relieve the emphasis on asters and dendranthema.

Some forms of Michaelmas daisy, such as the modern *Aster novi-belgii* hybrids, are prone to mildew and insect attack and will need regular spraying with a fungicide. If the plants suffer badly, it is best to cut out affected stems, water well and continue the spraying regime.

Here they are planted together in a border that is more a demonstration garden, showing the range of colours available. In your own border, they can be combined and colour-coordinated with other late-

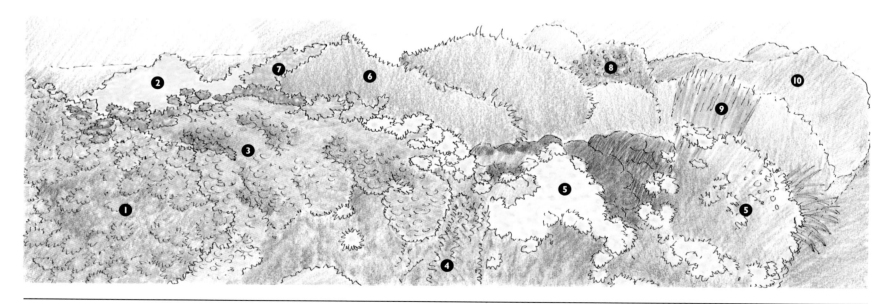

flowering autumn dazzlers including the white-flowered *Anemone japonica* 'Honorine Jobert' and the sunny yellow-flowered *Rudbeckia* 'Goldsturm'. The white-flowered *Achillea ptarmica* 'The Pearl' and *Campanula lactiflora,* with its branching flower stems in blue, white and sometimes pink blooms, are also good choices to prolong the flowering of the late summer border into autumn.

For the foreground, instead of sedum and penstemon, substitute hostas. *Hosta* 'Honeybells' and *H.* 'Green Fountain' provide particularly glowing foliage and useful flowers. For the background, the tall *Cephalaria gigantea* makes a bold display.

Left: *Their pink-mauve flowers blending so well together, the iceplant* Sedum x spectabile *'Brilliant' and* Dendranthema *'Raquel' provide colour at the front of the border over a long period during the autumn.*

Below: *At the Royal Horticultural Society Garden, Wisley, England, the late autumn border holds its own mellow display with Japanese anemone, penstemons, dendranthema and asters.*

Winter Shades

Even in winter's depths there are shrubs and herbaceous perennials that will lighten the gloomiest of days and bring the border to life.

Now that summer and autumnal abundance are past, the border can no longer depend on flowers alone for its richness of colour. Instead, bark, stems, foliage, berries, hips and seedheads, as well as the evergreen framework of hedges, are the factors that impress during this season.

Conifers, in a range of green, gold and even blue needle colour, such as x *Cupressocyparis leylandii* 'Castlewellan', together with box, holly, privet and yew, provide the specimen plantings, as well as hedging and edging for the winter garden. But for flaming, glowing colour, the winter stems of dogwood offer the brightest focus. Depending on form, there are stems in many shades of yellow-green and deep red. To ensure that they make the maximum impact, the plants should be stooled or cut back in spring, once their winter display is over. This encourages the growth of new stems throughout the season that will make the display so good the following winter, once their leaves have fallen.

Good stem colour is also available from the ghost bramble, *Rubus cockburnianus* and *Rubus biflorus,* which make a frosty white tracery if planted in the border. Cut back in spring to encourage new growth, and to keep the plants in hand, although the ghost bramble is not as vigorous as the hedgerow bramble.

If there is space in the garden for trees, within or near the border, maples and birches offer a wonderful range of bark colours and textures.

In a winter border, the most important effect is that of light. In this border, the glow of ground-hugging ivy, *Hedera helix* 'Sagittifolia Variegata', lights the foreground. Moving upwards, the flower bracts of *Helleborus foetidus* take the brightness above their glossy, toothed leaves to the linear stems of the dogwoods, *Cornus alba* 'Sibirica' and *C. stolonifera* 'Flaviramea'.

For floral effects, winter-flowering heathers, such as *Erica*

Left: *Flaming fiery colours of witch hazel,* Hamamelis x intermedia *'Jelena' are criss-crossed by the frosty stems of the ghost bramble,* Rubus biflorus. *In the foreground the little blue stem grass makes its autumn red foliage display, while* Erica x darleyensis *and* Eranthis hyemalis *provide the floral effects.*

Opposite: *In the foreground, the variegated foliage of* Hedera helix *'Sagittifolia Variegata' makes a light carpet for* Erica carnea *'C. J. Backhouse'. Rising in a shimmering row above their dark green shining foliage, the flower bracts of* Helleborous foetidus *take the glowing colour effect to the linear stems of two dogwoods. The light lemon-green of* Cornus stolonifera *'Flaviramea' and the red stems of* Cornus alba *'Sibirica' should be cut to ground level in spring to ensure a good growth of new stems for next winter's show.*

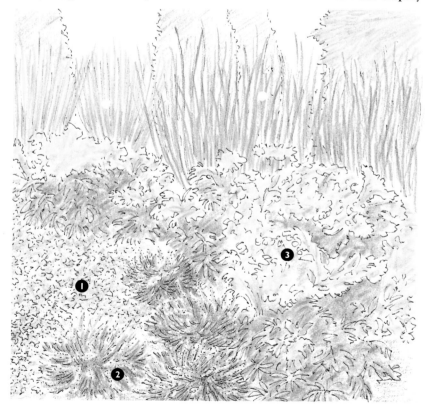

PLANT LIST

1 *Hedera helix* 'Sagittifolia Variegata'
2 *Erica carnea* 'C. J. Backhouse'
3 *Helleborus foetidus*

x *darleyensis* 'Darley Dale' or
E. carnea 'C. J. Backhouse' with
slightly differing mauve bell-
shaped flowers, provide good
ground cover and colour at the
base of trees and in the
foreground of a border.

Small trees and shrubs that
carry the floral effect through the
season are useful in the border.
The pink flowers of *Prunus* x
subhirtella 'Autumnalis' float
across this border, to make a
high level floral focus. In the
border there are many winter-
flowering viburnums such as
Viburnum x *bodnantense* with
its fragrant flowers. For the most
dazzling effects of all, witch
hazels offer a sparkling firework
display with their finely cut
flowers in shades of orange,
bronze and yellow.

Grasses, too, offer good
colour in winter. Some, such as
the little blue stem grass,
Schizachyrium scoparium, have
foliage and stems that change
colour. The spring and summer
blue-green of this grass's stems
and foliage turns red in autumn
and winter, and if planted fairly
densely, will make a strong
impact in an informal border.

Incidental effects are also
part of the winter display.
Seedheads, foliage, stems and
evergreen hedging and edging
are all transformed into a winter
wonderland when the first frost
occurs. Then the real bones and
framework of the garden are
highlighted by a delicate, but
ephemeral tracery.

Rose Border

Roses once used to be grown in separate borders devoted solely to their cultivation. In such a border, their summer glory could be admired, but after flowering, their thorny, bare stems and falling foliage in autumn looked unattractive.

Today in most domestic gardens the rose has come in from the cold and joined the party in the flower border with other plants. Old roses, in particular, need good herbaceous partners. Beautiful and fragrant they may be when in flower during high summer, but their season of beauty is short and soon they need the cluster of companions to disguise their own shortfalls.

However, while they are in flower there are so many herbaceous perennials, as well as annuals, that look attractive with them, that it is worthwhile choosing plants to complement and harmonize with the full fragrant blooms of the old roses. The range of plants that mix happily with roses is wide. Ground-covering, softly pastel-flowered geraniums such as *Geranium endressii, Geranium pratense* 'Mrs Kendal Clarke' and *Geranium phaeum* in its white or purple form, and *Alchemilla mollis* and primulas are good companions in season.

Tall spires of white or mauve foxgloves are the romantic's choice for a rose border, but for lower cover around the roses, the red, button-like flower of *Knautia macedonica* on long thin stems is attractive. Lamium with its streaky silver-leaved and pink-hooded flowers is good at ground level, while phlox in white or shades of pink and penstemon in pink, mauve and burgundy make a pleasing contribution at mid-height.

In this border, a romantic, painterly look has been created using delicately coloured annuals. The natural, simple flowers of corn cockle, *Agrostemma githago,* which grows to 95cm (3ft) and carries its pastel flowers on will-o-the-wisp stalks, rise above the white blooms of *Rosa* 'Iceberg'. Taking up the same pastel shades, but with a metallic finish, are the delicate papery blooms of the poppy, *Papaver rhoeas* 'Mother of Pearl'. Taller perennials such as *Thalictrum aquilegiifolium*, with its silvery foliage and frothy flowers, rise

The soft full blooms of Rosa *'Comte de Chambord' are enhanced by the edging of upright, blue spikes of* Lavandula *'Hidcote'.*

PLANT LIST

1 *Agrostemma githago*
2 *Papaver rhoeas* 'Mother of Pearl'
3 *Rosa* 'Iceberg'
4 *Thalictrum aquilegiifolium*

Right: *A painterly image is created by mixing corn cockle* Agrostemma githago *with the metallic poppies 'Mother of Pearl' and sowing them into the same border as delicately scented white* Rosa *'Iceberg'*.

even higher above the cultivated former cornfield flowers and roses. Hollyhocks, dame's violet and silene are also planted in the border and there are low-growing miniature roses to enjoy at a lower level in the mixed herbaceous border. Unlike old roses, the miniatures will flower over a long period, and some, depending on the species and type, offer small, often bronze-edged foliage.

Although the under- and inter-planting of roses with many other plants may make rose maintenance slightly more difficult, it is worthwhile for the longer flowering and the harmonious combinations which can be achieved. Spring bulbs, including crocus and snowdrops, and spring bedding such as aubrietia and violas will also suit the base of roses.

Roses will thrive if they can be mulched around their roots in spring, so avoid planting them too closely. If you need to spray during the growing season, avoid doing so on hot or windy days as you may damage the surrounding plants. Regular deadheading, and for old roses, cutting out of suckers and tying or shortening of whippy new growth, is necessary. Old roses also look attractive if their stems are arched and tied down to encourage more flower stems to break along the branch.

Foliage Border

Shape, colour, texture, architectural stature and delicate accents are just some of the ornamental offerings that plants grown more for their foliage than their flowers make to the border's beauty.

Sometimes the foliage effects come from plants that do not flower, or whose flowers are considered secondary, such as those of the plantain lily or hosta. In most cases, plants are chosen for a combination of their attributes, but those with good foliage earn their place in the border with great ease.

Evergreen foliage in its various colours and variegations makes up the permanent framework in the planting scheme. But plants such as ferns or hostas, whose fronds and leaves die down each year, offer an extra dimension. As they unfurl, the curving fronds or, in the case of hosta, rolled leaves, provide a sort of foretaste of their future size and texture. Later, when it is fully open and mature, hosta foliage makes an architectural impact. Ferns, so useful in shady, damp areas, offer a more delicate tracery.

Hostas are used here to make a bold, shapely block of colour and are available in a variety of leaf colours including golden, waxy-blue and variegated creamy white and green. They make a ruff-like edge to the border, shaping it and screening the feet of neighbouring plants.

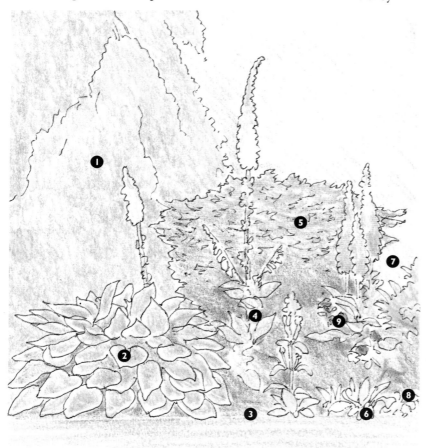

PLANT LIST

1 *Betula pendula* 'Youngii'
2 *Hosta fortunei* 'Aureomarginata'
3 *Sedum maximum* 'Atropurpureum'
4 *Digitalis purpurea* 'Alba'
5 *Acer palmatum atropurpureum*
6 *Stachys lanata*
7 *Iris foetidissima*
8 *Heuchera* 'Pewter Moon'
9 *Geranium* 'Johnson's Blue'

Above: *Layer on layer of hosta foliage crowds the edge of the border, making a strong architectural impact through the growing season.*

Opposite: *Although there are flowering plants in this section of the border, the main impact comes from the colour and shapes of the plant foliage.*

Good foliage effects can be had from plants with coloured leaves. Purple foliage from the smoke bush, *Cotinus coggygria*, purple sage, dwarf berberis clipped into formal shapes and the deep purples of acers all offer excitement and good foliage accents to the border. Likewise, golden foliage provides colour and texture. Some golden-leaved plants such as golden marjoram need to be grown in shade to protect their foliage from sun scorch.

Midway between green and gold, the lemony-green, furry leaves of *Alchemilla mollis* have an extra delight. At each leaf's centre there is a small depression, and this holds drops of dew, like a little cup. Once this dew was thought to be the purest for washing the face.

In autumn, the real show-stoppers in the border come out in force. Acers, grasses and small trees and shrubs take on their seasonal colour before losing their leaves. In this border, the purple-leaved *Acer palmatum atropurpureum* becomes fiery red and if it is planted so that it is backlit with the low-setting sun, it becomes almost incandescent. Some forms of *Acer palmatum* turn gold, others orange or red. Hostas lose the chlorophyll in their leaves and become an attractive yellow.

In this border, the foliage of the hostas cools down the purple of the acer and makes a good contrast for the small leaves of the weeping birch whose shape and bark are such strong features in the border. In autumn, the yellow of the hosta and red of the acer fight it out in the fading sunlight, glowing when all the herbaceous perennials have been cut back.

Circular Border

Sometimes the form of a border is as breathtaking as the plant combinations that fill it, and here the concept of a border in the round is taken beyond the limits of simply an island of plants.

PLANT LIST

1 *Clematis* 'Victoria'
2 *Miscanthus sinensis* 'Cascade'
3 *Veronica virginica*
4 *Phlox paniculata* 'Elizabeth Arden'
5 *Monarda* 'Balance'
6 *Tradescantia* 'Zwanenburg Blue'
7 *Delphinium* 'Piccolo'
8 *Thalictrum aquilegifiolium*
9 *Monarda* 'Scorpion'
10 *Galega hartlandii* 'Lady Wilson'

One of the many sitting places in the garden has a view over the inner pool area.

The inner triangular paths seem to be as curved as the outer path, but it is actually an illusion created by the circular retaining wall and the soft overspilling of the plants.

The photograph (right) shows a section of a circular border with a concentric circular path going nearly all the way round it. A concentric border, 1.8m (6ft) deep, planted with colours that correspond to those of the inner circle, lies inside the path. The circles are further emphasized by the 36-pole pergola circle and the circular retaining wall and pond terrace at the centre of the garden. The inner circular border, large in its scope but treated in essence like a long border that has been curved back on itself, is crossed by two sets of paths that make their own contrasting double triangular shape on the design.

On paper, the intellectual geometry of the border is easy to grasp and once it is filled with the plants, combined so well and on so many different levels, the extraordinary harmony and symmetry of the garden reveals an overlay of colour, texture and fragrance. There are nine distinct colour schemes in the inner circle. The starting point for the different colour schemes are the colours of the six *Buddleja davidii* planted at intervals on the inside of the pergola. They include 'Empire Blue', 'Pink Beauty', 'White Cloud', 'Black Knight', 'Summer Beauty' and 'Purple Prince'.

Each section is colour- co-ordinated with its neighbouring section, so that although the sections are distinct, they also

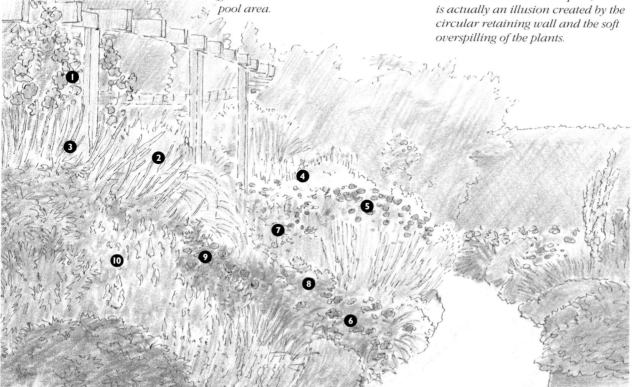

merge with each other. Plants in the outer sections are tall or medium-tall in height, so that as you curve along the circular path, outside the border, you can only see in to a certain level. Beyond the screen of plants is the rest of the border, but from the outside you can only guess at it, so retaining an element of surprise and interest in what is to come.

When you have criss-crossed the circular garden on the triangular paths, and walked the whole of the curved exterior path, there are numerous seats to find, as well as the sunken terrace at the garden's heart.

In this lower terrace there are some plants, mostly sun-loving Mediterranean varieties, grouped together in pots. The space in this area, the ability to look back at the border from an area without plants and the enjoyment of the small pool, make a tranquil garden.

As you walk along the curved outer path, only two borders are visible: the exterior one and the low- to medium-height plants of the outer section of the circular border. The taller plants at the foot of the pergola, and those that clothe the pergola itself, act as a screen to protect the privacy of the inner part of the garden.

Herbaceous Border

Herbaceous plants need to be chosen with care. Some well-behaved, no-fuss but showy plants are suggested here but there are many more. If in doubt, always find out whether the plant needs staking, how fast it spreads and whether it is prone to pests and diseases. Border phlox and perennial asters are prone to mildew, for example.

PLANTING A BORDER

After the initial planting, your border will need little care to keep it looking good.

1 Always make sure the pots have been watered before planting, otherwise the rootball may remain dry as water runs off it when watering after planting.

2 Space the plants out in their pots before you start to plant, as changes are easy at this stage. Try to visualize the plants at their final height and spread, and don't be tempted to plant them close together.

3 Knock the plant out of its pot only when you are ready to plant, so that the roots are not exposed unnecessarily to the drying air. Carefully tease out some of the roots.

4 Plant small plants with a trowel, large ones with a spade, and always work methodically from the back, or from one end of the border.

5 Return the soil and make sure the plant is at its original depth or just a little deeper. Firm it with your hands or a heel to expel large pockets of air in the soil.

6 Water thoroughly unless the weather is wet. Be prepared to water regularly in dry weather for at least the first few weeks after planting.

RELIABLE AND EASY PLANTS

It's worth including some of the following plants on your shopping list, but add others to suit the size of your border and to reflect your own taste.

Agapanthus (not for cold areas)
Alchemilla mollis (may self-sow so be prepared for seedlings)
Anemone hybrida
Anthemis tinctoria
Astilbe
Bergenia (a non-woody evergreen)
Catananche caerulea
Dianthus (a non-woody evergreen)
Dicentra spectabilis
Echinops ritro
Erigeron
Hemerocallis
Kniphofia
Liatris spicata
Lilium (not if lily beetles are a problem in your area)
Liriope muscari
Polemonium caeruleum
Schizostylis coccinea
Veronica spicata

GARDENER'S TIP

You can buy pot-grown herbaceous plants at any time of the year, but spring or autumn are the best times to plant.

Herbaceous borders will need less care if you plant large clumps of fewer kinds rather than lots of different ones that will need more frequent attention.

Romantic Border

Soft colours, fragrance, walls draped with swags of abundant blooms and beds filled with all the choicest of summer-flowering roses, peonies and iris are just some of the pointers to an informal and romantic style.

Although formal in their individual shapes, the character of the borders in this small walled garden is one of soft, romantic informality. Nearly all the wall space surrounding the borders is covered with climbers or wall plants such as *Ceanothus* 'Cascade', the white-flowered potato climber *Solanum jasminoides* and numerous clematis, all softening the texture of the hard landscaping. The impression is of a wall hung with generously draped, floral-printed textiles. The plants in each of the beds echo the colours of the "wall hangings"

becoming more like soft furnishings than plants.

In spring, the box-edged beds are filled with single colour tulips, pink double early flowering *Tulipa* 'Angelique' and *Tulipa* 'White Triumphator', as well as Barnhaven primulas and numerous irises including 'Jane Phillips', 'Black Hills' and 'Braithwaite'. In early summer, peonies, including 'Duchesse de Nemours', 'Mrs Perry' and 'Cedric Morris', and roses come to the fore. Lavender takes the floral fragrance forward until the lilies, including 'Journey's End' and 'Sans Souci', open their

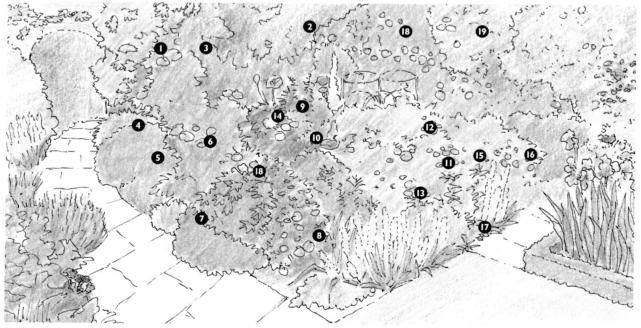

PLANT LIST

1 *Clematis*
2 *Ceanothus* 'Cascade'
3 *Abelia grandiflora*
4 *Senecio* 'White Diamond'
5 *Hebe* 'Red Edge'
6 *Rosa* 'Gertrude Jekyll'
7 *Lavandula* 'Hidcote'
8 *Rosa* 'Queen of Denmark'
9 *Papaver orientale* 'Mrs Perry'
10 *Papaver* 'Cedric Morris'
11 *Rosa* 'Magenta'
12 *Buddleja* 'Nanho Blue'
13 *Artemisia ludoviciana*
14 *Juniperus scopulorum* 'Skyrocket'
15 *Rosa* 'Reine Victoire'
16 *Rosa* 'Heritage'
17 *Sisyrinchium striatum*
18 *Rosa* 'Constance Spry'
19 *Rosa* 'Mme Albert Carrière'

sumptuous blooms to overwhelm with their beauty and fragrance.

The softness of the blooms and shapes of the old roses within the beds is contrasted with the tall upright flower spikes of foxgloves in white and purple, and the creamy yellow of *Sisyrinchium striatum*. The contrasting nature of the soft foliage of roses and lavender, and the spiky foliage of sisyrinchium, as well as the iris, keep the style from becoming too sentimental. Similarly,

anchoring the generous nature of the blooms in each of the beds, are plants with silver foliage. These plants are highly textured and they add to the already heady romance of the style, with their metallic colouring offering a glint of something rather more steely.

In keeping with the feel of the plants, the white-painted wrought-iron bench offer the garden visitor a view into a less hurried and more indulgent world. On the surface, such a style looks easy to maintain, but

behind the relaxed exterior there is a routine of regular maintenance.

In autumn, once plants die down they are cut back and tidied and manure is dug in around the plants, especially the roses. Old roses are cut back if their new growth is spindly, and lavenders are trimmed back, as are the box hedges. Clematis, depending on their flowering time, are cut back in autumn and spring and all climbing plants are tied in as they grow during the spring and summer.

Opposite: *The weathered statue of Flora is well-placed among sumptuous blooms of clematis, roses and geraniums.*

Below: *Evoking the essence of romance, of long summer nights and days. Fragrant roses, wall plants and pastel-coloured perennials combine well to make a very particular garden style.*

Meditation Border

Depending on the mixture of plants and style, borders have varying effects on our senses. Some combinations of plants excite and stimulate, while others offer peace and calm – such as this border, created to be a place of meditation.

To create the right ambience for quiet repose only a few plants are necessary. Their large-scale planting does not allow for the visual or mental stimulation in the same way that a vibrant and floriferous border does and it allows the mind to be free, as is the eye, to roam back and forth along the edges of the paths, and there is plenty of space for thoughts and stillness.

This tranquil garden room is framed by high evergreen hedges of yew, *Taxus baccata,* on two sides and the conifer, *Thuja plicata* on one side (the fourth side is a wall of Kentish ragstone bricks or old Kent reds). The aim is to play down the senses and the energy that borders normally offer. Entering the garden is like coming upon a quiet, cloistered green room, set apart from the rest of the world. Even the seat, which is stonework from an old churchyard, contributes to the feeling of other worldliness.

The linear shapes of the paths and beds also contribute to the peaceful nature of the border. The tranquil planting is achieved by using *Alchemilla mollis* to line the border and to spill out onto the paths. Inside the lady's mantle edging are masses of Irish ivy, *Hedera helix* 'Hibernica'. The glossy leaves of the ivy contrast well with the soft and furry texture of the alchemilla leaves. The ivy is planted at a density of 30 plants per side and they took nearly three years to cover the ground allotted to them. Once or twice a year, they attempt to over-reach the space, and that is the time when they are cut back with a sharp spade.

The alchemilla was planted at a similar density and it is prevented from flopping over the path by a support of 38cm (15in) canes (stakes) and garden twine. The flowers are cut off, which is a back-breaking exercise, in mid-July and new mounds of green leaves form. Although the alchemilla flowers offer a lime-yellow colour, it is the calm of the green ivy that predominates in this garden.

In the two box-edged rectangles at the end of the meditation garden, *Viola cornuta* is used as a ground cover and, when they are better established, the two variegated box plants in the centre are to be trained as topiary columns.

In the late evening when the sun is setting, its rays light up the axis of the paths right up to the stone seat, giving the impression that it is more altar than seat. In the early morning too, the meditation garden has its special effects as the dew, held in the cupped foliage of *Alchemilla mollis*, dances with light.

PLANT LIST

1 *Alchemilla mollis*
2 *Hedera helix* 'Hibernica'
3 *Buxus sempervirens*
4 *Viola cornuta*

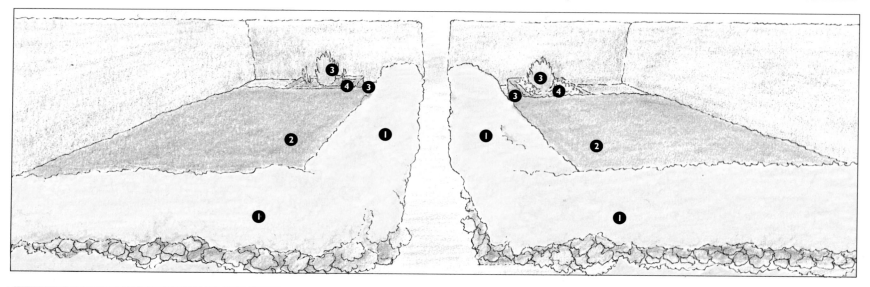

Right: *A simple plan of light and dark green plants, massed together, provides the inspiration for the meditation garden below.*

Below: *With no vibrant colours nor any dramatic changes in tempo or focus, the massed alchemilla and ivy plants allow for a calming of the senses and provide the precious time for quiet reflection.*

Mixed Border

Don't be too rigid about the plants that you use or mix in beds and borders. Herbaceous and non-woody evergreens can be useful ground cover around shrubs, while some shrubs, such as rue, can often be mistaken for herbaceous plants when used among them. Sometimes a mixed border containing both shrubs and herbaceous plants can bring out the best in both. If there are any gaps left, don't hesitate to sow bright annuals instead of leaving bare soil for weeds to colonize.

This very narrow bed shows how charmingly shrubs and herbaceous plants may be combined. However, if slugs are a problem in your garden, you may find the hostas an unwise choice.

Astilbe chinensis pumila

Hostas have been planted at the front of this mixed border. The height differential means that you have the benefit of two borders in one, as the hostas in front do not mask the tall plants behind.

Right: *Plants such as Astilbe and Potentilla add colour to mixed borders and can largely be left to their own devices.*

Potentilla 'Tangerine'

Right: *This narrow border is only about 1.2m (4ft) wide, but herbaceous perennials have been allowed to tumble over at the front to provide useful colour contrasts with the yellow shrub behind. This is the evergreen* Choisya ternata *'Sundance' with* Aster novi-belgii *'Audrey' (left) and 'Jenny' (right) and a pink chrysanthemum in the centre. In front is a pink-flowered rock rose that would have bloomed in late spring and early summer.*

Sensational Shrubs

A garden without shrubs would be inconceivable. They not only provide colour, both in their flowers and their foliage, but structure, shape, texture and scent. They also provide a natural habitat for wildlife, offering food and shelter as well as nesting sites. Gardening with shrubs can be a great adventure – they offer maximum reward for minimal effort – apart from a little pruning, most shrubs can be left to their own devices.

Left: Cotinus coggryia *with sun shining through its leaves.*

Above: *A newly established shrub border offers colour and textural interest.*

Designing with Shrubs

Of all aspects of gardening, designing a garden or border is probably one of the most exciting and, at the same time, one of the most difficult. It requires the ability to see things that are not yet there and to assemble whole groups of different plants in the mind's eye.

THE BASIC ELEMENTS

Most people have an awareness of the basic elements of garden design from other disciplines; most of us, for example, are adept at choosing what clothes to wear. We know what colours go together and what suits our shape and height. We are aware that certain fabrics add a touch of luxury to an outfit and that certain colours create a bright effect, while others produce a more subtle image. Similarly, most people are at least involved in decorating their home, where again the choice of colours, textures and finishes have become almost second nature over the years.

PERSONAL TASTE

The same principles we apply to choosing clothes and items for the home are used when designing in the garden, with many of the choices coming from an innate feeling for what the gardener likes and dislikes. This means that, like clothing, gardens are personal, with the fortunate result that each garden is different from the next. By all means be inspired by ideas seen in other gardens, but do not slavishly imitate another garden: the chances are that it will not work in your situation – the climate might be slightly different or the soil might be wrong. There are no definite rules with regard to design; there is no ultimate garden. However, there are a few guidelines that the experience of many centuries of gardening have produced, and it is worth bearing these in mind.

THE SHAPE OF THE BORDER

A border can be any shape, to suit the garden. Curved edges tend to create a more informal, relaxed feeling, while straight edges are more formal. The one point to remember is that the border should not be too narrow. Shrubs look better in a border where they have room to spread without being too crowded. A border that is only wide enough to take one shrub at a time has a habit of looking more like a hedge than a border. A wider border also allows the gardener to build up a structure of planting, which is more visually satisfying.

Left: *An attractive border filled with a mixture of shrubs and herbaceous plants designed to provide interest over a long period of time. Shrubs in flower include the blue* Ceanothus, *white* Olearia, *purple* Lavandula stoechas *and the white* Prostanthera cuneata, *with a purple rhododendron in the background.*

PART OF THE SCHEME

Shrubs need not be confined to borders – they can become part of the overall scheme of the garden. This is particularly important where the garden is small and there is little room for formal borders. Shrubs can be mixed with other plants or simply used in isolation, as focal points that draw the eye. They can be taken out of the ground and used in pots or other containers, or grown against walls and fences. Besides being part of the design, they can have a sense of purpose, perhaps to screen a dustbin (trash can) or to create a perfumed area near where people sit in the evening.

HEIGHT AND SHAPE

Shrubs have a lot to offer the designer as there is such a wide choice of attributes that can be applied to them. Shrubs come in all sorts of shapes and sizes, from tiny dwarf ones to those that are difficult to distinguish from trees. The general principle of design is to put the tallest at the back and smallest at the front. This must not be rigidly adhered to or the the border will begin to look like choir stalls. Bring a few of the taller ones forward and place some of the shorter ones in gaps between bigger ones. This makes the border more interesting and prevents the viewer from taking in the whole border at a glance.

The different shapes of the plants also add variety. Some are tall and thin, others short and spreading. The latter are particularly useful as ground cover and can be woven in and out of other shrubs as if they were "poured" there. Heathers are especially useful for this.

In this small garden, shrubs are not only used to make an interesting background of different textures, shapes and colours, but are also planted in containers to break up the foreground. To complete the picture, formal hedges hold the whole scheme together.

Right: *This attractive border builds up beautifully from the front but, at the same time, is not regimented as the heights vary along its length. It demonstrates well the effectiveness of differently-shaped shrubs and other plants while, at the same time, illustrating the importance of colour and leaf shapes.*

Mixing Shrubs

Shrub borders or shrubberies have died out as gardens have become smaller. In many ways, the border devoted to only shrubs would be a labour-saving form of gardening, but being able to mix in a few other plants helps to make it more interesting.

GROWING SHRUBS WITH PERENNIALS AND ANNUALS

Mixing shrubs and other plants creates a greater variety of different habitats in the garden for a greater range of plants. For example, there are many herbaceous plants, many coming from wooded or hedgerow habitats in the wild, that need a shady position in which to grow. Where better than under shrubs? Many of these, such as the wood anemone, *Anemone nemorosa*, appear, flower and die back in early spring before the leaves appear on the shrubs, thus taking up a space that would be unavailable later in the season once the foliage has obscured the ground beneath the shrub.

Herbaceous plants can also be used to enliven a scene where all the shrubs have already finished flowering. For example, if you have a number of rhododendrons, most will have finished flowering by early summer and will be comparatively plain for the rest of the year. Plant a few herbaceous plants between them and retain interest for the rest of the year.

Herbaceous plants also extend the range of design possibilities. For example, it might not be possible to find a shrub of the right height that blooms at the right time with the right-coloured flowers. One of

the thousands of hardy perennials may offer the perfect solution. Similarly, the combination of textures and shapes might not be available in shrubs, so look to see if there are herbaceous or annual plants that will help solve the problem.

In the early stages of the establishment of a shrub border or a mixed border, the shrubs are not likely to fill their allotted space. To make the border look attractive in the meantime, plant annuals or perennials in the gaps. These can be removed as the shrubs expand.

WOODLAND PLANTS FOR GROWING UNDER SHRUBS

Anemone nemorosa (wood anemone)
Brunnera macrophylla
Campanula latifolia
Convallaria majalis (lily of the valley)
Cyclamen hederifolium
Eranthis hyemalis
Euphorbia amygdaloides robbiae (wood spurge)
Galanthus (snowdrop)
Geranium
Helleborus (Christmas rose)
Polygonatum
Primula

This Lychnis chalcedonica *adds the final touch to a good combination of foliage. Without it, the grouping might seem dull compared with other parts of the garden in the summer.*

The geranium in the foreground is the right height and colour to match the roses and the ceanothus behind. It would be hard to find a shrub to fit in with this combination.

Left: *Sometimes, one startling combination acts as a focal point and draws the eye straight to it. This combination of the blue flowers of a ceanothus and the silver bark of the eucalyptus is extraordinarily beautiful. There are many such combinations that the gardener can seek and this is one of the things that makes gardening so satisfying and even, at times, exhilarating.*

Above: *A good combination of textures, shapes and colours is achieved here with the cardoon* (Cynara cardunculus) *providing interesting colour and structure, while the* Salvia sclarea *in the front provides the subtle flower colour.*

Planting Shrubs

There is nothing difficult about planting a shrub, except possibly making the decision as to where to plant it. One thing that must always be borne in mind is that shrubs *do* grow, and it is a common mistake to underestimate by how much. The result is that shrubs are often planted too close together and then the gardener is faced with the heart-rending decision as to which to dig out so that the others can continue to grow. Avoid this by finding out how big the plant will grow and allowing for this when planting. This means there will be gaps between the shrubs for the first few years but these can be temporarily filled with herbaceous perennials and annuals.

PLANTING CARE

If you are planting more than one shrub at a time, stand them all, still in their pots, on the bed in the places where you wish to plant them, so that you can check that they will all fit in and that the arrangement is a good one. Make any adjustments before you plant, as it does the shrub no good to be dug up and replanted several times because it is in the wrong place.

The actual planting is not a difficult process but looking after the plant once it is planted is important. Water it well until it becomes established. If the site is a windy one, protect either the whole bed or individual shrubs with windbreak netting, until they are firmly established. In really hot weather, light shading will help relieve stress on the plant as its new roots struggle to get enough moisture to supply the rapidly transpiring leaves.

PLANTING TIMES

The recommended time for planting shrubs is at any time between autumn and early spring provided that the weather allows you to do so. Planting should not take place if the weather is too wet or too cold or if the ground is waterlogged or frozen.

However this advice is basically for bare-rooted plants – that is, those dug up from nursery beds. Although container-grown plants are easier to establish if planted at the same time, it is possible to plant out at any time of the year as long as the rootball is not disturbed. If planting takes place in the summer, then avoid doing it during very hot or dry weather. The plants will need constant watering and protection from the effects of drying winds and strong sun.

1 Before you start planting, check that the plant has been watered. If not, give it a thorough soaking, preferably at least an hour before planting.

2 If the soil has not been recently prepared, fork it over, removing any weeds. Add a slow-acting fertilizer, such as bonemeal, and fork this in.

3 Dig the hole, preferably much wider than the rootball of the shrub. Place the plant, still in its pot, in the hole and check that the hole is deep enough by placing a stick or cane (stakes) across the hole: the top of the pot should align with the top of the soil. Adjust the depth of the hole accordingly.

4 Remove the plant from its pot, being careful not to disturb the rootball. If it is in a plastic bag, cut the bag away rather than trying to pull it off. Place the shrub in the hole and pull the earth back around it. Firm the soil down well around the plant with the heel of your boot and water well.

5 Finally, mulch all around the shrub, covering the soil with 7.5–10cm (3–4in) of bark or similar material. This will not only help to preserve the moisture but will also help to prevent weeds from germinating.

White frothy mounds of flowers are produced by Spiraea 'Arguta' *during the spring. Since it produces its flowers before many other shrubs come into leaf, it can be planted towards the back of the border where it will show up while in flower but then merge into the background for the rest of the year when it is not so striking.*

Moving a Shrub

The ideal, when planting shrubs, is to place them in the right position first time round, but, occasionally, it becomes necessary to move one. If the shrub has only been in the ground a few weeks, this is not a problem: simply dig around the plant, lifting it with as big a ball of earth as possible on the spade and move it to a ready-prepared new hole. Moving a well-established shrub requires more thought and planning.

1 If possible, root-prune the shrub a few months before moving, to encourage the formation of new fibrous roots. Water the plant well the day before moving it.

MOVING A SHRUB

If the move is part of a long-term plan, there may well be time to root-prune the shrub first, a few months before you intend to move it. This involves digging a trench or simply slicing a sharp spade into the soil around the shrub, to sever the roots. This encourages the shrub to produce fibrous feeding roots on the remaining roots and makes it easier for it to become established once it is moved.

Once you have moved the shrub, keep it well-watered and, as with all newly-planted shrubs, if it is in a windy situation, protect it with windbreak netting to prevent excessive transpiration. Shrubs that have been moved are vulnerable to wind-rock, so stake them firmly.

A shrub with a large ball of earth around its roots is very unwieldy to move. This can be a recipe for a back injury, so be very careful. Always get somebody to help, if possible. This will also ensure you don't drop the plant, which makes it far more difficult to re-establish.

2 Dig a trench around the plant, leaving a rootball that two people can comfortably lift. Sever any roots you encounter to release the rootball.

3 Dig under the shrub, cutting through any tap roots that hold it in place.

4 Rock the plant to one side and insert some hessian (burlap) sacking or strong plastic sheeting as far under the plant as you can. Push several folds of material under the rootball.

5 Rock it in the opposite direction and pull the hessian sacking or plastic sheeting through, so that it is completely under the plant.

6 Pull the sheeting round the rootball so that it completely encloses the soil and tie it firmly around the neck of the plant. The shrub is now ready to move. If it is a small plant, one person may be able to lift it out of the hole and transfer it to its new site.

7 If the plant plus the soil is heavy, it is best moved by two people. This can be made much easier by tying a bar of wood or metal to the trunk of the shrub or to the sacking. With one person at each end, lift the shrub out of the hole.

8 Prepare the ground and hole as for a new shrub and lower the transplanted shrub into it. Follow the reverse procedure, unwrapping and removing the sheeting from the rootball. Ensure the plant is in the right position and refill the hole.

Once the shrub has been replanted in its new position, water it thoroughly and mulch the soil around it. In more exposed positions place netting round it to prevent winds from drying the plant out and scorching it. It may also need protection from fierce sun. Moving a shrub in autumn or winter, as long as it is not too cold or wet, will allow it to become established in time for its first summer.

Staking a Standard Shrub

In a well protected garden or in a border where a new shrub is surrounded by other supportive shrubs or plants, it may be unnecessary to stake, but where the wind is likely to catch a shrub it is important to stake it until it is established.

SHORT AND TALL STAKING

The aim of staking a shrub is to allow the new roots to move out into the soil while anchoring the plant firmly. If the wind rocks the plant, the ball of soil that came with the plant is likely to move as well, severing the new roots that are trying to spread out into the surrounding soil. The modern technique for staking trees and shrubs is to ensure that the base of the shrub is firmly anchored, preventing the rootball from moving, while the top is free to move in the wind, which will strengthen it. Thus, only a short stake is required, with a single tie about 25cm (10in) or so above the ground. If the shrub is top-heavy – for example, a standard rose – it is important to use a taller stake and tie it in two places, or the top of the shrub may well snap off. Unlike other forms of staking, this support should be left in place rather than removed once the shrub is established.

USEFUL SUPPORTS

A number of items can be used as stakes for shrubs. You can buy a variety of specially-designed plastic or wire supports from your local garden centre ; alternatively, twiggy sticks pushed into the ground around a plant can be effective. Use short garden canes for fragile plants, tall canes (stakes) for plants with tall, flowering stems and thicker pieces of wood for shrubs that need a stronger or more permanent means of support.

Both short and tall staking is best done when first planting the shrub so that the roots can be seen. If the stake is knocked in afterwards it is likely to sever unseen roots. If it becomes necessary to stake a mature or already-planted shrub, use two stakes set some way out on either side of the shrub, with a crossbar to tie the stems to.

STAKING A STANDARD SHRUB

1 For a standard shrub, make sure you use a strong stake. It should be of a rot-resistant wood or one that has been treated with preservative. Firmly place the stake in the planting hole, knocking it into the soil so that it cannot move.

2 Plant the shrub, pushing the rootball up against the stake, so that the stem and stake are approximately 7.5–10cm (3–4in) apart.

3 Firm the soil down around the plant with the heel of your boot.

4 Although it is possible to use string, a proper rose or tree tie provides the best support. Fix the lower one 15cm (6in) above the soil.

5 Then fix the second tie near the top of the stake, just below the head of the standard shrub.

6 Water the ground around the plant thoroughly and mulch with a chipped bark or similar material.

Regularly check the ties, to make certain they are not too tight; otherwise they will begin to cut into the wood as the stems of the shrub increase in girth.

Ground Cover

One of the most valuable uses of shrubs is as ground cover. Ground cover is what its name implies, planting that covers the ground so that no bare earth shows. While there are obvious visual attractions in doing this, the main benefit is that ground cover prevents new weeds from germinating and therefore reduces the amount of maintenance required.

PLANTS FOR COVER

In the main, ground-covering plants are low-growing, but there is no reason why they should not be quite large as long as they do the job. Large rhododendron bushes form a perfect ground cover, for example, as nothing can grow under them.

Some ground-covering plants have flowers to enhance their appearance – heather (*Erica* and *Calluna*) and *Hypericum calycinum*, for example – while others depend on their attractive foliage – ivy (*Hedera*) and euonymus are examples.

Ground cover will not stop established weeds from coming through; it does inhibit the introduction of new weeds by creating a shade that is too dense for the seed to germinate and that starves any seedlings that do manage to appear.

SHRUBS SUITABLE FOR PLANTING AS GROUND COVER

Arctostaphylos uva-ursi
Calluna vulgaris (heather)
Cistus (rock rose)
Cornus canadensis
Cotoneaster dammeri
Cotoneaster horizontalis
Erica (heather)
Euonymus fortunei
Hebe pinguifolia 'Pagei'
Hedera (ivy)
Helianthemum nummularium
Hypericum calycinum
Juniperus communis 'Repanda'
Juniperus sabina
   'Tamariscifolia'
Juniperus squamata
   'Blue Carpet'
Lithodora diffusa
Pachysandra terminalis
Salix repens
Vinca minor (periwinkle)

A solid block of gold shimmers above the soil. The evergreen Euonymus fortunei *'Emerald 'n' Gold' makes a perfect ground cover plant because it is colourful and dense.*

Prostrate conifers perform well. One plant can cover a large area and the texture and colour of the foliage makes it a welcome feature. They have the advantage of being evergreen and thus provide good cover all year round.

The periwinkles, especially Vinca minor, *make good ground cover. They are evergreen and will thrive in quite dense shade. However, if you want them to flower well it is better that they are planted more in the open.*

In the rock garden, the ground-hugging Salix repens *rapidly covers a lot of territory. It needs to be cut back from time to time, to prevent it from spreading too far.*

Above: Lithodora diffusa *is one of those plants that straddles the divide between hardy perennials and shrubs, because it is classed as a subshrub. It provides a very dense ground cover for the rock garden and, in the early spring, makes a wonderful carpet of blue.*

Right: *By late summer and into autumn, much ground cover is looking a bit tired and jaded. However,* Ceratostigma plumbaginoides *is still flowering and presents a good choice of plant for providing colour at this time of year.*

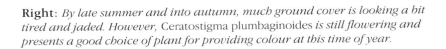

Dwarf Shrubs

In the small garden and the rock garden, dwarf shrubs are much more in keeping with the scale of things than large plants. Being small, they also have the advantage that you can grow more varieties in the same space.

USING DWARF SHRUBS

Dwarf shrubs are treated in exactly the same way as the larger ones. They can be used by themselves in rock gardens or separate beds. Or they can be mixed in with taller shrubs. Many dwarf shrubs make very good ground cover plants. They can also be used in pots and other containers, either in groups or as specimen plants.

ROCK GARDEN SHRUBS

Very small dwarf shrubs are usually grown in rock gardens and even in troughs. Many are no more than a few centimetres high. They too are grown for their foliage and flowers. Some are perfect miniatures of larger plants. *Juniperus communis* 'Compressa', for example, could be a large conifer seen through the reverse end of a telescope.

For those who like bright colours, nothing could fit the bill better than Genista lydia. *In spring, it is absolutely covered with a mound of bright, gold-coloured, pea-like flowers. It looks good tumbling over rocks or a wall but can be used anywhere. It requires very little attention.*

Most ceanothus are large shrubs, often needing wall protection to bring them through the winter. C. 'Pin Cushion' is a miniature version for the rock garden. It still retains both the good foliage and the blue flowers that attract so many gardeners to this group of plants and has the advantage that it needs little attention.

As well as the more common dwarf shrubs, there are many varieties that will appeal to those who may want to start a collection of unusual shrubs: x Halimiocistus revolii (x H. sahucii) is one example. This beautiful plant spreads to form a mat of dark green leaves, dotted with white flowers in midsummer. It likes a well-drained soil but needs little attention.

The rock rose (Helianthemum) is one of the great joys of dwarf shrubs. There are many different varieties, with a wide range of colours, some bright while others are more subtle. The colour of their foliage also varies, from silver to bright green. Rock roses are suitable for the rock garden, raised beds or mixed borders. They spread to make large sheets, but rarely get tall. They need to be sheared over after flowering, to prevent them from becoming too sprawling.

There are a number of dwarf willows of which this, Salix helvetica, *is one of the best. It forms a compact shrub with very good silver foliage. It can be used in a rock garden or wherever dwarf shrubs are required. It looks especially good with geraniums – G. sanguineum, for example – growing through it. This willow needs very little attention.*

Left: *The group of dwarf conifers growing in this rock garden is* Juniperus communis *'Compressa'. This is one of the very best varieties of dwarf conifer, because it never grows very high, usually not more than 45cm (18in), and it takes many years to reach that height. Their slow growth rate means they are useful for alpine troughs and they have the advantage that they need very little attention.*

Above: *Using a few dwarf shrubs and conifers in a trough or sink adds to the height of the planting, giving it more structure and interest than if it were simply filled with low-growing alpine plants.*

Shrubs with Coloured Foliage

Most foliage is green, but the number of different greens is almost infinite. A lot can be done by careful arrangement of these various greens, but even more can be achieved by incorporating into the garden the large number of shrubs that have foliage in other colours besides green.

VARYING SHADES OF GREEN

Leaves need green chlorophyll to function, so they are never completely devoid of green, even though another colour may dominate. Yellow foliage still has a green tinge to it and purple likewise. Scrape back the hairs that make a leaf look silver or grey and there will be green. When grown out of the sun, particularly later in the season, this green becomes more apparent. Occasionally, stems bearing paper-white leaves appear on some shrubs.

MAINTAINING THE COLOUR

Purple leaves need the sun to retain their colour. Silver-leaved plants must always be grown in the sun; they will not survive for long in shade. Golden and yellow foliage often need a dappled shade – too much sun and the leaves are scorched. However, too much shade and the leaves turn greener. Avoid the midday sun.

Growing coloured-leaved shrubs is the same as for any other shrub – they need the same pruning. If a reversion occurs, this must be cut out.

As well as shrubs with single-coloured foliage, there are shrubs with foliage in two or more colours, known as "variegated" foliage, and shrubs which are planted for their autumn foliage – just two other interesting aspects of the colouration of shrubs.

SILVER FOLIAGE

Caryopteris x *clandonensis*
Convolvulus cneorum
Elaeagnus 'Quicksilver'
Hebe pinguifolia 'Pagei'
Hippophaë rhamnoides
Lavandula angustifolia
Pyrus salicifolia 'Pendula'
Rosa glauca
Salix lanata
Santolina chamaecyparissus
Santolina pinnata neapolitana

BETTER FOLIAGE

Coppicing or pollarding some coloured-leaved shrubs improves the quality of the leaves. It produces bigger and often richer-coloured foliage. Cut the plants back in the early spring, before growth begins. They will quickly regain their original size but the foliage will be bigger and better. *Sambucus* (elder), *Cotinus* (smoke tree) and *Rosa glauca* all benefit from this.

Rosa glauca has the most wonderful glaucous (grey- or blue-green) foliage with a purple-blue tint which contrasts well with the pink and white flowers. The foliage is improved by coppicing or pollarding.

COPPICING

1 Cut back the stems to very short stubs, leaving perhaps one or two buds on each stem to grow. The treatment looks a bit drastic, but a mass of new shoots will be produced during the summer, with colourful stems in winter.

2 A head of brightly-coloured branches will stem from the base in the winter as on this *Salix alba* 'Britzensis'.

Left: *Silver foliage is very desirable. All silver plants need a sunny position and a well drained soil, this cotton lavender,* Santolina chamaecyparis *being no exception. Shear the plant over in the spring, just as new growth begins, to keep it compact. Many gardeners also prefer to cut off the flowering stems, because they find the sharp yellow flowers too harsh.*

Below: *This shrub grows in areas that are too dry to grow many other plants. It has had many names over the years and is now called* Brachyglottis *(Dunedin Group)* 'Sunshine'.

The silver leaves of plants can often set off the colour of their flowers beautifully. Here, the silvery-grey leaves of Helianthemum *'Wisley Pink' are a perfect foil for its pink flowers. Shear over the plant after flowering, to keep it from becoming straggly.*

A favourite silver-leaved shrub is Elaeagnus *'Quicksilver' which in the sunshine looks like burnished pewter. During the spring, the leaves are supplemented by masses of small, pale primrose-yellow flowers which, as well as being attractive, have a delicious scent that wafts all over the garden.*

Shrubs with Variegated Foliage

There has been a steady increase of interest in variegated shrubs and today they can be seen in one form or another in most gardens. This increase of interest is welcome, because it has stimulated the search for more types of variegated plants and now there are many more from which to choose.

TYPES OF VARIEGATION

Most variegations in shrubs are gold, followed very closely by cream and white. These have the effect of lightening any group of plants they are planted with. They are particularly useful in shade or in a dark corner, because they shine out, creating interest where it is often difficult to do so. Other colours include different shades of green. Again, these have a lightening effect. On the other hand, variegation that involves purples often introduces a more sombre mood. Sometimes, there are more than two colours in a variegation and this leads to a sense of gaiety, even if combined with sombre colours.

When looked at closely there are several different patterns of variegation. From a distance the differences blur and the leaves just register as variegated, but if you get closer you can see how the variegation can alter the appearance of the leaves. In some cases, it is the edges of the leaves that are variegated, sometimes as a ribbon and in others as an irregular margin, perhaps penetrating almost to the centre of the leaves. Another common type is where the centre of the leaves are variegated. Sometimes this is an irregular patch in the centre and in others the variegation follows the veins of the leaf. Yet a third form of variegation is where the leaves are splashed with an alternative colour, as though paint has been flicked onto their surface. A final type is where the variegation appears as long parallel strips down the leaves.

All these are attractive and it is worth looking out for and collecting at least one of each type. The more one looks at this group of plants, the more fascinating they become.

SILVER AND WHITE VARIEGATION

Cornus alternifolia 'Argentea'
Cornus alba 'Elegantissima'
Cornus controversa 'Variegata'
Euonymus fortunei 'Emerald Gaiety'
Euonymus fortunei 'Silver Queen'
Euonymus fortunei 'Variegatus'
Euonymus japonicus 'Macrophyllus Albus'
Fuchsia magellanica 'Variegata'
Prunus lusitanica 'Variegata'
Rhamnus alaternus 'Argenteovariegata'
Vinca minor 'Argenteovariegata'

The variegated Weigela florida *'Albomarginata' is seen here against a spiraea. The white-striped leaves blend well with the white flowers of the spiraea in spring, and in summer the interest is continued because the weigela produces pink flowers.*

Left and below: *Use variegated leaves to draw attention to particular areas of the garden.*

Left: Rhamnus alaternus *'Argenteovariegatus', as its name implies, has a silver variegation. This is present as stripes down the margins of the leaves and sets the whole shrub shimmering. It can grow into quite a large shrub, up to 3.5–4.5m (12–15ft) high.*

CUTTING OUT REVERSION IN SHRUBS

Variegation is an abnormality that comes about in a number of different ways. Frequently, the process is reversed and the variegated leaves revert to their original green form. These green-leaved stems are more vigorous than the variegated ones, because they contain more chlorophyll for photosynthesis and thus produce more food. If these vigorous shoots are left, they will soon dominate the shrub and it may eventually all revert to green. The way to prevent this is to cut out the shoots as soon as they are seen.

Above: *Green-leaved shoots have appeared in this* Spiraea japonica *'Goldflame'. If left, they may take over the whole plant. The remedy is simple. Remove the affected shoots back to that part of the stem or shoot where the reversion begins.*

Shrubs with Fragrant Foliage

There are a surprising number of shrubs with fragrant foliage. Some fragrances might not be immediately apparent, because they need some stimulant to produce it. Rosemary, for example, does not perfume the air until it is touched. Some of the rock roses (*Cistus*) produce a wonderfully aromatic scent after they have been washed with rain. Similarly, the sweet-briar rose (*Rosa rubiginosa*) and its hybrids, such as 'Lady Penzance', produce a delightful scent after rain.

WHERE TO PLANT

It is a good idea to plant shrubs with aromatic foliage near where you walk, so that when you brush against them they give out a delicious aroma. Few gardeners can resist running their fingers through rosemary foliage as they pass, and a lavender path is a pleasure to walk along, because the soothing smells of the herb are gently released along the path as you go.

For hot, dry gardens, *Camphorosma monspeliaca* is one of the best plants to grow, because it smells of camphor when the new shoots are touched. Thyme planted in the ground may be too low to touch with the hands, but it releases its fine fragrance if it is walked on in paving. Many conifers have a pleasant, resinous smell when they are rubbed. Juniper, in particular, is good.

Above right: *While it is sensible to plant thyme used for the kitchen in a more hygienic position, it does make a wonderful herb for planting between paving stones because when crushed by the feet it produces a delicious fragrance – and trampling on it does not seem to harm the plant. Beware of doing so in bare feet though, because there may well be bees on the thyme.*

SHRUBS WITH FRAGRANT FOLIAGE

Aloysia triphylla
Laurus nobilis (bay)
Lavandula (lavender)
Myrica
Myrtus communis (myrtle)
Perovskia
Rosmarinus (rosemary)
Salvia officinalis (sage)
Santolina

Right: Prostanthera cuneata *is an evergreen shrub that has leaves with a curious aromatic scent that is very appealing. In spring, and again in the summer, white, scented flowers are produced, which look very attractive against the dark foliage.*

One of the most beguiling of garden scents is that of rosemary, another culinary herb. If given a sunny well-drained site, this shrub will go on growing for many years, until its trunk is completely gnarled and ancient looking.

Culinary herbs are a great source of scented foliage. Sage, for example, has a dry sort of herby smell, which will usually evoke in the passer-by thoughts of delicious stuffing mixtures. This is an evergreen and provides fragrance all year round.

Right: Hebe cupressoides, *like so many plants, has a smell that is characteristically its own. It is a resinous type of fragrance that is reminiscent of the cypresses after which it is named.*

Shrubs with Berries and Fruit

It is not just the leaves and flowers that make a shrub worth growing. Flowering usually produces some form of seed, which is often carried in an attractive casing of fruit or berry. Two of the oldest fruiting shrubs to be appreciated, are the holly and the mistletoe.

THE APPEAL OF FRUIT

Fruit enhances the appearance of a shrub, especially if the fruit is brightly-coloured. Fruit bushes, such as gooseberries and redcurrants, can be fan-trained or grown as standards. Many have been specially bred to increase the range of colours. The firethorn *(Pyracantha)* can now be found with red, orange or yellow berries.

Berries and fruit are attractive to birds and other animals, so if you want to keep the berries buy a shrub like skimmia which will not be eaten by them.

Bear in mind that the male and female flowers may be on separate plants. Although they will both flower, only the female will bear fruit. So if you want fruit or berries, buy both.

BERRIED SHRUBS

Chaenomeles (japonica)
Cotoneaster
Crataegus (hawthorn)
Euonymus europaeus
Gaultheria (pernettya)
Hippophaë rhamnoides
Ilex (holly)
Ligustrum
Rosa
Symphoricarpos
Viburnum opulus

Left: *Pyracantha makes a very decorative display of berries in the autumn. There are several varieties to choose from, with the berry colour varying from yellow, through orange to red. The berries are not only attractive but good food for the birds.*

Below: *It is important when buying pernettyas* (Gaultheria mucronata) *that you buy both a male and a female plant to ensure that pollination takes place. One male will suffice for several females that carry the berries.*

Right: Piptanthus *is not totally hardy and is normally grown against a wall for protection. After its yellow flowers in spring, it produces these attractive pods, which decorate the plant in midsummer.*

Left: *When buying holly, ensure that you buy a berry-bearing form as not all carry them. Seen here in flower is* Ilex aquifolium *'Ferox Argentea'.*

Right: *Skimmias are good plants for the winter garden as they have very large, glossy berries, with the advantage that the birds do not like them, so they remain for a long period. Ensure you get a berrying form and buy a male to pollinate them.*

Below: *The cotoneasters produce a brilliant display of berries, as well as having attractive leaves and flowers. The berries are not too popular with birds and are often left until all the other berries have been eaten.*

Rose heps or hips provide an extension to the rose's season. The colour varies from variety to variety, with some being red and others orange, and some, such as R. pimpinellifolia, *bearing black berries.*

Shrubs for Topiary

Most shrubs are grown naturally. They may be cut back if they get too big, or trimmed if they are part of a hedge, but their natural shape is not generally altered. However, there is one class of shrub-growing in which the shape is drastically altered, so much so that it takes a close look to identify the plants involved. These are topiaries.

PRODUCING A SHAPE

Topiaries can be cut to any shape. They can be formed into abstract or geometrical shapes, such as balls, cones or pyramids, or something more intricate, perhaps depicting a bird, a person or even a teapot. There is no limit to what the imagination can produce.

Tight, slow-growing shrubs are the ones to choose for topiary, with yew and box being the best. Holly (*Ilex*), privet (*Ligustrum*) and box-leaf honeysuckle (*Lonicera nitida*) are also recommended. Several others can also be used, but they need a lot more attention to keep them neat.

The simplest topiaries are "carved" out of solid shrubs, particularly if they are yew or box, because these will easily regenerate and slowly fill out to their new shape. However, the most satisfactory way to produce topiary is to train the shrubs to their shape from the very beginning. A metal or wooden former or template helps with this. The shoots are tied in and trimmed as they grow, until the shrub has acquired the desired shape. Some formers are just a rough guide to the shape, intended to hold the main pieces in position, especially if

they are vulnerable, but others are shaped like the finished work and can be used as a trimming guide when the work is complete.

Topiaries can take several years to reach completion, so do not get too impatient. Several projects can be started in pots at the same time, so there is always something going on to keep the interest alive.

TOOLS FOR TOPIARY

Unless the topiary is on a large scale, avoid using powered tools. It is too easy to lose concentration or momentary control. Use hand tools which give you more control. For cutting thicker stems, especially in the initial training, use secateurs (pruners), snipping out one stem at a time. Once the shape has been formed, trim it over with normal hedging shears or a pair of clippers of the type usually used for sheep-shearing. The latter give excellent control, but can only be used for light trimming, such as removing the tips of new growth. If the topiary is made from a shrub with large leaves, use secateurs to avoid cutting the leaves in half, otherwise they will die back with a brown edge.

In this topiary a four-masted ship in full sail glides across the garden. Here, the complicated design is slightly obscured by other topiaries in the background.

This practical piece of topiary has a wooden seat worked into the bottom of the shrub, supported on a metal frame. A complete set round a table would be a novel feature for a barbecue or outdoor meal.

These simple shapes worked in box can be used to advantage in a wide variety of positions in the garden. They will take several years of dedication to produce, but the effort is definitely worth it.

Gardens do not always have to be serious: there is a sense of fun about this jolly witch, sitting around her cauldron with her cat and its mouse, which would cheer up anybody looking at it.

Topiary shapes can be as precise or as free as you wish. In this free interpretation of a simple windmill, cut from yew, you can sense the pleasure of the person who created it.

Glorious Climbers

Climbers can be used in many different ways. They can decorate buildings by covering the walls, transforming their appearance. This is particularly useful if the building is unsightly, such as a concrete garage, or if its lines need to be softened. Walls covered in plants in this way also provide an interesting backdrop for the rest of the garden. If they are grown on trellises, climbers can be used as boundaries, to provide privacy, or add screen cover.

Left: *Clematis provides a burst of colour – a beautiful backdrop to plant other shrubs against.*

Above: *Climbers can be trained to provide screens and shelter.*

Planting Climbers

There are so many different types of climbers that you are bound to be able to choose one that is suitable for any place in the garden. As always, though, the trick is to match up the plant and the planting position correctly.

CHOOSING A POSITION

Probably the most important thing to remember about planting a climber is that it is essential to pause and consider whether you are planting it in the right place. Once planted, with the roots spreading and the stems attached to their supports, it is very difficult to move a climber successfully. Once it has grown to its full size, if you realise that you have got the site wrong, you will have a choice of living with your mistake or scrapping the plant and starting all over again with another one. So, think carefully about the position of any climber you plan to introduce.

As well as considering how the climber looks in its intended position, there is a practical consideration. If you are planting against a wall or fence, the plant should be set a distance away, as the ground immediately adjacent to such structures is usually very dry. Similarly, if a pole or post has been concreted in or simply surrounded with rammed earth, it is best for the roots of your climber to be planted a short distance out and the stems led to the support with canes (stakes) or sticks.

Most plants should be planted at the same depth as they were in their pot or in the nursery bed (usually indicated by the soil line on the stem). The main exception is clematis, which should be planted 5cm (2in) deeper, so that the base of the stems is covered.

Mulching around the climber helps to preserve moisture and to keep the weeds down. A variety of methods can be used for mulching; any of them will be of benefit at this stage in helping the climber to establish itself quickly.

PLANTING TIMES

Traditionally, climbers were planted, when the weather allowed, between mid-autumn and mid-spring, but most climbers are now sold as container-grown plants and these can be planted at any time of the year, as long as the weather is not too extreme. Bare-rooted climbers have the best chance of survival if planted at the traditional time. Avoid planting any climber when the weather is very hot and dry, or when there are drying winds. In winter, avoid times when the ground is waterlogged or frozen.

1 Dig over the proposed site for the climber, loosening the soil and removing any weeds that have grown since the ground was prepared. If the ground has not recently been prepared, work some well-rotted organic material into the soil to improve soil texture and fertility.

2 Before planting, add a general or specialist shrub fertilizer to the soil at the dosage recommended on the packet. Work the fertilizer into the soil around the planting area with a fork. A slow-acting organic fertilizer is best.

3 Water the plant in the pot. Dig a hole that is much wider than the rootball of the plant. Place the soil evenly around the hole, so that it can easily be worked in around the plant. The hole should be away from any compacted soil, near a support and at least 30cm (12in) away from a wall or fence. Before removing the plant from its pot, stand it in the hole, to make certain that the depth and width are correct.

4 Place a cane (stake) or stick across the hole; the top of the rootball should be at the same level. Dig deeper or add soil to the bottom of the hole, as necessary, to bring it up to the correct height. Remove the plant from the pot, being careful that none of the soil falls away from the rootball. If the plant is in a polythene (plastic) container rather than a pot, cut the bag away rather than pulling it off. Holding the plant steady, pull in the soil from around the hole, filling in around the rootball. Firm as you go, with your hands, and then finally firm down all around the plant with your foot, making certain that there are no cavities or large air pockets.

5 Train the stems of the climber up individual canes to their main support. Tie the stems in with string or plastic ties. Even twining plants or plants with tendrils will need this initial help. Spread them out, so that they ultimately cover the whole of their support. Water the plant in well.

6 Put a layer of mulch around the plant, to help preserve the moisture and prevent weed growth.

Right: *The delicate bells of* Clematis viticella *hang suspended in mid-air.*

Using Climbers

A screen, whether a trellis or a hedge, will look more interesting throughout the year if other plants are used to liven it up. There is at least one climbing plant in flower during every month of the year and combining these with the screen will add an extra dimension.

ENHANCING SCREENS

Many of the plants that have the best screening qualities, are fairly consistent in their appearance all year round. While this means that the screen is highly effective, it can be a little monotonous. Climbers can be trained into it, to grow through and be supported by it. The flowers of the climber then peep through, with the plain foliage of the screen acting as a foil to their colour. A large screen can act as host to several climbers, with flowering periods that follow on from each other, so that the screen is colourful for most of the year. If the climber produces interesting seedheads as well as attractive flowers, you have even more scope. Such is the case with *Clematis tangutica*, the seedheads of which persist into winter.

Some climbers are more vigorous than others, so it is important to choose ones that are compatible with the plants forming the screen. The screen needs to be established and growing well before the climbers are introduced, or it will not be big enough to give the climbers the support they need.

Where the screen is made of timber or plastic, there is no need to wait before plants are placed against it, unless the wood has recently been treated with a wood preservative. Place the plants at the base of the screen, about 15cm (6in) out into the border, and use a cane to guide the stems towards the screen. As the stems begin to grow, weave them into the screen until they become established. Against a fence, the stems will need to be held in place with a system of wires and ties.

CLIMBERS TO GROW THROUGH TREES OR HEDGES

Akebia quinata
Aristolochia macrophylla
Celastius orbiculatus
Clematis alpina 'Frances Rivis'
Clematis macropetala 'Markham's Pink'
Clematis montana 'Elizabeth'
Clematis tangutica
Eccremocarpus scaber
Humulus lupulus 'Aureus'
Jasminum officinale 'Aureum'
Lathyrus latifolius
Lonicera x heckrotii
Passiflora caerulea
Rosa 'Kiftsgate'
Rosa 'Wedding Day'
Rosa 'Zéphirine Drouhin'
Tropaeolum speciosum
Vitis 'Brant'
Vitis coignetiae

Above: *Climbing roses have been trained over an arch, providing a screen from one part of the garden to the next, and creating an illusion of space.*

Below left: *Bougainvillea is a beautiful climber suitable if you garden in a warm country.*

Below: Clematis *'Perle d'Azur' provides a gorgeous splash of colour in the garden.*

TYING IN

1 Tie in the stems, spreading them out rather than tying them in a tight column of stems. If possible, spread at least some of the stems horizontally: this will not only produce a better wall or trellis cover but also encourage flowering.

At their peak, roses are amongst the loveliest of climbing plants. Here the rambling Rosa 'Excelsa' *is seen climbing up a pillar.*

Training Methods 1

Training is an important aspect of growing climbers. The general shape and well-being of the plant is taken care of by pruning, but how it is trained and where it is positioned are the most important things to consider when thinking about how your climber will look.

POSITIONING THE PLANT

The overall shape of the plant depends on its position. Those against a wall, for example, need to be tied in so that they do not protrude too far. Similarly, climbers over arches must be constrained on at least the inner side, so that they do not catch people walking through the arch. In some places, the plants can be left to show off the way they froth out over their supports. Vigorous climbers covering large trees, for example, are best left natural and untrained. Plants on trellis can be allowed a certain amount of ebullient freedom but they may also need some restraint.

SPREADING OUT THE STEMS

The climber's natural tendency is to go straight up through its support or host until it reaches the light. This frequently means that the climber forms a tight column without much deviation on either side. To make a good display the gardener should spread out the stems at as early a stage as possible so that the main stems fan out, covering the wall, fence or trellis. This not only means that the climber covers a wider area but also that its stems all receive a good amount of light, and thus flowering is encouraged at a lower level.

EARLY DAYS

At the time of planting it can be a good policy to train individual stems along canes (stakes) until they reach the wires, trellis or whatever the support may be. This will prevent them from all clustering together, making it difficult to train them at a later stage. Once the plant starts to put on growth, tie this in rather than tucking it behind the trellis or wires. This will enable you to release it at a later stage to re-organize it.

Above: *Tying in climbers under overhanging tiles can be a problem, because it may be difficult to find anchor points. A criss-cross arrangement of vertical wires can normally be fixed between the end of the eaves and the wall below the tiles; it makes an attractive feature in its own right. Here,* Rosa 'Zéphirine Drouhin' *is supported on wires.*

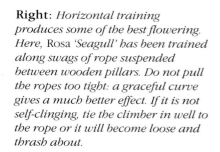

Right: *Horizontal training produces some of the best flowering. Here,* Rosa 'Seagull' *has been trained along swags of rope suspended between wooden pillars. Do not pull the ropes too tight: a graceful curve gives a much better effect. If it is not self-clinging, tie the climber in well to the rope or it will become loose and thrash about.*

Above: *A similar effect to climbing on ropes can be had by training the climber along poles attached to pillars. These form a rustic trellis and can look very effective, even during the winter when the climber is not in leaf. Here, Rosa 'Felicia' clambers over the structure.*

Right: *Vigorous climbers, such as rambling roses, some clematis and Russian vines, can be grown through trees. This is an easy way of training because, once the plant has been pointed in the right direction (by tying it to a cane (stake) angled into the tree), it can be left to its own devices. Make certain that the tree can support the weight of the climber, especially in high winds. Here Rosa 'Paul's Himalayan Musk' begins its ascent.*

Training Methods 2

ENCOURAGING FLOWERS

Once the climber has thrown up some nice long shoots, bend these over in a curving arc and attach them to the wires or trellis. From these will come new shoots which should be treated in the same manner so that the wall, fence or trellis is covered in an increasing series of arching stems. This method has the advantage, besides creating a good coverage of the wall, of making the plant produce plenty of flowers. The chemistry of the stems is such that flower buds are laid down on the top edge of the curving branches. Roses, in particular, benefit greatly from this method of training.

Curving branches over to encourage growth can also be used for climbers growing around tripods or round a series of hooped sticks, where the stems are tied around the structure rather than in a vertical position. This will encourage a much thicker coverage and many more blooms as well as allowing you to use vigorous plants in a limited space.

CHOOSING YOUR METHOD OF TRAINING

There are endless possibilities for training your climber. The choice will be affected by the constraints of the garden and personal choice. You may have something particular in mind that you want to construct, or you may have simply bought a climber you took a fancy to and now want to find a good place for it where it will flourish and add to the beauty of the garden.

TRAINING CLIMBERS OVER EYESORES

Climbers that grow quickly and produce lots of flowers are well-suited to covering unsightly features in the garden such as refuse areas, grey concrete walls belonging to a neighbouring property or ugly fences you are not allowed to pull down.

CLIMBERS TO TRAIN OVER EYESORES

Clematis montana
Clematis rehderiana
Fallopia baldschuanica (Russian vine)
Hedera (ivy)
Humulus (hops)
Hydrangea anomala petiolaris
Lonicera (honeysuckles)
Vitis coignetiae (crimson glory

CLIMBERS AND WALL SHRUBS FOR NORTH- AND EAST-FACING WALLS

Akebia quinata
Camellia
Chaenomeles (Japonica or ornamental quince)
Clematis 'Marie Boisselot'
Clematis 'Nelly Moser'
Euonymous fortunei
Hedera (Ivy)
Hydrangea anomala petiolaris
Jasminum nudiflorum
Lonicera x *tellemanniana*
Parthenocissus (Boston ivy or virginia creeper)
Pyracantha (Firethorn)
Rosa 'New Dawn'
Schizophragma

Above: *Rosa 'New Dawn' has a very long flowering period and has the added benefit that it can be grown on a north-facing wall. Here it has been tied into trellising on a wall.*

Left: *Climbers planted near doorways should be kept under control to avoid injury. Clematis, such as this C. 'Rouge Cardinal', are safer than roses as they have no thorns to catch the unwary.*

When roses are well-trained they can produce an abundance of flowers. The curiously coloured R. 'Veilchenblau', shown here growing up a wooden trellis, puts on a fine show during midsummer.

Above: *If possible, train climbers that have scented flowers near open windows, so that their fragrance can be appreciated indoors. Here* Rosa *'Albertine' is in full flower, while beyond is a wisteria that has finished flowering.*

Right: *To obtain extra height for the more vigorous roses a trellis can be erected on top of a wall. When well-trained they present a backdrop of colour against which to view the border in front and below.*

Growing Climbers on Wires

If a large area of wall is to be covered with non-clinging climbers, wires are the only realistic way of supporting them. Alternative methods, such as covering the whole wall with wooden trellis, are expensive and, if the wall is at all attractive, may detract from its appearance.

HOW TO USE WIRES

Wires can be used for most types of climbers, except for clinging ones, which should be able to cling directly to the surface of the wall. If the wires are too far apart, however, plants with tendrils may have difficulty finding the next wire up and may need to be tied in. Wires are also suitable for wall shrubs, which while not needing support, benefit from being tied in to prevent them from being blown forward by wind rebounding from the wall. Wires are unobtrusive and can be painted the same colour as the wall, to make them even less visible. Galvanized wire is best, as it will not rust. Rusty wires are not only liable to break but may also cause unsightly rust marks that may show up on the wall. Plastic-covered wire can be used but the coating is not as permanent as a galvanized one.

Do not use too thin a wire or it will stretch under the weight of the plants. If there is a chance that the wires will stretch, use bottle screws or tension bolts at one end. These can be tightened as the wire slackens.

1 Before it is fixed to wires, the young plant is loose and growing in all directions.

2 The wires are supported by vine eyes, which are fastened into the wall. Although you might be able to hammer them directly into soft brickwork, it is usually easier to drill a pilot hole.

3 If you are using vine eyes with a screw fixing, you need to insert a plastic or wooden plug in the wall first. The eye is then screwed into the plug. This type of vine eye varies in length, the long ones being necessary for those climbers, such as wisteria, that grow large and need wires further from the wall.

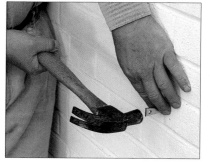

4 The simplest vine eyes are wedge shaped. Hammer them directly into the masonry and then feed the wire through a hole. While wedge-shaped eyes are suitable for brick and stone walls, the screw type are better for wooden fences and posts.

5 Thread the galvanized wire through the hole in the vine eye and wrap it round itself, forming a firm fixing. Thread the other end through the intermediate eyes (set at no more than 1.8m/6ft intervals and preferably closer) and then fasten the wire round the end eye, keeping it as taut as possible.

6 Curve over the long stems and attach them to the wires, using either plastic ties or string. Tie at several points, if necessary, so that the stems lie flat against the wall and do not flap about.

7 When all the stems are tied in, you should have a series of arches. Tying them in like this, rather than straight up the wall, covers the wall better and encourages the plant to produce flowering buds all along the top edge of the stems.

Climbers such as roses and clematis can be trained up the whole side of a house with wires. Here Rosa *'Madame Isaac Pereire' completely covers its wires.*

Fixing Trellis to Walls

Permanent wooden trellis, fixed to a wall, is not only a strong method of supporting climbers but also an attractive one. However, large areas of trellis can look overpowering, especially on house walls; wires are a better choice for these situations. Apart from self-clinging plants, which support themselves, any type of climber can be held up by such trellis.

HOW TO USE TRELLIS

The trellis should be well fixed to the wall, preferably with screws. It should be held a short distance from the brickwork or masonry, so that the stems of the climber can easily pass up behind it. This can be simply achieved by using spacers – wooden blocks will do – between the trellis and the wall.

If the wall is a painted one, or might need future attention for other reasons, it is possible to make the trellis detachable. The best method is to fix hinges along the bottom edge of the trellis. This allows the framework to be gently eased away from the wall, bringing the climber with it, so that maintenance can take place. The top is held by a catch. Alternatively, the trellis can be held in position by a series of clips or catches. This is not so easy to manoeuvre as one held on hinges, however.

Any shape of trellis can be used, such as square, rectangular or fan shaped, depending on the climber and the effect of the shape on the building or wall. It is possible to be more imaginative and devise other shapes, perhaps creating a two-dimensional topiary. The mesh can be either square or diagonal, the former being better with brickwork, because the lines of the trellis then follow those of the brick courses rather than contradicting them.

CLIMBERS FOR TRELLIS

Akebia
Clematis
Cobaea scandens (cathedral bells)
Humulus (hop)
Ipomoea (morning glory)
Jasminum officinale
Lathyrus odoratus (sweet peas)
Lonicera (honeysuckle)
Rosa (roses)
Solanum crispum
Solanum jasminoides
Tropaeolum (nasturtiums)
Vitis (vines)

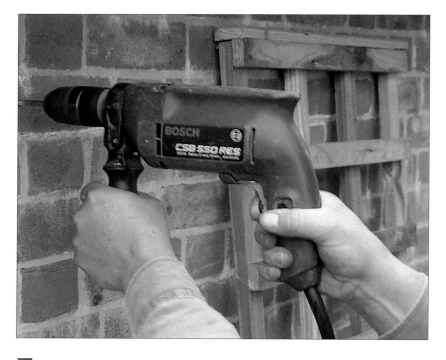

1 Take the trellis to the wall and mark its position. Drill holes for fixing the spacers and insert plastic or wooden plugs.

2 Drill the equivalent holes in the wooden batten (lath) and secure it to the wall, checking with a spirit level (carpenters level) that it is horizontal. Use a piece of wood that holds the trellis at least 2.5cm (1 in) from the wall. Fix a similar batten at the base and one halfway up for trellis above 1.2m (4ft) high.

3 Drill and screw the trellis to the battens, first fixing the top and then working downwards. Check that the trellis is not crooked.

4 The finished trellis should be tightly fixed to the wall, so that the weight of the climber, and any wind that blows on it, will not pull it away from its fixings.

The rose 'Dublin Bay' here climbs up a wooden trellis secured to the wall. This rose is fragrant and flowers over a very long period.

Growing Climbers on Netting

A cheap but effective method of providing support for climbers on a wall is to use a rigid plastic netting. This can be used for large areas but it is more effective for smaller climbers, where a limited area is covered.

HOW TO USE NETTING

Rigid plastic netting is suitable for covering brick or stone walls as well as wooden walls and panel fences. It can also be wrapped around poles or pillars, to give plants something to grip. You can string netting between upright posts, as a temporary support for annual climbing plants such as sweet peas, but it is not really suitable for a permanent structure of this sort.

Netting is readily available from garden centres (supply stores) and nurseries. It is also possible to buy special clips, which make fixing the netting to a surface very simple.

The clips are designed to be used either with masonry nails or with screws. They have the advantage that they hold the netting away from the wall, so that there is room for the plant to climb through it or wrap its tendrils round the mesh, whereas if the netting is nailed directly to the wall there is no space between them.

A further advantage of this method of fixing is that the net can be unclipped and eased away from the wall, allowing the latter to be painted or treated with preservative before the net is clipped back into position.

Plastic netting can be used either with plants that support themselves with tendrils or by twining, or with plants that need to be tied in. It does not look as attractive as the more expensive wooden trellising but, once it has been covered with the climber, it is not noticeable, especially if the right colour has been chosen. After a few years you will not be able to see the netting at all; it will be covered in a mass of foliage and flowers.

1 Position the first clip just below the top of where the net will be and drive in a masonry nail. Alternatively, drill a hole, plug it and screw the clip into it.

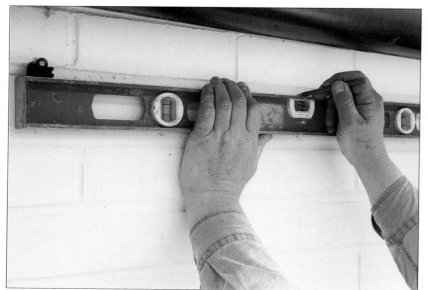

2 With a spirit level (carpenter's level), mark the position of the other upper clip, so that it is level with the first. Fix the second clip.

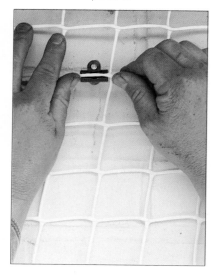

3 Place the top of the net in position, with one horizontal strand in the jaw of the clip. Press it home so it is securely fastened. Repeat with the other clip.

4 Smooth the net down against the wall and mark where the next set of clips will come. They should be at about 60cm (2ft) intervals down the wall. Move the net out of the way, fix the clips and press the net into the clips. Follow the same procedure with the bottom clips.

5 When the netting is securely in place, train the climber up into it. Even those that are self-supporting may need tying in to get them going. If the plant is a little way out from the wall, train it towards the netting along canes (stakes).

Netting is rather ugly and it is best used with vigorous climbers that will soon cover it. Here, the netting has only been used well above the ground, where the main support is needed. Unsightly supports won't show around the base of the climbers, where the main stems make an attractive feature in their own right.

General Maintenance

Climbers are relatively maintenance-free and look after themselves, apart from one or two essential things. These essentials are, however, crucial not only to ensuring a good "performance" from your climbers, but also in making your garden safe for you and other users; so don't neglect these jobs, as they are important.

ESSENTIAL JOBS

Make regular checks that the main supports are still secure to the wall or that posts have not rotted or loosened in the wind.

Tie in any stray stems as they appear. If they are left, the wind may damage them. A worse situation can arise with thorned climbers, such as roses, whose thrashing stems may damage other plants or even passers-by. If they are not essential, cut off any stray stems to keep the climber neat and safe.

Throughout the flowering season, a climbing plant's appearance is improved by removing old flowerheads. Dead-heading also prevents the plant from channelling vital resources into seed production, and thus frees energy for more flowering and growth.

WINTER PROTECTION

In winter, it may be important to protect the more tender climbers from the weather. Walls give a great deal of protection and may be sufficient for many plants but, even here, some plants may need extra protection if there is the possibility of a severe winter. One way is simply to drape hessian (burlap) or shade netting over the plant, to give temporary protection against frosts. For more prolonged periods, first protect the climber with straw and then cover this with hessian.

Watch climbers with variegated foliage, as some have the habit of reverting back to their normal green. If the stems bearing these leaves are not removed, the whole climber may eventually revert, losing its attractive foliage.

ROUTINE CARE

1 When vigorous climbers are grown against a house wall, they can become a nuisance once they have reached roof level.

4 Most climbers will produce stems that float around in space and that will need attention to prevent them being damaged or causing damage to other plants or passers-by. This *Solanum* definitely needs some attention.

5 Regularly tie in any stray stems to the main supports. In some cases, it will be easier to attach them to other stems, rather than the supports. Always consider the overall shape of the climber and how you want to encourage it to grow in the future.

6 Sometimes it is better to cut off stray stems, either because there are already ample in that area or because they are becoming a nuisance. Trim them off neatly back to a bud or a branch. Sometimes, such stems will make useful cutting material from which to grow new plants.

2 At least once a year, cut back the new growth to below the level of the gutters and around the windows.

3 Dead-head regularly. If the dead flower is part of a truss, just nip out that flower; if the whole truss has finished, cut back the stem to a bud or leaf.

7 For light protection, especially against unseasonal frosts, hang shade netting or hessian (burlap) around the climber.

8 If the plant is against a wall, hang the shade netting or hessian from the gutter or from some similar support. This is a useful method of protecting new shoots and early flowers. For really tender plants, put a layer of straw around the stems of the climber and then hold it in place with shade netting or hessian. Remove as soon as the plant begins to grow.

The overall effect of tying-in will be a neater and more satisfying shape. If possible, spread out the stems so that the climber looks fuller and less crowded.

Annual Climbers

When considering climbers, most gardeners automatically think of woody climbing plants, such as clematis or roses, and forget about the annuals. However, annual climbers are extremely useful plants and should never be overlooked.

ANNUAL CLIMBERS

Asarina
Cobaea scandens (cathedral bells)
Eccremocarpus scaber
Gourds
Ipomoea (morning glory)
Ipopoea lobata (syn. *Mina lobata*)
Lablab purpureus (syn. *Dolichos lablab*)
Lathyrus odoratus (sweet peas)
Rhodochiton atrosanguineus
Thunbergia alata (black-eyed Susan)
Tropaeolum peregrinum (syn. *T. canariensis*)
Tropaeolum majus (nasturtium)

INSTANT COLOUR

One of the great virtues of annual climbers is that they are temporary; they allow the gardener the opportunity of changing the plants or changing their position every year. This means that it is possible to fill gaps at short notice or simply to change your mind as to the way the garden should look.

Another virtue of annuals is that they come in a wide range of colours, some of which are not so readily available in other climbers. The "hot" colours – red, orange, yellow – in particular, are of great use. Annuals, on the whole, have a very long flowering season, much longer than most perennials. This also makes them very useful.

The one drawback of annuals is that they must be raised afresh each year. Many can be bought as young plants from garden centres but all can be raised from seed. This doesn't require a lot of time or space: the majority will germinate quite happily on a kitchen windowsill. With the exception of sweet peas, which are hardy and should be sown in winter, most annuals should be sown in spring, pricked out into pots, hardened off and then planted out in the open ground as soon as the threat of frosts has passed.

Annuals can be grown up any type of support, both permanent and temporary. Although they are only in place for a few months, some, such as *Cobaea scandens* (cathedral bells), can cover a very large area. *Nasturtiums* (*Tropaeolum*) are also annuals that can put on a lot of growth in a season.

Many climbers can be used as trailing plants as well as climbing ones. Annual nasturtiums are a good example of this. Here the nasturtium 'Jewel of Africa' is seen around a purple-leaved Canna *'Wyoming'.*

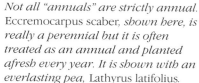

Not all "annuals" are strictly annual. Eccremocarpus scaber, *shown here, is really a perennial but it is often treated as an annual and planted afresh every year. It is shown with an everlasting pea,* Lathyrus latifolius.

Annuals are not restricted to just flowers. Many vegetables also make attractive climbers as well as being productive. Here, scarlet runner beans are grown up a wigwam (tepee) of canes (stakes). This is not only attractive but allows the gardener to produce quite a large crop in a small space.

Sweet peas are amongst everyone's favourite climbers. Not only do they look good in the garden; they are also wonderful flowers for cutting for the house. Most have a delicious scent.

Right: Cobaea scandens *is a vigorous annual climber. For success it must be planted in a warm position, preferably against a wall, and given as long a growing season as possible.*

Left: *The morning glories,* Ipomoea, *are just that, glorious. Soak seeds overnight before sowing and germinate in a warm place or propagator. Harden off thoroughly before planting or they are unlikely to do well. Plant them in a sheltered sunny position.*

Evergreen Climbers

Climbing plants are valued for their flowers, but there are a few that hold their place in the garden because of their evergreen foliage – the best known is ivy. Its glossy, three-pointed leaves make a permanent cover for whatever they climb up.

FOLIAGE SCREENS

One of the best uses of evergreens is as a cover for eyesores. They can be grown directly over an ugly wall or allowed to clamber over trellising judiciously positioned to hide a fuel tank or messy utility area. There are some places in the garden, moreover, where it is preferable that the appearance does not change with the seasons. A gateway, perhaps, may be surrounded by an evergreen climber over an arch, so that it presents the same familiar image to the visitor all year round.

From a design point of view, evergreen climbers provide a permanent point of reference within the garden. They form part of the structure, around which the rest of the garden changes season by season.

Plain green can be a little uninspiring; green works extremely well, however, as a backdrop against which to see other, more colourful, plants. Climbers such as ivy have glossy leaves, which reflect the light, giving a shimmering effect as they move. Evergreen leaves can vary in shape, and they can also be variegated, providing contrasting tones of green and sometimes colour variation.

Laurus nobilis *provides attractive green foliage.*

EVERGREEN CLIMBERS

Clematis armandii
Clematis cirrhosa
Fremontodendron californicum
Hedera (ivy)
Lonicera japonica
Solanum crispum
Solanum jasminoides
Vinca major (periwinkle)

EVERGREEN WALL SHRUBS

Azara
Callistemon citrinus
Carpenteria californica
Ceanothus (some)
Coronilla glauca
Cotoneaster
Desfontainea spinosa
Elaeagnus x *ebbingei*
Elaeagnus pungens
Escallonia
Euonymus fortunei
Euonymus japonicus
Garrya elliptica
Itea ilicifolia
Laurus nobilis
Magnolia grandiflora
Piptanthus laburnifolius
Pyracantha (firethorn)
Teucrium fruticans

Above: *Variegated ivies can make a big impact. Those with golden variegation are excellent for lighting up dark corners and they are especially good in helping to brighten the grey days of winter.*

Above: *Although the flowers of ivy are insignificant, the evergreen leaves make a valuable contribution to the garden. Here, three different varieties make a dense screen.*

Right: *This* Solanum crispum *'Glasnevin' is one of the very best climbers. Unless the weather gets very cold, it retains its shiny leaves throughout the winter and then is covered with its blue flowers from late spring right through to the autumn. The leaves may drop during severe winters, but they soon recover.*

Above: Vinca major *(periwinkle) can be considered a shrub if it is kept rigorously under control by cutting back, but it is often used as a climber, scrambling through shrubs and hedges, as here. It retains its glossy green leaves throughout the winter and produces bright blue flowers from midwinter onwards.*

Below: *There is a brightly variegated periwinkle, 'Variegata', which looks good against dark hedges.*

Fragrant Climbers

When choosing plants, the main consideration is, often, what the flowers are like, followed by the foliage. Something that is often forgotten, or just considered as a bonus, is fragrance; and yet it is something that most people enjoy and it enhances the pleasure of all uses of the garden.

USING FRAGRANCE

Climbers include some of the loveliest and most scented plants in the garden. Some of them, such as honeysuckle or jasmine, will perfume the air over a long distance. They are always worth growing on house walls near windows that are often open, so that the beautiful smells waft in and fill the rooms. Another good place to locate fragrant climbers is over an arbor or where there is a seat. Fragrance can be a tremendous aid to relaxation: think of sitting in the evening, after a hard day, with the air filled with the smell of honeysuckle.

Most scented climbers are at their best in the evening. This is a bonus if you are at work all day and, again, makes them very suitable for planting where you relax or have your evening meal. Some scented climbers, such as sweet peas, make ideal flowers for cutting to bring indoors.

Check carefully that a climber is fragrant. Honeysuckles (*Lonicera*) are amongst the most fragrant of climbers, but not all of them are scented, by any means. *Lonicera tragophylla* and *L.* x *tellmanniana* are both very attractive honeysuckles, but neither has any smell at all. Roses, too, vary in the intensity of their scent, and it is worth finding out which ones you like

best. Beware that not all smells are nice. The privets (*Ligustrum*), sometimes used as wall shrubs, have a smell that many people find revolting.

FRAGRANT CLIMBERS AND WALL SHRUBS

Azara
Akebia quinata
Clematis montana
Itea ilicifolia
Jasminum (jasmine)
Lathyrus odoratus
    (sweet peas)
Lonicera (honeysuckle)
Magnolia grandiflora
Osmanthus
Rosa (roses)

The fragrance of this Rosa 'Wedding Day' *climbing through a tree will be carried far in the warm summer evenings.*

Above: *Honeysuckle has a very heady perfume, from flowers that first appear in spring and then continue through the summer; odd flowers are still being produced in autumn.*

Left: *Not all honeysuckles are fragrant but* Lonicera periclymenum *and its varieties are amongst the best. They can be vigorous growers and need strong supports.*

Growing Rosa *'Zéphirine Drouhin' around a summerhouse is ideal. This rose has a delightful perfume and flowers on and off throughout the summer and well into the autumn. It has the advantage that it is thornless and so is safe to use near places where people are sitting or walking.*

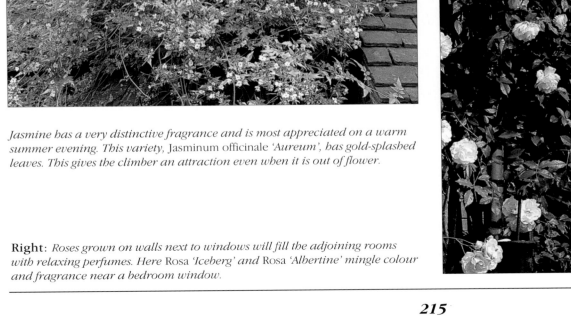

Jasmine has a very distinctive fragrance and is most appreciated on a warm summer evening. This variety, Jasminum officinale *'Aureum', has gold-splashed leaves. This gives the climber an attraction even when it is out of flower.*

Right: *Roses grown on walls next to windows will fill the adjoining rooms with relaxing perfumes. Here* Rosa *'Iceberg' and* Rosa *'Albertine' mingle colour and fragrance near a bedroom window.*

Wall Shrubs

Not all plants that one sees climbing up walls or supported on trellis are true climbers. Many are just ordinary shrubs that are growing against a wall for a variety of reasons. In the wild, some of these might scramble through others if they are next to them, but, generally, they are free-standing shrubs. These shrubs are used as surrogate climbers in the garden, partly because they look good in positions where climbers are grown and partly because some need the protection that walls and fences provide.

WALL SHRUBS	
Abutilon	*Ficus carica* (fig)
Azara	*Fremontodendron californicum*
Carpenteria californica	(fremontia)
Ceanothus (Californian lilac)	*Garrya elliptica*
Chaenomeles (japonica,	*Itea ilicifolia*
ornamental quince)	*Jasminum* (jasmine)
Clianthus puniceus	*Magnolia grandiflora*
(parrot's bill)	*Pyracantha* (firethorn)
Cotoneaster	*Teucrium fruticans*
Euonymus fortunei	(shrubby germander)

ADVANTAGES OF WALL SHRUBS
Wall shrubs are often more compact and controllable than climbers. They can be used in smaller spaces, which climbers would soon outgrow. They can be clipped into topiary shapes and will retain their shape for some time, unlike climbers, which have a constant tendency to throw out new shoots. Wall shrubs increase the range of colours and periods available to the gardener, as well as offering a greater range of foliage effects.

Walls offer winter protection to many shrubs that could otherwise not be grown. The warmth that comes from a house wall offers the opportunity to grow plants, such as *Ceanothus*, which might otherwise succumb to the cold weather and die.

It is sometimes difficult to tell what is a climber and what is a wall shrub. *Pyracantha* cut tight against a wall, for example, has every appearance of being a climber, as has a large *Magnolia* grandiflora. *Euonymus fortunei*, which grows like any other shrub in the open ground, will, given the chance, shin up a wall as if that were its normal habitat. But, in fact, the difference between climbers and wall shrubs does not matter. Sad would be the case if a plant were banished from a wall or some other support simply because it was not, strictly speaking, a climber.

Above: Piptanthus nepalensis *blooms in the spring, producing bright yellow, pea-like flowers. As summer moves on, so these attractive pods are formed, adding yet another dimension to the plant. Both the flowers and pods show up well against a brick wall.*

Left: Fremontodendron californicum *is usually grown against a wall. Wear gloves and a mask when pruning or handling as the stems are covered with fine hairs that can get into the lungs or irritate the skin.*

Right: *Although most frequently used as a free-standing shrub,* Euonymus fortunei *'Emerald 'n' Gold' will happily climb up a wall or fence.*

Above: Carpenteria californica *with its large white flowers, surmounted by a boss of yellow stamens is set off well by the dark green foliage. This plant is usually grown as a wall shrub, because it is slightly tender.*

Left: Calistemon citrinus, *with its curious, bottle-brush-like flowers, is a tender shrub that needs the warm protection of a wall if it is to survive. It flowers during the summer months.*

Above: Ceanothus *produces some of the best blue flowers of any wall shrubs. Many can be grown free-standing, but most do best if grown against a wall or a fence as here.*

Climbers with Spring Interest

Spring is one of the most joyous times of the year in the garden; the winter is over and ahead lie the glories of summer. Many of the plants that flower at this time of year have a freshness about them that almost defies definition.

PROTECTING FROM FROST

Spring is a time of varying weather and plants can suffer badly from late frosts. This is made worse when frosts are preceded by a warm spell, in which a lot of new growth appears. These young shoots are susceptible to sudden cold weather and can be burnt off. Buds are also likely to be harmed and it is not uncommon to see a *Clematis montana*, for example, covered in buds and full of promise one day, only to be denuded of buds the next after a night of hard frost. This, should never deter you from growing spring-flowering climbers; such frosts do not occur every year and, in most springs, these climbers perform at their best. If frosts are forecast, guard against them.

Many tender early-flowering shrubs need walls for protection and are usually grown as wall shrubs. Shrubs such as camellias are particularly prone to frost damage.

Once they have finished flowering, many spring-flowering climbers are a bit dreary for the rest of the year. One way to enliven them is to grow another, later-flowering, climber through their stems. This is very useful where space is limited.

SPRING-FLOWERING CLIMBERS AND WALL SHRUBS

Abeliophyllum distichum
Akebia quinata
Akebia trifoliata
Azara serrata
Ceanothus arboreus
    'Trewithen Blue'
Chaenomeles (japonica or
    ornamental quince)
Clematis alpina
Clematis armandii
Clematis macropetala
Clematis montana
Forsythia suspensa
Garrya elliptica
Lonicera (honeysuckles) (some)
Piptanthus laburnifolius
Ribes laurifolium
Rosa (early roses)
Schisandra
Wisteria

Above: *Spring is the time when all plants are beginning to burst forth. Clematis are some of the earliest climbers, one of the earliest and most impressive being* C. montana, *which frequently has so much bloom that the leaves cannot be seen.*

Right: Clematis armandii *is one of the few evergreen clematis. It is also one of the earliest to flower, doing so in late winter or early spring.*

Above: *Another early clematis, more delicate in appearance, is* C. macropetala. *It is here seen with* C. montana, *which will flower a week or so later.*

Above: *Honeysuckles (Lonicera) are a great feature of spring and summer. This one (L. periclymenum) is in a natural habitat – scrambling through a bush. In this case, the supporting plant is a berberis, whose purple-bronze leaves make a good contrast to the yellow flowers.*

Left: Rosa *'Maigold' is one of the many roses that although strictly a shrub, have a tendency to climb. They can be used as low climbers up pillars, as here, or on tripods, trellis or low walls. It starts flowering early in the season and often repeats later in the year.*

Right: *When in full flower, wisteria must be one of the most beautiful of climbers. It can be grown as a free-standing tree but it is best supported on a wall or pergola. Walls help to protect it against late frosts which can damage the flower buds.*

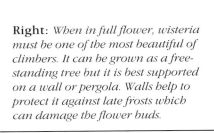

Summer Interest

Summer is when many climbers are at their best. Clematis and roses, in particular, produce plenty of blooms, covering pergolas and arches as well as climbing up walls and through trees and shrubs. They make a valuable contribution to the summer scene, giving vertical emphasis to a garden that would otherwise be flat and less interesting.

SUMMER CLIMBERS

Campsis
Clematis
Cobaea scandens (cathedral bells)
Eccremocarpus scaber (Chilean glory flower)
Fallopia baldschuanica (Russian vine)
Ipomoea (morning glories)
Jasminum (jasmines)
Lapageria rosea
Lathyrus (peas)
Lonicera (honeysuckles)

Passiflora (passion-flowers)
Phaseolus coccineus (runner beans)
Rosa (roses)
Schisandra
Schizophragma
Solanum crispum 'Glasnevin'
Solanum jasminoides
Thunbergia alata (black-eyed Susan)

SHADE AND FRAGRANCE

During hot, sunny summers, climbers are most welcome for providing dappled shade as they cover arbors and pergolas. There is nothing better than to sit on a summer's day in the shade of an arbor or relax there with a meal or a drink in the evening after work. Relaxation is further enhanced if the climbers are fragrant – and many are. Roses, honeysuckle and jasmine are three of the most popular scented climbers.

Many shrubs and trees are spring-flowering and climbers can be used to enliven them during the summer months, when they are, perhaps, at their dullest. *Clematis viticella* is probably the best to use for this purpose; because it is cut back almost to the ground during the winter, it doesn't smother the tree or shrub when it is in flower. Later in the season, when the tree or shrub has finished flowering, the clematis grows up through its branches and produces its own colour, usually over a long period.

Similarly, climbers can be used in herbaceous borders, where there are gaps left by perennials that flower early in the season and are then cut back. Clematis can be left to scramble through the border, either without any support or over a simple twig framework.

Above: Campsis radicans *is a beautiful climber for the second half of the summer. Its large tubular flowers, here just opening, contrast well with the green of the foliage. It is not a common climber but it is not difficult to find or to grow.*

Above: Clematis florida *'Sieboldii' is a very distinct clematis, with creamy white outer petals and an inner button of purple ones. It is a beautiful flower even when still in bud and while opening.*

Right: Clematis *'Perle d'Azur' must be one of the best of the blue clematis. It produces flowers of a delicate lilac blue in tremendous profusion around midsummer.*

Above: *Bougainvillea is a climber that grows in hot climates. In more temperate areas, it has to be grown under glass, but, in warmer districts, it can be grown outside. Its brilliant colours continue for months as it is the papery bracts rather than the flowers that provide the colour.*

Right: *Scrambling plants are a neglected area. There are very many of them and they can provide a lot of vertical interest through the summer months. Here a* Euonymus fortunei *'Emerald Gaiety' scrambles up through a large bush, with* Geranium x oxonianum *pushing its way up through both.*

Autumn Interest

Most climbers have finished flowering by the time the autumn arrives but many have qualities that make them still desirable in the garden at this time of year.

FOLIAGE AND BERRIES

Perhaps the biggest attraction of autumn climbers is the change in colour of the leaves, prior to their fall. Many take on autumnal tints, some of the most fiery red. This will completely transform the appearance of the climber itself and, often, that of the surrounding area. Another benefit that some climbers have to offer is that they produce berries or fruit. Most produce seed of some kind or other but these are often visually insignificant; others produce an abundance of bright berries – honeysuckle (*Lonicera*), for example – or large luxurious fruit, such as the passion flowers (*Passiflora*). Others carry their seeds in a different but, none the less, very attractive way. The fluffy or silky seed heads of clematis, for example, always make an interesting feature.

As well as providing an important visual element in the garden, the berries and other forms of seed are also a good source of food for birds. Birds will be attracted to the fruit for as long as they last, which may be well beyond the autumn and into the winter. Not only birds like fruit: man also likes the garden's edible bounty. Many fruiting plants, ranging from currants and gooseberries to apples, plums, pears and apricots, can be grown against a wall, which provides not only support but also warmth and protection. Fruiting trees, such as apples and pears, also make good plants to train up and over arches and pergolas.

AUTUMNAL-FOLIAGE CLIMBERS

Actinidia (kiwi fruit)
Akebia quinata
Campsis
Chaenomeles (japonica or flowering quince)
Clematis alpina
Clematis flammula
Clematis tibetana vernayi
Cotoneaster
Fallopia baldschuanica (Russian vine)
Hydrangea anomala petiolaris
Hydrangea aspera
Hydrangea quercifolia
Jasminum officinale (jasmine)
Lonicera tragophylla (honeysuckle)
Parthenocissus (Boston ivy or Virginia creeper)
Passiflora (passion-flower)
Ribes speciosum
Rosa (roses)
Tropaeolum (nasturtium)
Vitis (grapevine)

BERRIED AND FRUITING CLIMBERS AND WALL SHRUBS

Actinidia (kiwi fruit)
Akebia
Clematis
Cotoneaster
Hedera (ivy)
Humulus lupulus (hop)
Ilex (holly)
Lonicera (honeysuckle)
Malus (crab apple)
Passiflora (passion-flower)
Prunus (plums, apricots, peaches)
Pyracantha (firethorn)
Pyrus (pears)
Rosa (roses)
Vitis (grapevine)

Above: Clematis cirrhosa *flowers in late autumn and carries its fluffy seed heads well into winter.*

Left: *The berries of* Cotoneaster horizontalis *are set off well against the foliage of* Helleborus foetidus.

Right: Pyracantha *offers the choice of yellow, red or orange berries, depending on the variety. This is* P. *'Orange Charmer'.*

Above and right: Parthenocissus henryana *is seen here in both its summer and autumn colours.*

Left: Some clematis *display a mass of silky heads throughout the autumn.*

Below: *Fruit trees are attractive as wall shrubs as they carry blossom in spring and fruit in the autumn.*

Winter Interest

While there are not many climbers that are interesting in winter, they are still a group of plants that are worth thinking about. Valuable wall space should not be taken up with plants that do not earn their keep for the greater part of the year, but it is often possible to find space for at least one that brightens up the winter scene.

Hedera colchica 'Dentata Variegata' is in perfect condition even in these frosty conditions. The gold variegation is good for lightening up dark winter days.

The winter jasmine, Jasminum nudiflorum, flowers throughout winter, supplying cut flowers for indoors and decorating walls and fences outside.

WINTER-FLOWERING CLIMBERS

Surprisingly, there is one clematis that is in full flower during the bleaker winter months. *Clematis cirrhosa* is available in several forms, some with red blotches on their bell-shaped flowers. *Clematis armandii* appears towards the end of winter and heralds the beginning of a new season. There are three honeysuckles that flower in the winter and, although they are, strictly speaking, shrubs, they can be grown against a wall. As an added bonus, these are very strongly scented and they will flower throughout the whole of the winter. Another wall shrub that flowers early is *Garrya elliptica*, with its long, silver catkins. This is the more valuable because it will grow on a north-facing wall.

One of the most commonly grown wall shrubs is the winter jasmine, *Jasminum nudiflorum*, which produces a wonderful display of bright yellow flowers.

EVERGREEN CLIMBERS

While not so attractive as the flowering plants, evergreen climbers, such as ivy (*Hedera*), can be used as winter cover both for walls and for other supports. These evergreen climbers afford valuable winter protection for birds and insects, especially if grown by a warm wall. Different green tones and, especially, variegated leaves, can add a surprising amount of winter cheer, even on dark days.

Climbers and wall shrubs that still carry berries from the previous autumn can add interest in the winter. Cotoneaster and pyracantha are good examples.

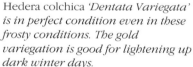

WINTER CLIMBERS AND WALL SHRUBS

Chaenomeles (japonica or
  flowering quince)
Clematis armandii
Clematis cirrhosa
Garrya elliptica
Hedera (ivy)
Jasminum nudiflorum
  (winter jasmine)
Lonicera fragrantissima
  (winter honeysuckle)

Right: Clematis armandii *flowers in late winter, with a wonderful display of pure-white flowers.*

Above: Garrya elliptica *is an excellent plant for winter. It has beautiful silver catkins and is one of the few plants suitable for growing on north-facing walls.*

Above: Clematis cirrhosa *is the earliest clematis to flower, starting in early winter and continuing until spring. The many varieties include this one, 'Balearica'.*

Right: Chaenomeles, *known as* japonica, *or Japanese or ornamental quince, flowers from midwinter to spring, then has hard fruit that often lasts through until the next spring.*

Easy-care Options

Gardens should always be objects of beauty and give an immense sense of satisfaction, but they can also be demanding, and there is often a fine line between one that is a source of pleasure and one that becomes a worry or even a burden. Taking the easy way out does not mean cutting down your aspirations. A garden that requires just a little of your precious leisure time can be every bit as enticing and attractive as one that is demanding in upkeep.

Left: *Evergreen shrubs and trees set the backdrop against which flowers with seasonal interest can be planted.*

Above: *Once established, conifers will look after themselves.*

Gravel Beds

Gravel makes a splendid backdrop for plants, and it's easy to keep weed-free. Dwarf alpines and large architectural plants like yuccas or red-hot pokers look equally good. The plants that look best in a gravel bed, however, are those that naturally grow in dry or stony conditions.

You can plant in any area of gravel, but if you want to make a feature where plants predominate, you may prefer to set the feature in an area of grass.

GRAVEL BEDS IN GRASS
You should be able to find space for a gravel bed like this even in a small garden.

Above: *A gravel bed will make an excellent setting for a variety of plants, such as this sedum.*

I Mark out the bed with rope, a hoe, or by sprinkling sand where you think the outline should be. If the lawn is large, a long and winding ribbon of gravel can look very effective. This is sometimes referred to as a dry-riverbed style. If the garden is smaller, a more compact shape, perhaps oval or kidney-shaped might be more appropriate.

2 Cut the outline of the bed using a half-moon edger. A spade will do, but this does not produce such a crisp edge.

4 Spread a generous quantity of garden compost or rotted manure over the surface, and a slow-release or controlled-release fertilizer. Then fork this in to loosen and enrich the soil. If the ground is poorly drained and you want to grow "dry soil" plants, work in plenty of coarse grit too. This is an important stage as it is difficult to improve the soil once the gravel is in place.

3 Lift the grass with a space, removing about 10cm (4in) from the surface. The finished bed must be several centimetres (a few inches) below the grass, otherwise the gravel will spill onto the lawn and damage the lawnmower.

5 Spread about 5cm (2in) of gravel over the soil, making sure it is kept off the lawn and does not threaten to spill over onto it.

PLANTS TO USE
Although many plants will grow well in a gravel bed, for a low-maintenance garden you should choose drought-resistant plants that you won't need to water, even in dry spells.

PLANTING

To plant, just draw back the gravel in that area and plant normally, but avoid planting deeply as the gravel will be drawn back around the plant afterwards. For most plants this will do no harm, but if necessary just keep the gravel away from the immediate area around the stem.

6 Try adding a few boulders or beach pebbles. These create interest and make the bed look more natural.

Right: *A gravelled area. Gravel beds can be heavily planted with a combination of drought-resistant plants and the weed-suppressing gravel will mean they mainly look after themselves.*

Flowers that Sow Themselves

Plants that germinate readily from self-sown seeds can be a problem in the wrong place, but you can use them freely in areas that have a natural boundary, such as a bed in a lawn.

Opposite: *These* Aquilegia alpina *have sown themselves, and all the gardener had to do was a little thinning and weeding in the spring.*

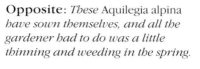

HOW TO START THEM OFF

Decide on a position where the plants can multiply freely without becoming a nuisance. Suitable places are among shrubs and herbaceous plants, especially in a mixed bed, or in beds restrained by clear boundaries. Don't sow them where you will have to keep weeding out the seedlings where they're not wanted.

SELF-SOWING ANNUALS

Calendula (pot marigold)
Eschscholtzia (Californian poppies)
Limnanthes (poached egg plant)
Linaria (toad flax)

SELF-SOWING PERENNIALS

Aquilegia (columbine)
Digitalis (foxglove) (a biennial)
Foeniculum vulgare (fennel)
Lupinus (lupin)

1 Start with weed-free ground. Hoe off or pull out any weeds in the area you want to sow. Fork out any deep-rooted perennial weeds.

2 Annuals used for this purpose are best scattered randomly rather than sown in rows. Avoid sowing too thickly or you'll have more thinning to do.

3 Perennials, like lupins and columbines, should be sown in small pinches about 45cm (1 1/2ft) apart, instead of being scattered randomly.

4 Simply rake the annual seeds in, first in one direction and then the other if possible. Pull some soil over the perennials sown in spaced pinches. Keep watered until they germinate and are growing well.

5 After initial sowing, and each subsequent year, pull out any weed seedlings before they compete with the sown seedlings. You should be able to identify the desirable seedlings by the larger number with the same kind of leaf.

6 As the seedlings become larger, hoe between them to control weeds. Once the plants meet, you should be able to stop weeding.

Easy Bedding

If you like the cheerful brightness of seasonal bedding rather than the permanent but predictable show from shrubs and border plants, you can compromise by using a mixture of seasonal and permanent plants. This will reduce the amount of regular replanting and save on cost as well as time.

If you do want to use traditional summer bedding plants, choose those that flower prolifically over a long period without deadheading. Some of the most trouble-free and spectacular bedding plants to use are suggested opposite.

ECONOMICAL WITH ANNUALS

These pictures show how imaginatively you can use summer bedding plants in combination with perennials. The plants you choose should reflect your own preferences, but the concept is easy to adapt to your own needs.

PLANTING A PERMANENT EDGING

Perennials will form the basis of the edging, with bedding plants added for variety.

1 Always dig over the ground and clear it of weeds before planting.

2 Rake in a general fertilizer before planting. (Wait until spring to apply the fertilizer if planting in autumn or winter.) This will encourage vigorous early growth and help the plants to knit together more quickly.

3 Space out the plants in their pots first, in case you have to adjust them to go evenly around the bed.

4 Plant with a trowel, adjusting the spacing to suit the plant. About 15cm (6in) apart is suitable for most plants if you want quick cover, further apart if you don't mind waiting a little longer for a carpeting effect.

5 Firm in to remove large pockets of air, then water thoroughly. Keep well watered for the first few weeks. The bed may be planted immediately with spring or summer bedding plants or bulbs as appropriate. When they have finished, lift them but leave the perennial edging.

Begonia *'White Devil'*

Impatiens *(busy Lizzie)*

Left: Impatiens *(busy Lizzie) and begonias are popular choices for colourful beds.*

NO-FUSS SUMMER BEDDING PLANTS

The following will continue to flower for many months without dead-heading, regular attention or watering.

Begonia semperflorens
Impatiens (busy Lizzie)
Lavatera trimestris
Osteospermums
Pelargoniums (bedding geraniums)
Petunias
Tagetes patula (French marigolds)

Right: *This edging is the perennial* Sedum spurium *but many other carpeting plants can be used (beware of very invasive sedums, however). This provides a neat year-round edging that you don't have to replace and at most needs an annual trim to keep it neat. Fill the centre of the bed with spring and summer bedding plants.*

Make the Most of Bulbs

Some bulbs will flower reliably year after year with the clumps improving all the time. Whether it's spring-flowering daffodils, summer alliums, or autumn colchicums, there are plenty of bulbs that you can plant and forget.

Most summer-flowering bulbs, such as alliums and lilies are best planted in groups in a border, but the easiest way to grow many spring-flowering and autumn-flowering bulbs is to naturalize them in the grass. Don't cut the grass until the leaves die down (colchicums flower in autumn but the leaves do not appear until spring).

NATURALIZING LARGE BULBS
Tulips and daffodils can be planted in this way.

1 To create a natural effect, scatter the bulbs on the grass and plant them where they fall. It is better to keep your naturalized bulbs to one small area of the lawn so that the rest can be cut normally and it won't look too untidy.

2 You can plant with a trowel, but a bulb planter is quicker and more convenient. Insertion will be easier if the ground is moist.

3 Crumble some soil from the bottom of the core. Drop some of this into the hole to fall around the bulb and make sure it is not suspended in a pocket of air. Then press the core back into position.

1 For small bulbs and corms it is sometimes easier to lift and then replace the grass. Use a half-moon edger (edging iron), or a spade, where you want to lift the grass. Use a spade to slice beneath the grass, then roll it back for planting.

2 Loosen the soil with a fork, and work in a slow fertilizer release.

3 Scatter the bulbs randomly. Very small ones can be left on the surface; larger ones are best buried slightly. Aim to cover the bulbs with twice their own depth of soil under the grass. Roll back the grass, firm it well, and water.

NATURALIZING SMALL BULBS
Plant snowdrops or crocuses in the lawn for spring flowering.

Right: *Naturalizing bulbs in grass eliminates the need for annual replanting and means you don't have to cut that part of the lawn until the leaves have died down naturally.*

Living Carpets

Ground cover is one of the labour-saving gardener's best weapons. It suppresses weeds, covers bare soil, and makes a worthwhile visual contribution. Some of the flowering ground-cover plants are both colourful and beautiful.

Opposite: Convallaria majalis *(lily of the valley) takes a few years to become established, but then makes an effective as well as a fragrant ground cover.*

NON-WOODY GROUND COVER

Ajuga reptans (E)
Alchemilla mollis
Anthemis nobilis (E)
Bergenia species *(E)*
Cerastium tomentosum (E)
Geranium endressii
Lamium maculatum
Pulmonaria species
Tiarella cordifolia(E)
Waldsteinia ternata (E)

PLANTING GROUND COVER
Ground cover initially needs protection from weeds.

1 Clear the ground of weeds first. Annual weeds can be hoed off or killed with a herbicide. Some perennial weeds will have to be dug out by hand or killed by several applications of weed-killer, as regrowth occurs.

2 Fork in as much rotted manure or garden compost (soil mix) as you can spare, then apply a slow-release or controlled-release balanced fertilizer at the rate recommended by the manufacturer, and rake it in.

3 Unless planting a ground cover that spreads by underground stems or rooting prostrate stems on the surface, it is best to plant through a mulching sheet to control weeds while the plants are becoming established.

4 Spread out the mulching sheet. Using scissors or a sharp knife, cut a cross where the plant is to be positioned. Plant in staggered rows, at spacings appropriate for the plants.

5 Provided you use small plants, it should be easy to plant through the slits with a trowel. If using large ground-cover plants it may be better to omit the mulching sheet and plant with a spade.

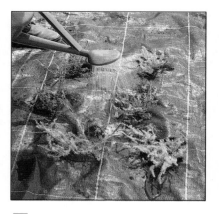

6 Be sure to water thoroughly after planting, and in dry weather throughout the first year.

7 It will probably take several seasons before the plants knit together to form a living carpet so, although not essential, you may prefer to use a decorative mulch such as chipped bark to improve the overall appearance.

Going Wild

Most of us like to tempt wildlife into the garden. You can encourage wildlife simply by feeding the birds, making a pond, and growing plants that butterflies are attracted to. A true wildlife enthusiast will want to go one step further, however, and design the garden with wildlife in mind. Whether this kind of gardening appeals depends on whether you can look at buttercups and daisies and see them as attractive wild flowers, or only as weeds.

A more acceptable compromise for many are normal flower borders given over mainly to wild flowers. Here various poppies and forget-me-nots have self-seeded to provide an undisturbed wild area that is visually attractive and easily managed. Some weeding may be necessary to prevent particularly rampant weeds taking over the bed or border, but generally a bed like this will look after itself.

It is worth clearing the area of weeds first, leaving it for weed seedlings to germinate before weeding again, then sowing a wild flower seed mixture. In this way you are more likely to have a bed with a good range of attractive wild flowers rather than the dominant local weeds.

A wildlife pond usually looks rather overgrown, but that's how it should be. Wildlife is less attracted to large areas of clear water with fountains and cascades than to areas of still water almost congested with plant growth.

It is also important to have some shelter close to the pond, such as a border, an area with bog plants, or even a hedge. Wildlife is much more vulnerable in an open position, but choose a bright position rather than one in dense shade.

Although shape is relatively unimportant, some shallow beach edges are crucial, so that amphibians and other creatures can gain access to the water easily, and climb out without difficulty. An area of shallow water will also encourage birds and other animals to use the pond for drinking.

Whether you could live with this as part of your back lawn depends on the relative appeal of gardening against wildlife. If you like a neat and tidy garden with lots of flowerbeds, this kind of wildlife feature will not appeal. But even a small area of long grass like this will encourage a wide range of birds (especially when seeds ripen), insects and mammals. You should also be able to introduce many attractive wild flowers into an area like this, and of course there is less lawn to mow!

Many common garden plants will attract butterflies, especially Buddleja davidii, *the butterfly-bush. Other common flowers attract butterflies too: this is a Small Tortoiseshell on a hyacinth.*

Left: *With a wild garden, you need only cut the long grass areas once or twice a year, and let nature do the rest. If there are rare flowers among the buttercups and daisies, you will have to time any cutting carefully to avoid interfering with their natural growth cycles; some parts can be left completely uncultivated. This will attract a wide range of wildlife, most of which will venture into the more ornamental part of the garden.*

Self-sufficient Shrubs

Some of the most popular shrubs – like roses and buddlejas – need a lot of attention if they are to remain looking good. Pruning is a regular requirement for many of them, and those prone to pests and diseases are bad news unless you are prepared to spend time spraying or dusting too. But for every shrub that is a potential problem for the low-maintenance gardener, there are many more that are just as attractive and almost totally trouble-free.

There are hundreds of well-behaved compact shrubs that will not demand frequent pruning or hacking back. If in doubt, check with your garden centre (supply store) to make sure the shrubs you choose don't need regular pruning, won't become bare and leggy at the base with all the flowers at the top, and aren't susceptible to diseases.

PLANTING SHRUBS

Shrubs will be in position for many years, so take your time over planting and prepare the ground thoroughly.

1 Water the pots thoroughly and let them drain, then position them where you think they should be in the border. Check the likely size on the label or in a book, then revise your spacing if necessary. If the spacing seems excessive initially, you can always plant a few extra inexpensive shrubs between them to discard when they become overcrowded.

2 Fork over the area and remove any weeds. Then fork in as much rotted manure or garden compost (soil mix) as you can spare, or use a proprietary planting mix.

3 Excavate a hole large enough to take the rootball. Stand the pot in the hole and use a cane (stake) or stick to check that the plant will be at its original depth in the soil when planted. Add or remove soil as necessary.

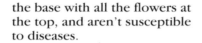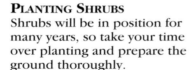

4 Carefully tease out some of the roots if they are tightly wound around the inside of the pot. This will encourage them to grow out into the surrounding soil more quickly.

5 Return the soil and firm it well around the roots to steady the shrub in wind and to prevent large pockets of air that might allow the roots to dry out. Pressing the earth in with your heel is the most effective way of firming the soil around a shrub.

6 Apply a balanced fertilizer according to the manufacturer's instructions, if planting in spring or summer. Hoe or rake it into the surface, then water thoroughly.

Right: *A border like this is planted with* Choisya ternata *'Sundance' a low-maintenance shrub, and Michaelmas daisies, yet it remains bright and beautiful for many months of the year.*

SELF-SUFFICIENT FLOWERING SHRUBS

Cistus
Escallonia
Hibiscus syriacus
Hypericum
Mahonia
Olearia x *haastii*
Yucca

SELF-SUFFICIENT FOLIAGE SHRUBS

Aucuba japonica
Berberis thunbergii
Choisya ternata
Elaegnus pungens 'Maculata'
Euonymous fortunei
Ruscus aculeatus
Viburnum davidii

Using Grasses

A grass lawn can be high maintenance, but a grass bed can make a striking feature that will not take up much of your time. Grasses can also be used in mixed beds and borders, but be careful as some of them will try to take-over and can be difficult to eradicate. Choose well-behaved clump-forming species or plant in a container as shown below.

PLANTING GRASSES
Groups of grasses are refreshingly different, but beware of the rampant species.

1 Grasses often work best as a low-maintenance feature in a bed of their own. There are many kinds to grow, from compact dwarfs for the edge to huge plants 2.4m (8ft) or even taller. Study a specialist catalogue, and when you have bought the plants space them out to see how they will look.

2 Make sure the plants have been well watered beforehand, then knock out of the pot and plant in well-prepared, weed-free soil. If there are a lot of roots tightly wound around the edge of the pot, gently tease out some of them.

3 Firm the soil around the roots, using your hand or heel, then water in thoroughly. Keep watered in dry spells until the plants are well established.

4 If planting a spreading grass in a border, or even if using a rampant species in a grasses-only bed, plant it in a container to restrain its spread. This method is not suitable for very large grasses, but you are unlikely to be using these in a small border. Excavate a hole large enough to take the container, which must have drainage holes in it.

5 Partly fill the container with soil then plant normally, with the rootball at the correct level. Firm the plant well, and add more compost if necessary.

6 Make sure the rim is flush with the surrounding soil (but not below it, otherwise the most rampant grasses will escape), and for a more natural appearance make sure that the soil is flush with the rim. Water thoroughly.

Opposite: *Grasses can be attractive plants to use in a border. Some can be used as an edging but most are used mid- or back-border.*

Fern Gardens

Most people dismiss garden ferns as boring and uninteresting, but anyone who has grown ferns as houseplants will know how fascinating and beautiful they can be. What they lack in colour they make up for in elegance.

Don't be deterred from trying garden ferns if you have had trouble keeping indoor ferns happy and healthy. Provided they have suitable conditions (shade for most of them), they will thrive without any help on your part.

Use ferns in a shady position where the more colourful flowers fail to thrive. If you are worried about bare ground in winter, choose mainly evergreen species, but a mixture of shapes and sizes will make your fern garden more interesting.

PLANTING A FERN GARDEN
Ferns are easy to grow but most prefer a moist, shady or partially shaded position, and it pays dividends to prepare the ground thoroughly. Spring is a good time to plant.

1 Most ferns need a moist, humus-rich soil, so fork in as much garden compost (soil mix) or rotted manure as possible. This is especially important if the area is shaded by trees or a wall that also cast a "rain shadow", where the soil is usually dry as a result.

2 If the soil is impoverished, add a balanced fertilizer and rake it into the surface. If planting in late summer, autumn or winter, do not use a quick-acting fertilizer. Wait until spring to apply, or use a controlled-release fertilizer that will only release the nutrients when the weather is warm enough for growth.

Dryopteris affinis syn. D *pseudomas* 'Cristata The King'

3 It is very important that ferns do not dry out, especially when newly planted. Water the pots thoroughly about half an hour before planting, to make sure the rootball is wet to start with.

4 Make a hole large enough to take the rootball, but if the roots are very tightly wound around the pot, carefully tease out some of them first. This will encourage them to grow out into the surrounding soil. If the plant is in a large pot, you may have to use a spade instead of a trowel.

5 Firm in carefully to eliminate any large air pockets that could allow the roots to dry out. Then water thoroughly so that the surrounding soil is moist down to the depth of the rootball.

Asplenium scolopendrim (hart's-tongue fern)

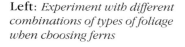

Left: *Experiment with different combinations of types of foliage when choosing ferns*

Because ferns are subtle rather than bright, they can be used very effectively to soften a focal point like this ornament. This simple combination can transform an otherwise potentially dull corner of the garden.

6 To help conserve moisture and maintain a high level of organic material in the soil, mulch thickly with peat, a peat substitute or a garden compost. Top up the mulch each spring.

Heathers

Heathers make excellent low-maintenance beds, with a guarantee of evergreen cover and – depending on the varieties used – colourful flowers practically the year round. Many have attractive golden foliage that looks good for twelve months of the year.

Use them with dwarf conifers if you want to add height, or alone for a carpet of living colour. You could use them as a ground cover around the base of a birch tree with silver bark – winter-flowering varieties will look stunning.

Calluna vulgaris 'Blazeaway'

PLANTING A HEATHER BED
Prepare the soil thoroughly as some heathers have special needs. Although heathers will suppress weeds after they have been established for a couple of years or so, you will have to control weeds for the first few seasons.

1 Dig the soil thoroughly, and pull up as many deep-rooted or difficult perennial weeds as possible. Add plenty of organic material such as garden compost or rotted manure, especially if the soil is dry or impoverished.

2 If planting in spring or summer, rake in a balanced general fertilizer. If planting in autumn or winter wait until spring to apply fertilizer.

Erica carnea

A combination of heathers, such as Erica carnea *and* Calluna vulgaris, *will provide interesting colour variations, even when not in flower.*

3 Some heathers, such as the winter-flowering *Erica carnea* varieties will grow on a neutral or even slightly alkaline soil. Many others, such as *Calluna vulgaris*, need an acid soil. Adding peat to the planting area will benefit all types.

4 Start planting at one end or at the back of the bed. Space the plants about 30–45cm (1–1½ft) apart, but the planting distance will vary with species and even variety, so check first.

5 Use a mulch to help suppress weeds, conserve moisture, and improve the appearance of the bare soil while the plants are young. Peat is useful for this, but you may prefer to use a renewable alternative such as chipped bark.

Heathers make happy companions for conifers, and if you choose winter-flowering varieties like these Erica carnea, *the garden will always be bright.*

PLANTING THROUGH PLASTIC
This method will cut down weeding to the absolute minimum.

1 Cover the whole area with black plastic or a plastic mulching sheet. Make cross-shaped slits in the plastic.

2 Plant through the slits in the sheet.

3 If you don't like the visual appearance of the plastic, cover it with a mulch of chipped bark.

Dwarf Conifers

Dwarf conifers need little attention after their first year, but to look effective they are best grown as a group with contrasting shapes, sizes and colours, or with carpeters such as heathers.

PLANTING A CONIFER BED
A good garden centre (supply store) will have a bewildering array of dwarf and slow-growing conifers, but it is best to consult a good specialist catalogue or book before you buy. Some described as dwarf may reach 2.4m (8ft) or so in time, and those described as slow-growing may be even larger eventually. Make sure your dwarf conifers really are dwarf if space is at a premium.

Chamaecyparis obtusa *'Aurea'*

Chamaecyparis lawsonia *'Silver Threads'*

These varieties are among many that need little care, but provide year-round colour.

1 Dwarf conifers look good in a small bed or border. If you find it difficult to plan beds and borders on paper, stand the pots where you think the plants will look good, and be prepared to shuffle them around until they look right. Bear in mind the eventual height and spread.

2 Dig a hole larger and deeper than the rootball. Stand the pot in the hole to make sure it is large enough.

3 Fork in as much rotted manure, garden compost or planting mixture as you can spare. This is especially important on very dry soils, or near a fence or wall.

4 Add a controlled-release or slow-release fertilizer to the planting hole, using the manufacturer's recommended rate, and work in with a fork or trowel.

5 Make sure the soil in the pot is moist, then knock the plant out and check the roots. If they are very tightly wound around the inside of the pot, carefully tease some of them out so that they will grow into the surrounding soil.

6 Check the planting depth by standing the rootball in the hole, and using a cane (stake) or piece of wood to make sure it will be at its original depth when the soil is returned. Add or remove soil as necessary.

This bed shows how bright and colourful a conifer and heather bed can be, and it really is a low-maintenance combination.

7 Firm in to eliminate large air pockets that might cause the roots to dry out, then water thoroughly.

8 Mulch with a decorative material such as chipped bark. Make sure the mulch is at least 5cm (2in) thick so that it will suppress weeds effectively.

Make the Most of Trees

Trees largely look after themselves, and make attractive features as specimens set in a lawn, or planted towards the back of a shrub border.

Trees in a border are generally less trouble because falling leaves drop almost unnoticed onto the soil and are quickly recycled. Leaves on a lawn usually have to be raked up, and mowing beneath a low-hanging tree or up to a trunk can also cause difficulties. Don't be deterred from trying a tree in a lawn, but choose one with small or evergreen leaves, and try some of the tips suggested below to make mowing and cultivating around the base easier.

TREES IN LAWNS

Mowing will be frustratingly difficult if you take the grass right up to the trunk of the tree, especially as it becomes larger. Lawn trees are generally better planted in a bed cut into the grass, which you can plant with some ground-cover plants, or cover with a decorative mulch to suppress weeds.

TREES IN BORDERS

The best way to cover the ground beneath trees in a border is with ground-covering plants that will tolerate shade and dry soil. If the tree is very large, or has large leaves, you may have to rake them off the plants when they fall, but most of them usually work their way between the plants and soon rot down. If you use a ground cover that dies down in winter, falling leaves will not matter.

HOW TO PLANT A LAWN TREE

Trees often look best planted in isolation in a lawn.

1 With sand, mark a circle on the grass about 90–120cm (3–4ft) across. Lift the grass with a spade, and remove about 15cm (6in) of soil with it. Fork in garden compost or manure.

2 Insert a short stake before you plant, placing it on the side of the prevailing wind. Place it off-centre, to allow space for the rootball. A short stake is preferable to a long one.

3 If planting a bare-root tree, spread out the roots. Place the tree in the hole and use a cane (stake) to check that the soil mark on the stem will be at final soil level, about 5cm (2in) below the grass.

4 Return the soil, and firm in well. Water thoroughly and secure with a tree-tie. Use a thick ornamental organic mulch to suppress weeds and make the bed look more attractive.

Right: *Once established* Hedera colchica *'Dentata Variegata' will form an attractive evergreen carpet that will suppress weeds and needs practically no attention.*

Left: *Use beach pebbles instead of an organic mulch to make an attractive feature. They will prevent weed growth and can look very ornamental.*

A RAISED EDGE

Raising the edge makes more of a feature of the bed, but you won't easily be able to mow up to the edge unless you also make a mowing strip. A sunken border about 10–15cm (4–6in) wide all round will enable you to mow over the edge without striking the raised edge.

Creative Containers

Gardening in containers is the quickest, simplest and most economical way to transform your garden, especially when space is at a premium. A wide range of good-quality plants is available to every gardener all the year round, so that no corner need ever be overlooked or dull. There is no rule restricting you to plastic and earthenware pots, and this versatility, coupled with mobility, makes containers an inspirational resource for expert and novice alike.

Left: *Grouping containers together with imagination and flair can transform the plainest of spots.*

Above: *Less obvious containers such as this copper boiler make superb and unusual displays.*

Using Containers

Using pots, troughs and urns in the garden will soften hard edges, extend the growing area and can create spectacular focal points. Displays of containers are an attractive and varied means of harmonizing the soft landscaping of the garden with the hard surfaces of the patio or courtyard.

ADAPTABLE DISPLAYS

Containers come in an enormous range of shapes, sizes and colours, and in a variety of different materials. In addition, they can be chosen or easily customized with a paint effect to match other accessories within the garden.

Introducing containers into a small garden means that all of the available space can be used to the full; it also allows the creation of movable displays in a way that is simply not possible in the garden. Plants can be grown with ease without relying on the local growing environment.

Arrangements can be changed seasonally, moved around to provide an instant display in a particular area or simply placed to make the most of the available light. You have more flexibility in

the choice of plants destined for a container, enabling you to grow those with a definite soil pH preference (such as rhododendrons or camellias), or those that prefer a dry site, in areas where the natural soil would not be suitable.

It is important to view plants in containers as integral parts of the garden, rather than as separate entities, and use them to extend the growing area into the hard-surface area. To this end, the plants chosen should include a mixture of both foliage and flowering varieties, so that the arrangement has structure as well as colour.

Position the pots around the entrance way or to edge stairs and paths to link the garden with the inside of the house.

PLANTING A CONTAINER

1 Cover the base of the container with a layer of coarse gravel or polystyrene (plastic), to help drainage.

2 Cover the drainage material with a layer of compost (soil mix) until the container is about half full.

3 Arrange the plant(s) inside the container and place compost around each to hold in position. Add and firm more compost around the plants, but leave a gap of about 1 cm (1/2 in).

4 Water the container thoroughly. Cover the surface of the compost with a layer of coarse grit or gravel, to act as a decorative mulch.

Left: *Container-grown plants can be enhanced by the choice of pot used. Remember this is not a low-maintenance option as the plants will not be able to draw as much nourishment or water from the surrounding soil.*

Opposite: *Arrangements of pots will enable you to grow plants with specific soil requirements, and the combinations can be varied as required.*

PERMANENT PLANTS FOR CONTAINERS

Arundinaria murieliae
    (*Fargesia murieliae*)
Arundinaria viridstraita
    (*Pleioblastus auricomus*)
Aucuba japonica (any
    variegated variety)
Buxus sempervirens (box)
Camellia
Choisya ternata 'Sundance'
Cordyline australis
Fatsia japonica'

Hakonechloa macra
    'Alboaurea'
Hostas
Houttuynia cordata
    'Chameleon'
Hydrangea macrophylla
Laurus nobilis
Lilium (most dwarf hybrids are
    suitable)
Mahonia 'Charity'
Rhododendron yakushimanum

Choosing Containers

The vast range of containers available means that they can be chosen to match the situation and the budget. Most containers can be customized and can do a great deal to improve the most unpromising environments.

TYPES OF CONTAINER

There are a multitude of containers on the market, made from a wide range of materials, and of varying quality and durability. One of the oldest is terracotta, either glazed or unglazed, which produces a rough, earthy container; terracotta will blend well in most gardens. It is reasonably durable, as long as it was guaranteed frost-proof when it was bought, otherwise it may shatter. Terracotta is used for pots, strawberry tubs, troughs and wall pots.

Wooden containers, such as half-barrels, tubs and troughs, have a rural look, are natural insulators (keeping plant roots warmer than stone or plastic) and are ideal for an informal setting. Those square wooden planters often called "Versailles", however, can be used very successfully in formal gardens and are particularly effective with very architectural plants, such as topiary, used in pairs to frame an entrance. How durable wooden containers are will depend upon how well they have been treated and seasoned, and they will probably need continued care as time goes on.

Reconstituted stone is used for larger pots, urns and troughs, and is much heavier than terracotta or wood. For this reason, it is a good choice where the container is likely to be left in position for a long time. These containers are usually highly ornamental, and suit a formal position near the house, or at the entrance to a seating area or walkway.

Concrete pots, urns and troughs are similar to reconstituted stone ones, and are equally heavy. Both concrete and reconstituted stone pots should be allowed to weather for several months before lime-hating plants are planted into them.

Plastic pots come in a wide variety of shapes, sizes and colours, are cheap and light to handle, and unlike the other materials, are not porous, so that water is not lost through the sides. Improvements are constantly being made to increase the durability, but they are still likely to crack if they are kept in strong sunlight.

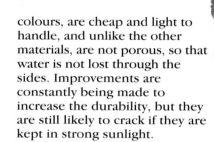

Top: Baskets can be made of traditional material or of wire.

Above: Galvanized tin is used for beautiful planters.

Left: Terracotta pots are available in all styles and sizes.

Opposite: A wheelbarrow was given a distressed paint effect, then filled with wooden trug baskets and terracotta pots.

COMPOST (SOIL MIX) FOR CONTAINERS

The two main types of compost (soil mix) available for use in containers are soilless and soil-based. Soilless composts are based on peat, or a peat-substitute such as coir fibre, and are light and easy to handle. They contain sufficient nutrients for at least one growing season, and are suitable for plants that will only be in the container for a maximum of 12 months before being repotted or discarded. They are free-draining and, once they dry out, they can be very difficult to re-wet.

Soil-based composts contain a lot of natural soil, so they are heavier to handle but much better at hanging on to both water and nutrients. Larger or older plants, or those which are to remain in the same pots for a long period of time, will benefit from the stability offered by this type.

A Basket of Spring Flowers

Miniature daffodils, deep blue pansies, yellow polyanthus and variegated ivy are planted together to make a hanging basket that will flower for many weeks in early spring.

Plant in autumn if growing daffodils from bulb and late winter or early spring for ready-grown daffodils.

MATERIALS
30cm (12in) hanging basket
Sphagnum moss
Compost (soil mix)
Slow-release plant food
    granules

PLANTS
3 variegated ivies
5 miniature daffodil bulbs 'Tête-
    à-Tête', or similar
3 blue pansies (*Viola*)
2 yellow polyanthus

variegated ivy

polyanthus

pansy

*miniature
daffodils*

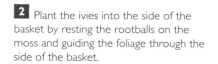

1 Line the lower half of the basket with moss.

2 Plant the ivies into the side of the basket by resting the rootballs on the moss and guiding the foliage through the side of the basket.

3 Line the rest of the basket with moss and add a layer of compost (soil mix) to the bottom of the basket. Push the daffodil bulbs into the compost.

4 Fill the remainder of the basket with compost, mixing a teaspoon of slow-release plant food granules into the top layer. Plant the pansies in the top of the basket.

5 Plant the polyanthus between the pansies.

Spring Display in a Copper Boiler

An old wash boiler makes an attractive container for a display of white tulips underplanted with purple violets and evergreen periwinkles.

MATERIALS AND TOOLS
Copper boiler, 60cm (24in) diameter
Plastic pot, 20cm (8in) diameter
Compost (soil mix)
Trowel

PLANTS
20 white tulip bulbs or tulips in bud
5 purple violets
2 periwinkles (*Vinca major* was used here)

tulip

periwinkle

violet

1 Place an upturned 20cm (8in) pot in the base of the boiler before filling it with soil mix.

4 Plant one violet in the centre and four around the edges. Scoop out the soil by hand to avoid damaging the growing tips of the tulips beneath the soil.

2 If you are planting tulip bulbs, half-fill the container with soil mix, arrange the bulbs evenly over the surface and then cover them with a good 15cm (6in) of soil mix. This should be done in late autumn.

3 Do the underplanting in the early spring. The soil mix will have settled in the container and should be topped up to within 8cm (3in) of the rim. Remove the violets from their pots. Gently squeeze the rootballs and loosen the roots to aid the plants' growth.

5 Plant a periwinkle at each side of the central violet, again loosening the rootballs.

GARDENER'S TIP

Lift the tulips when they have
finished flowering and hang
them up to dry in a cool airy
place. They can be replanted
later in the winter to flower
again next year. Provided you
pick off the dead flowers the
violet will flower all summer.
For a summer display, lift the
central violet and plant a
standard white marguerite in the
centre of the container.

Plant bulbs in autumn or plants in
bud in spring. Plant the violets and
periwinkle in spring.

6 Alternatively, if you are planting
tulips in bud, the whole scheme should
be planted at the same time. Work from
one side of the pot to the other,
interplanting the tulips with the violets
and periwinkles. Press down firmly
around the tulips or they will work
themselves loose in windy weather.
Position in sun or partial shade.

Terracotta Planter of Spring Bulbs

This container of bright yellow tulips and daffodils will brighten the dullest spring day. The variegated ivies conceal the soil and pleasantly soften the edge of the planter.

MATERIALS AND TOOLS
Planter, 60cm (24in) long
Crocks or drainage material
Standard soil mix
Trowel

PLANTS
10 tulips
6 pots of miniature daffodils
6 variegated ivies

tulip

miniature daffodil

GARDENER'S TIP
Plant in early spring.

1 Fill the bottom of the planter with drainage material. Be especially careful to cover the drainage holes so that they do not become clogged with soil mix.

2 Remove the tulips from their pots and carefully separate the bulbs. Plant them in a staggered double row down the length of the planter.

3 Interplant the container with miniature daffodils.

4 Finally plant the ivies around the edge of the planter. Remember that if you are using a planter like this as a window box, the back of the arrangement should look just as good as the front.

Tinware Planter of Lily of the Valley

Lily of the valley grow well in containers and will thrive in the shade where their delicate scented flowers stand out among the greenery. Surrounding the plants with sheet moss is practical and will stop the soil splashing back onto the leaves and flowers during spring showers.

MATERIALS AND TOOLS
Tinware planter
Clay capsules
Compost (soil mix)
Spaghnum moss
Trowel

PLANTS
6–8 pots of lily of the valley

lily of the valley

1 Fill the bottom of the planter with 5cm (2in) of clay granules.

2 Cover the granules with a layer of soil mix and place the lily of the valley plants on the soil mix.

3 Fill in around the plants with more soil mix, and press firmly around the plants so that they won't rock about in the wind. Cover the soil with moss, fitting it around the stems of the lily of the valley, so that it will keep the plants upright.

GARDENER'S TIP

If you want to bring your planter indoors to enjoy the scent of the flowers, use a planter without drainage holes in the base, but be very careful not to overwater. Once the plants have finished flowering replant them in a pot with normal drainage holes or in the garden. They are woodland plants and will be quite happy under trees.

Plant early in spring.

Sweet Peas, Geranium and Chives

This large basket is filled with sweet peas surrounding a geranium *(Pelargonium)* and interplanted with chives to provide contrasting leaves.

GARDENER'S TIP
Sweet peas will flower longer if you keep picking the flowers and remove any seed pods. Similarly, chives grow longer and stronger if you remove their flower heads before they seed.

Plant in late spring.

MATERIALS
40cm (16in) hanging basket
Sphagnum moss
Compost (soil mix)
Slow-release food granules

PLANTS
Geranium *(Pelargonium)*
2–3 small or low-growing sweet peas such as 'Snoopea'
3 chive plants

sweet peas

chives

geranium

1 Line the basket with moss, reserving a small amount.

2 Fill the basket with compost (soil mix) and mix a teaspoon of slow-release plant food granules into the top of the compost. Plant the geranium *(Pelargonium)* in the centre of the basket.

3 Gently divide the sweet peas into clumps of about eight plants each.

4 Plant the sweet pea clumps around the edge of the basket.

5 Plant the chives between the sweet peas and the geranium.

6 Fill any gaps with a little moss. Water well and hang in a sunny position.

Marguerites and Pimpernels

Anagallis, the less well-known blue relative of the wild scarlet pimpernel, has been planted to climb amongst the stems of the yellow marguerites and snapdragons. Blue-flowered variegated *Felicia* and golden *Helichrysum* complete the picture.

GARDENER'S TIP
Deadhead the marguerites, snapdragons and *Felicia* to keep them flowering all summer. When planting the marguerites, pinch out the growing tips to encourage bushy plants.

Plant in spring.

MATERIALS
76cm (30in) window box
Compost (soil mix)
Slow-release food granules

PLANTS
2 yellow marguerites
 (*Argyranthemum*) 'Jamaica
 Primrose'
4 blue *Anagallis*
3 variegated *Felicia*
3 *Helichrysum petiolare*
 'Aureum'
4 yellow snapdragons
 (*Antirrhinum*)

marguerite

Anagallis

Felicia

Helichrysum

snapdragon

1 Check the drainage holes are open in the base and, if not, drill or punch them open. Fill the window box with compost, mixing in 3 teaspoons of slow-release plant food granules.

2 Plant the marguerites on either side of the centre in the middle of the window box.

3 Plant two of the *Anagallis* in the back corners of the window box and the other two at the front, on either side of the marguerites.

4 Plant one *Felicia* in the centre of the box and the other two on either side of the *Anagallis*.

5 Plant the *Helichrysum* in the front corners of the window box.

6 Plant two of the snapdragons on either side of the central *Felicia* and the other two on either side of the marguerites. Water thoroughly, drain, and stand in a sunny or partially sunny position.

A Pastel Composition

Pure white geraniums emerge from a sea of blue *Felicia*, pinky-blue *Brachycome* daisies and verbena in this romantic basket.

MATERIALS
36cm (14in) hanging basket
Sphagnum moss
Compost (soil mix)
Slow-release food granules

PLANTS
2 pink verbena
2 pink *Brachycome*
Blue *Felicia*
White geranium (*Pelargonium*)

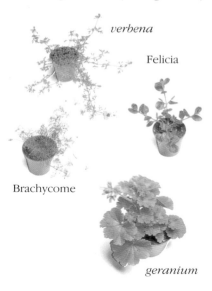

verbena

Felicia

Brachycome

geranium

I Line the basket with moss.

2 Fill the basket with compost (soil mix), adding a teaspoon of slow-release plant food granules into the top layer.

3 Plant the verbenas opposite each other at the edge of the basket, angling the rootballs to encourage the foliage to tumble over the sides.

4 Plant the *Brachycome* daisies around the edge of the basket.

GARDENER'S TIP
White geranium flowers discolour as they age; be sure to pick them off to keep the basket looking its best.

Plant in late spring or early summer.

5 Plant the *Felicia* off-centre in the middle of the basket.

6 Plant the geranium (*Pelargonium*) off-centre in the remaining space in the middle of the basket. Water thoroughly and hang in a sunny position.

An Antique Wall Basket

This old wirework basket is an attractive container for a planting scheme of deep pink pansies, a blue *Convolvulus,* a variegated-leaf geranium (*Pelargonium*) and deep pink alyssum.

GARDENER'S TIP
Wall baskets look good amongst climbing plants, but you will need to cut and tie back the surrounding foliage if it gets too exuberant.

Plant in late spring or early summer.

MATERIALS
30cm (12in) wall basket
Sphagnum moss
Compost (soil mix)
Slow-release food granules

PLANTS
5 rose-pink alyssum
Ivy-leaved geranium
    (*Pelargonium*) 'L'Elégante'
3 deep pink pansies
Convolvulus sabatius

alyssum

1 Line the back of the basket and the lower half of the front with moss. Plant the alyssum into the side of the basket by resting the rootballs on the moss and guiding the foliage through the wires.

2 Line the remainder of the basket with moss, fill with compost (soil mix), mixing a half-teaspoon of plant food granules into the top of the compost. Plant the geranium at the front.

3 Plant the pansies around the geranium.

geranium

pansy

Convolvulus

4 Plant the *Convolvulus* at the back of the basket, trailing its foliage through the other plants. Water well and hang in partial sun.

A Trough of Alpines

A selection of easy-to-grow alpine plants are grouped in a basket-weave stone planter to create a miniature garden. The mulch of gravel is both attractive and practical as it prevents soil splashing onto the leaves of the plants.

GARDENER'S TIP
Tidy the trough once a month, removing dead flowerheads and leaves and adding more gravel if necessary. A trough like this will last a number of years before it needs replanting.

Plant in spring.

MATERIALS
40cm (16in) stone trough
Suitable drainage material
Compost (soil mix)
Slow-release food granules
Gravel

PLANTS
Sempervivum
Alpine *Aquilegia*
White rock rose
 (*Helianthemum*)
Papaver alpinum
Alpine phlox
Pink saxifrage
White saxifrage

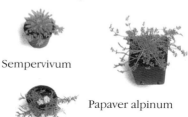

Sempervivum

Papaver alpinum

alpine phlox

rock rose

alpine Aquilegia

saxifrage

1 Cover the base of the trough with a layer of crocks.

2 Fill the container with compost (soil mix), adding in a teaspoon of slow-release plant food granules and extra gravel for improved drainage.

3 Before planting, arrange the plants, still in their pots, in the trough to decide on the most attractive arrangement.

4 Start planting from one end, working across the trough.

5 Complete the planting.

6 Scatter a good layer of gravel around the plants. Water thoroughly and stand in a sunny position.

Flowers for Late Summer

Although this window box is already looking good, towards the end of the summer it will really come into its own – by then the vibrant red and purple flowers of the geranium, *Salvia* and lavenders will be at their most prolific.

MATERIALS
60cm (24in) wooden planter, stained black
Polystyrene or other suitable drainage material
Compost (soil mix)
Slow-release plant food granules

PLANTS
Geranium (*Pelargonium*)
2 *Lavandula pinnata*
2 *Salvia* 'Raspberry Royal'
2 blue *Brachycome* daisies
Convolvulus sabatius
6 rose-pink alyssum

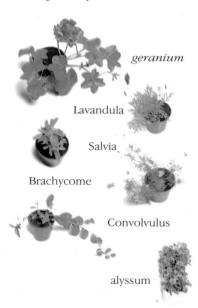

geranium

Lavandula

Salvia

Brachycome

Convolvulus

alyssum

1 Line the container base with polystyrene or similar. Fill the window box with compost (soil mix), adding in 3 teaspoons of food granules. Plant the geranium at the back of the window box, in the centre.

2 Plant the two lavenders in the rear corners of the box.

3 Plant the *Salvia* at the front of the box on either side of the geranium.

4 Plant the *Brachycome* daisies in the front corners of the box.

5 Plant the *Convolvulus* in the centre, in front of the geranium.

Both the lavenders and the *Salvia* are highly aromatic, so if possible position this box near a door or a path, so that you can enjoy the fragrance as you brush against the plants.

Plant in early summer.

6 Fill in the spaces with the alyssum. Water well and place in a sunny position.

Evergreens and Extra Colour

They may be easy to look after but all-year-round window boxes can start to look a bit lifeless after a couple of seasons. It does not take much trouble to add a few seasonal flowers and it can make all the difference.

MATERIALS
76cm (30in) window box
Compost (soil mix)
Slow-release food granules

PLANTS
Hebe 'Baby Marie'
Convolvulus cneorum
Potentilla 'Nunk'
Variegated ivies
2 *Diascia* 'Ruby Field'
Pink marguerite
    Argyranthemum) 'Flamingo'

Hebe

Convolvulus
cneorum

Potentilla

ivy

Diascia

marguerite

GARDENER'S TIP
At the end of the summer, remove the *Diascias* and marguerite, feed the remaining plants with more granules and fill the spaces with winter-flowering plants such as pansies or heathers.

Plant in spring.

1 Check the drainage holes are open in the base and, if not, drill or punch them open. Fill the window box with compost (soil mix), mixing in 3 teaspoons of slow-release plant food granules. Plant the *Hebe* in the centre.

2 Plant the *Convolvulus* near the right-hand end of the window box.

3 Plant the *Potentilla* near the left-hand end of the window box.

4 Plant the two ivies at the front corners of the window box.

5 Plant the *Diascias* on either side of the *Hebe* at the front of the window box.

6 Plant the marguerite between the *Hebe* and the *Convolvulus* at the back of the window box. Water well and stand in full or partial sun.

Autumn Colour

Long Tom pots were very popular in Victorian times. They are now being made and are available in a variety of colours. There is a wonderfully architectural quality to the outline of this cream Long Tom and the plants it contains.

MATERIALS AND TOOLS
Long Tom, 30cm (12in) pot
Crocks
Equal mix loam-based soil mix
    and standard soil mix
Clay saucer
Gravel
Slow-release food granules
Trowel or scoop

PLANTS
Caper figwort (*Phygelus*)
Day lily (*Hemerocallis dumortieri*)
Hardy fuchsia, preferably a
    variety with compact growth

day lily

Cape figwort

Fuchsia

1 Cover the drainage holes at the base of the pot with crocks.

2 Position the largest plant first. You will probably have to loosen the soil around the rootballs of the plants to fit them all in the pot. Gently squeeze the soil and tease the roots loose.

3 Add the other two plants, again loosening the soil if necessary.

4 Fill any spaces between the plants with soil mix, and push the soil mix firmly down the sides of the pot so that no air spaces are left.

5 The shape of the container means that the soil will dry out quite quickly, especially when it is so densely planted. To counteract this, stand it in a clay saucer filled with wet gravel.

6 Scatter 2 tablespoon of plant food granules onto the soil mix and mix in. Water regularly and place in a sunny position.

Classic Winter Colours

Convolvulus cneorum is an attractive small shrub with eye-catching silver-grey leaves which last through winter. It has white flowers in spring and summer. Planted with ice-blue pansies, it makes a subtle display from autumn to spring.

MATERIALS
30cm (12in) hanging basket
Sphagnum moss
Compost (soil mix)

PLANTS
8 silver/blue pansies (*Viola*)
  'Silver Wings', or similar
Convolvulus cneorum

Convolvulus

pansies

GARDENER'S TIP
At the end of winter cut back any dead wood or straggly branches on the *Convolvulus cneorum* and give a liquid feed to encourage new growth. These small shrubs may be used in baskets for a season, but then need planting into a larger container or the border.

1 Half line the basket with moss and fill with compost (soil mix).

2 Plant 4 of the pansies into the side of the basket by placing their root-balls on the compost and gently guiding the leaves through the side of the basket.

Plant in autumn.

3 Line the rest of the basket with moss and top up with compost. Plant the *Convolvulus* in the centre of the basket.

4 Plant the remaining 4 pansies around the *Convolvulus*. Water well and hang in sun or partial shade.

Evergreen Garden

Evergreen plants come in many shapes, sizes and shades of green. Grouped together in containers they will provide you with year-round interest.

MATERIALS AND TOOLS

Terracotta containers of various
sizes
Crocks or similar drainage
material
Equal mix loam-based soil mix
and container soil mix
Saucers
Gravel
Trowel

PLANTS

False cypress
Silver *euonymus*
Darwin's barberry (*Berberis darwinii*)
Berberis thunbergii
'Atropurpurea Nana'
Cypress (*Chamaecyparis pisifera*)
Pachysandra terminalis
Bergenia

barberry

Bergenia

Pachysandra terminalis

1 Large plants, such as false cypress, should be potted into a proportionally large container. If it is at all potbound, tease the roots loose before planting in its new pot. Place plenty of crocks or similar drainage material at the base of the pot. Fill around the rootball with soil mix, pressing it down firmly around the edges of the pot.

2 Smaller plants, like Bergenia, should be planted in a pot slightly larger than its existing pot. Place crocks in the base of the pot, position the plant and then fill around the edges with soil mix.

3 Plants will stay most longer if they are stood in saucers of wet gravel. This group of plants will do well positioned in partial shade. Water regularly and feed with slow-release plant food granules in the spring and autumn.

GARDENER'S TIP

Include some golden or variegated foliage amongst your evergreens or the group will look rather dull and one dimensional. Experiment for yourself and see how the lighter colours "lift" a group of plants.

Plant at any time of the year.

Winter Cheer

Many window boxes are left unplanted through the winter, but you can soon brighten the house or garden for the winter season with this easy arrangement of pot-grown plants plunged in bark.

MATERIALS
40cm (16in) glazed window
    box
Bark

PLANTS
2 miniature conifers
2 red polyanthus
2 variegated ivies

1 Water all the plants. Place the conifers, still in their pots, at either end of the window box.

2 Half-fill the window box with bark.

3 Place the pots of polyanthus on the bark between the two conifers.

miniature conifer

ivy

polyanthus

4 Place the pots of ivy on the bark in the front corners of the window box. Add further bark to the container until all the pots are concealed. Water only when plants show signs of dryness. Stand in any position.

GARDENER'S TIP
When it is time to replant the window box, plunge the conifers, still in their pots, in a shady position in the garden. Water well through the spring and summer and they may be used again next year.

Plant in early winter.

An Evergreen Wall Basket

Pansies will flower throughout the winter. Even if they are flattened by rain, frost or snow, at the first sign of better weather their heads will pop up again to bring brightness to the dullest day. They have been planted with ivies to provide colour from early autumn through to late spring.

MATERIALS
30cm (12in) wall basket
Sphagnum moss
Compost (soil mix)

PLANTS
2 golden variegated ivies
2 copper pansies (*Viola*)
Yellow pansy (*Viola*)

pansy

ivy

GARDENER'S TIP
Winter baskets do not need regular feeding and should only be watered in very dry conditions. To prolong the flowering life of the pansies, dead-head regularly and pinch out any straggly stems to encourage new shoots from the base.

Plant in autumn.

1 Line the basket with moss.

2 Three-quarters fill the basket with compost (soil mix) and position the ivies with their rootballs resting on the compost. Guide the stems through the sides of the basket so that they trail downwards. Pack moss around the ivies and top up the basket with compost.

3 Plant the copper pansies at each end of the basket.

4 Plant the yellow pansy in the centre of the basket. Water well and hang in shade or semi-shade.

Trug of Winter Pansies

Winter pansies are wonderfully resilient and will bloom bravely throughout the winter as long as they are regularly deadheaded. This trug may be moved around to provide colour wherever it is needed and acts as a perfect antidote to mid-winter gloom.

MATERIALS AND TOOLS
Old wooden trug
Spagnum moss
Standard soil mix
Slow-release plant food granules
Trowel

PLANTS
15 winter-flowering pansies

winter-flowering pansies

GARDENER'S TIP
An old basket, colander, or an enamel bread bin could be used instead. Junk shops and flea markets are a great source of containers that are too battered for their original use, but great for planting.

Plant in autumn to flower in winter.

1 Line the trug with a generous layer of the spagnum moss.

2 Fill the moss lining with soil mix.

3 Plant the pansies by starting at one end and filling the spaces between the plants with soil mix as you go. Gently firm each plant into position and add a final layer of soil mix mixed with a tablespoon of plant food granules around the pansies. Water and place in a fairly sunny position.

The Apothecary Box

Many plants have healing qualities and, while they should always be used with caution, some of the more commonly used herbs have been successful country remedies for centuries.

GARDENER'S TIP
Herbs should not be used to treat an existing medical condition without first checking with your medical practitioner.

Plant in the spring.

MATERIALS
Wooden trug
Compost (soil mix)
2 teaspoons pelleted chicken manure or organic plant food

PLANTS
Lavender – for relaxing
Rosemary – for hair and scalp
Chamomile – for restful sleep
Fennel – for digestion
Feverfew – for migraine
3 pot marigolds (*Calendula*) – for healing

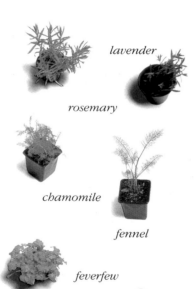

lavender

rosemary

chamomile

fennel

feverfew

pot marigold

1 Place a layer of drainage material in the trug and fill with compost, mixing in 2 teaspoons of fertilizer.

2 Plant the lavender in the centre of the trug and the rosemary in the front right-hand corner.

3 Plant the chamomile in the back left-hand corner.

4 Plant the fennel in the back right-hand corner.

5 Plant the feverfew in the front left-hand corner.

6 Plant the marigolds in the spaces between the other herbs. Water well and stand in full or partial sun.

Balconies and Roof Gardens

Of all the places to create a garden, a balcony or rooftop must be among the most challenging, especially if the site is exposed. The reward of a green haven high above the rest of the world is incentive enough to try, and it is much more relaxing to look out on to plants than on to bricks and concrete.

Trailing and climbing plants, lush foliage and bright flowers can all be brought into action to transform a plain, hard area into a delightful secret world, often invisible to those walking below.

Above: *Plants for small spaces should earn their keep. Always choose varieties with a long flowering season*

Left: *This terrace serves as an extension to the indoor living space and can be used for entertaining or simply relaxing.*

Exposure to Wind

Gusting wind and turbulence can be difficult for plants, but a well-placed windbreak can be disguised behind more tolerant plants, to shelter and protect delicate species.

CREATING WINDBREAKS

In built-up areas, the wind can really whistle between the "man-made canyons" of tall buildings, causing turbulence and destruction. Poorly fixed containers, light plants and furniture are all at risk of being dislodged. Plants with soft, tender foliage are likely to be scorched by the wind, resulting in poor growth.

Creating a windbreak will help minimize the problem; one which is partly permeable to the wind is much more effective than a solid one, where localized turbulence is created as the wind hits it and is deflected. Black windbreak netting becomes almost invisible if it is erected and then hidden behind a painted trellis, especially if plants are then grown up the trellis. This form of windbreak is both effective, and does not take up much room – an important consideration when space is at a premium. Where more room is available, a screen of tall, wind-tolerant shrubs installed along the most vulnerable side will act to shelter the area behind them; many plants will tolerate this kind of exposure while still providing colour and interest throughout the year. Using a broken windbreak rather than a solid one also allows full advantage to be taken of the view, so that even a windy day will not spoil the enjoyment of sitting out on the terrace.

WIND-TOLERANT SHRUBS

Some of these shrubs grow large in a garden, but in a container will remain much more compact.

Calluna vulgaris
Cornus alba 'Aurea'
Cotinus coggygria
Euonymus fortunei varieties
Hippophae rhamnoides
Hydrangea paniculata
Kalmia latifolia
Lavatera olbia
Lonicera pileata
Mahonia aquifolium
Pachysandra terminalis
Pieris floribunda
Spiraea japonica
Tamarix pentrandra
Taxus baccata
Thuja occidentalis
Viburnum tinus

ERECTING A WINDBREAK

- If required, paint the posts intended to support the netting and trellis. Attach securely to the railings or wall, with clamps or bolts.
- Attach black windbreak netting to the back of the posts.
- Fix trellis panels to the posts, in front of the netting.
- Train climbing plants to cover the trellis.

Bamboo panels act as a windbreak, while a parasol provides protection from the glare of the sun.

Lavatera *is a good choice for windy areas as it is strong and has an abundance of flowers in summer.*

Euonymus *will grow in unfavourable conditions and can be grown to screen more delicate plants.*

Opposite: *Here, strong fabric acts as a shield for plants while still allowing some light to penetrate.*

Overhead Screening

Used to make the area more secluded or simply to provide shade, overhead screening adds to the atmosphere of the balcony or roof garden by providing continuity with the living space inside.

ADAPTABLE SCREENING

Make sure the screening won't make rooms too dark. If this is likely to be a problem, a compromise in the form of a deciduous climber growing over a pergola may be the answer, providing cover during the summer but not the winter, when the light levels are lower.

Pergolas need to be sturdy to support the weight of the covering, but they are extremely versatile. The plants you grow up the sides can range from annuals like sweet peas to woody perennials such as grape-

vines, always bearing in mind the dimensions of the pergola. The sides can support cane or bamboo screens, if extra privacy is needed, and, if you don't want to grow plants over the top, you can pull over a canvas cover.

Pergolas can be made from anything from the usual rough timber to sleek bamboo poles. You need to choose carefully for the roof garden or balcony, according to how much extra weight can be introduced. Consider the prevailing wind direction, which may cause a

problem to a high structure if you don't give extra protection.

Canvas awnings are convenient to install, and can be designed to retract into a casing on the wall when not required. Unbleached sailcloth and lightweight muslin are natural-looking fabrics that will blend with most colours.

UMBRELLAS AND PARASOLS

Large, off-white canvas umbrellas are ideal for short-term cover where space allows, as long as the wind is not likely to gust and sweep them away.

Patio parasols are available in many colours so you can co-ordinate them with other fabrics. They will need to be anchored through the table into a base.

Above and opposite: *Parasols are an easy form of overhead screening, but may be less suitable for windy sites.*

Left: *A retractable canvas awning is a great solution for overhead screening, as it provides total shelter when required, but can be pulled back when no longer needed.*

Weight on the Balcony

Balconies vary considerably in their construction and appearance, from older, wrought-iron types to functional, modern brick ones. Roofs may not vary so much, but, if you are gardening on a flat-roofed extension, you need to be sure it is safe.

BUILDING STRUCTURE

Before you begin designing the garden, check the balcony or roof structurally, to make sure that it will bear the additional weight of the plants and containers you intend to bring in. A medium-sized tub, when planted up and watered, can weigh as much as 9kg (20lb), and you are likely to want many more than one. This is more likely to be a problem on an older building, where wear and tear may be taking their toll on the brickwork and mortar. The extra weight is difficult to judge, because it will not be constant, as the containers will weigh more when they have just been watered. This means that they may weigh more in winter than in summer, although this will also depend on local conditions and whether the plants have shed their leaves or not.

Consider the weight problem at the planning stage. How much extra load your roof or balcony can bear will depend on its construction and age; it is a wise precaution to explain the plans to a qualified builder or architect, and be guided by their opinion. Careful consideration of the materials to be used, however, can keep the extra weight to a minimum. Timber decking or tiles are lighter alternatives to paving slabs and require less effort to handle – a definite advantage for a roof garden, where everything has to be brought up from ground level. Screens of wattle, bamboo and plastic are lighter than timber fencing. Wooden trellis comes in a variety of weights, all of which are heavier than plastic.

Containers themselves also vary considerably in weight; plastic and wood weigh much less than reconstituted stone or concrete, or even terracotta. Even the compost (soil mix) can make a difference, because soil-based composts weigh a great deal more than soilless ones, even when these are wet. The addition of perlite or vermiculite to the compost reduces the weight still further, although it will also speed up drainage, so you may have to water more often. (Mixing water-retaining gel into the planting mixture when you plant up the containers helps it to retain water.) Every little helps: consider using broken expanded polystyrene (plastic foam) in the base of the container, rather than the traditional pieces of broken crockery.

Above: *Plastic is lighter than terracotta. Here, a plastic saucer is placed in the base of a fruit-picking basket (also lightweight). Plants in plastic pots can then be arranged in the basket, and the pots will be disguised.*

Expanded polystyrene (plastic foam) is a light option for drainage material. Place at the bottom of the pot before planting.

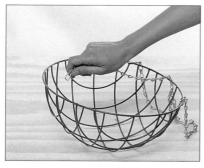

An open-weave wire hanging basket is a better option than stone or terracotta planters.

Baskets can be lined with moss or fibre-based proprietary liner, as here. A liner will absorb less water than a moss one.

Opposite: *If your balcony or terrace is relatively sheltered you can use lightweight material such as cane for furniture and screens.*

Watering and Drainage

Natural rainfall is not always sufficient for plants, even when they are growing in the garden, so it is particularly important to their health that watering is not neglected when they are growing in containers.

WATERING SYSTEMS

In their natural surroundings, many plants survive during periods of low rainfall by extending their roots deep into the earth in search of residual moisture. In containers, they are totally dependent on a regular supply of water to stay alive.

You can cut down on the need to water frequently by adding water-retaining gel to the compost. This swells up as it absorbs water, and releases it to the plants as they need it.

Irrigation systems that connect the water supply directly to the plants are an excellent way of cutting down on wasted water, because all the water is delivered exactly where

it is needed. These can be operated by timing devices to suit the needs of the plants.

You also need to consider how to get rid of rainwater. On a balcony, excess water can usually be drained away without a problem, but on a roof it may be more difficult. The surplus must drain off quickly, or the roof might not bear the weight.

If you are laying flooring, it must not interfere with the waterproof membrane covering the roof, and it is important that no damage occurs during installation that would cause water to seep into the rooms below. Ensure that canopies will not trap water during bad weather.

A drip-feed system is ideal for hanging baskets and window boxes. Watering will probably have to be programmed to operate at least a couple of times a day in hot weather.

Drip-feed systems can be used for plants in containers. Use a T-joint to run branches or tubes for individual drip feeds. Even in wet weather, containers under the "rain shadow" of a wall often need additional water to maximise growth.

A timing device will turn your watering system on and off automatically, yet can easily be de-activated if the weather is wet.

Left: *Use individual feed heads for watering containers. The special pegs will enable you to fix the tube in a suitable position.*

Opposite: *When installing the surface of the terrace make sure it does not interfere with the underlying structure of the roof.*

Plant Interest the Year Round

No garden need ever have a time when it looks dull or uninteresting, particularly a roof or balcony garden, which might well be visible all the time just outside the sitting room windows.

Above: *Colours in a summer scheme can be hot and vibrant or pale and cooling.*

Opposite: *Autumn flowers and foliage are complemented by orange gourds.*

PLANTS THAT EARN THEIR KEEP

In any garden, a plant should earn its place. One season of interest is acceptable if it is spectacular, but two are better and, if a particular plant has pretty flowers in spring or summer and then a wonderful blaze of autumn colour, it has definitely earned its keep.

Of course, not all plants do this; for foliage plants, which act as a foil to more dramatic flowering specimens, it is sufficient that they look gloriously lush throughout the season. One way of increasing the seasonal attraction of a woody shrub or small tree is to grow a second plant, a climbing or trailing one, through it. Choose a specimen to complement the colours of the host plant, whether it flowers at the same time as its host or separately, and one that will not outgrow or overwhelm the host.

By using the full range of plants available, it is possible to have colour in every season of the year. Then, even if the weather prevents work or relaxation outside, the garden still looks attractive.

Strong foliage can look spectacular in winter, when frost highlights the sharply toothed leaves of plants such as *Helleborus argutifolius* and mahonia, or makes the seed-heads of bronze fennel sparkle in the early mist. Birds appreciate the berries on plants like pyracantha, which persist on the plant throughout the winter if they are allowed.

Plant at all levels to make full use of the space. If the foliage of a herbaceous plant dies off in the autumn and does not return until late spring, fill the gap with early-flowering bulbs or corms, such as cyclamen (*C. hederifolium* or *C. coum*), crocus, snowdrop, dwarf narcissus, or dwarf iris, which will flower and die down again before the larger plant needs the room. They can be left in place throughout the year, even in a container, so that there is no root disturbance to plants nearby.

Above: Monarda *'Croftway Pink'* gives a beautiful show of colour in the summer.

PLANTS FOR YEAR-ROUND COLOUR

Winter
Cyclamen coum
Garrya elliptica 'James Roof'
Helleborus niger
Iris unguicularis
Mahonia x *media* 'Charity'

Spring
Berberis darwinii
Bergenia cordifolia
Forsythia
Galanthus nivalis
　(snowdrop)
Primula vulgaris

Summer
Argyranthemum dwarf dahlias
Lilium (dwarf hybrids)
Lonicera x *brownii*
　'Dropmore Scarlet'
Potentilla fruiticose varieties

Autumn
Aster novi-belgii (Michaelmas
　daisies), dwarf varieties
Clematis orientalis '
Nerine bowdenii
Rudbeckia fulgida var. *deamii*
Skimmia japonica ssp.
　reevesiana

Access to the Balcony or Roof Garden

Access routes to the balcony or roof garden are usually straightforward and should not present as many problems as found in front gardens. There are some special considerations for these areas, however. The most important point, which must be borne in mind at the initial planning stage, is that fire escapes need to be kept clear – especially when these are shared.

KEEP EXITS CLEAR

In an older property, where several flats are reached by means of a system of metal stairs and balconies, the whole appearance of the building can be altered and enhanced by allowing a tracery of climbing plants to grow along the metalwork. The building develops a character all its own and each individual balcony can then become a small garden for its owner, all different, but linked by the overall greenery. However, if the area in which the garden is being created constitutes part of a fire escape, it is essential for safety to keep it clear so people can descend quickly and easily in an emergency. This is particularly important for a communal balcony, where the same escape route is allocated to several flats – the last thing frightened people need in an emergency is to be falling over pots.

Top right: *Ensure easy access by keeping the area around the door clear of pots and other items.*

Right: *These pots, positioned outside the hand railings on a flight of stairs, are a clever compromise between practicality and decoration as they do not impede access.*

Left: *Climbing plants soften the metal stairs and hand rails.*

Safety on the Balcony or Roof Terrace

Safety considerations, such as checking the area has adequate structural strength for the added weight, should be taken care of before you plan your designs. After this, the main necessity is to carry out regular maintenance.

WEATHER

The weather is always an unpredictable element in any equation, simply because it is so variable. The following are the major factors to take into account.

All the fixtures and fittings on the balcony or roof will need to be secured against the possibility of a gust of wind knocking them over or off the edge. Many of the fittings, such as light furniture, can be taken indoors during the worst months of the year. Check permanent features like trellis screens, which will be expected to bear the brunt of the weather, to ensure that they are firmly fixed into position.

Bright sunlight will make plastic brittle after a few years, so plant supports such as trellises made out of this material may break away from the wall.

Excess water can usually be swept off a balcony, but on a roof, getting rid of the water depends on a good drainage system. You should install this first, before bringing in any structures, furniture, containers or plants, to prevent a build-up of water from causing damage to the structure.

Awnings and canopies made of fabric, especially those of natural fibres, are at least twice as heavy when they are wet as when they are dry. If they are stretched across a frame, they can trap large pools of water on top, which may result in the material ripping away from its fixing points, deluging whatever is underneath.

OVERHANGING THE STREET

Where the balcony directly overhangs the street, containers attached to railings must be firmly fixed. Likewise, position any pots on low walls around the edge of the roof garden where they will not cause damage if they over-balance.

Above left: *A small balcony will not need much maintenance. Fabric covered furniture should not be left outside during the winter months, and all fixtures should be checked regularly to make sure they have not come loose.*

Above: *A profusion of window boxes and pots adorning balconies are a delight to all who pass by. Make sure they are firmly fixed, with brackets if necessary, to ensure they are safe.*

Maintenance for Balconies and Roof Gardens

Keeping the balcony or roof garden in a good condition will enhance your enjoyment of it. You need to consider the structure, the plants, and the fixtures and fittings. The big advantage of the balcony and roof garden over the ground-level variety is that many of the back-breaking routine tasks, such as digging, are simply not necessary. However, other jobs are unique to these areas and must not be neglected.

PLANTS

In general, the plants will need weeding only if any seedlings happen to appear, and pruning only to keep them healthy and in shape. If any are tied against a wall, check the wires and nails periodically, to make sure they are not pulling away, and tie in new shoots. Occasionally, especially if the plants are protected from the rain, wipe any build-up of dust from the leaves; if dust is allowed to remain, it will interfere with photosynthesis, and the growth of the plant will be slower. As a matter of routine, remove dead leaves from the plants before they begin to rot.

FLOOR SURFACES

The balcony is probably the easiest to maintain, because, by its very nature as an extended part of the living area, it is usually easy to sweep clean or wash down.

Decking will need to be brushed with a stiff brush to remove any algae; then treat with an algae killer. In addition, treat softwood decks with a preservative every year.

Wash tiles periodically to reduce any build-up of algae; re-lay any tiles that work loose before they crack.

Concrete tends to suffer most damage from small cracks. If you overlook or ignore these, the action of the weather, or a stray seedling that grows in the crack, can enlarge it and cause considerable damage. Repair the hole with a stiff mixture of concrete containing an adhesive.

Regularly rake any gravel level; it should not need any other attention.

Left: *Many herbaceous plants look better if dead-headed, but large-flowered shrubs benefit as well. With shrubs, be careful to remove only the dead flower in case you inadvertently remove the buds for the shoots carrying next year's flowers.*

Maintain deck floors by brushing and washing down with an anti-algae treatment.

RAILINGS
Rub these down and repaint them with a weather-resistant paint when they show signs of damage.

ELECTRICAL FITTINGS
If electricity has been connected to the roof garden, for lights or a pond pump, it should be checked every year for signs of wear; this is best done by a qualified electrician, who can replace any damaged cables or connections.

Left: *Wooden furniture should be treated with wood preservative at the end of each season. Hardwood furniture needs little care but will benefit from being cleaned and oiled.*

Below: *Most containers will need little looking after but do check for signs of cracking before replanting in the spring.*

SEATING
Bring the cushions from upholstered furniture inside during wet or cold weather. Wash plastic frames with a detergent solution to remove the water marks left by rain.

Metal furniture can be left outside but it will need a scrub in spring with a detergent solution, to remove the dust and deposits of the winter. It will benefit from a new coat of weather-resistant paint every two or three years.

Treat softwood timber seating with a preservative or new coat of varnish every year. Hardwoods, such as teak, do not need preservative. A rub over with white spirit (mineral spirits), soap and water and, finally, teak oil will protect them for the year.

CONTAINERS
Most containers will need little maintenance. Weathering tends to enhance their appearance rather than detract from it. Any that have been painted may need another coat, and reconstituted stone containers may need to be brushed down.

TRELLISES AND PERGOLAS
Particularly where the trellis has been erected as a windbreak, the means of support will need regular checking to make sure it is still rigidly in place. The bottoms of posts are prone to rot. Treat them with preservative but, as many wood treatments are toxic to plants, it is usually better to detach the plants from their supports, and protect them before you begin applying the preservative.

Gardening Practicalities

While never the most enjoyable part of gardening, feeding, weeding, watering and pest control cannot be neglected. You need not, however, spend inordinate amounts of time on these jobs since there are many short cuts and labour-saving techniques which will not compromise the well-being of your plants. With these more mundane tasks under control, you will be free to enjoy your garden with peace of mind.

Left: *Evergreen shrubs and rock gardens are less demanding, but be careful not to neglect the needs of your other plants.*

Above: *Gravel is a labour-saving, and potentially attractive, alternative to the toil and trouble of maintaining a lawn.*

Soil Preparation

One of the most important of all gardening techniques is soil preparation. It is the foundation of all future growth and success. Neglect it and you are likely to face an uphill battle to produce any plants worth having.

REMOVING THE WEEDS

There are several important stages. The first is to rid the ground of weeds. Annual weeds are a nuisance but no more than this and, over a period, they will slowly be eliminated as their seed store in the ground is reduced. The real problem is persistent perennial weeds. In soft, friable soils, these can be removed by hand as the soil is dug. In heavier conditions, the only sure way is to use a chemical weedkiller. Modern herbicides are safe to use as long as the instructions on the packet are rigorously followed. If used properly, the weeds will be killed and, with good maintenance, there should be no need to use herbicides again.

CONDITIONING THE SOIL

It is important to improve the condition of the soil before you start to plant. Dig as much well-rotted organic material as possible into the soil. This will not only help break down the soil but will also provide nutrients for the shrubs' growth. It will also help the soil to provide a reservoir of moisture down around the shrubs' roots. The best organic material is garden compost. This can be prepared by piling up waste matter, such as leaves, the stems and dead flowers of herbaceous material, non-invasive weeds and grass clippings, together with uncooked waste from the kitchen, such as peelings, and allowing them to break down naturally. Woody stems, such as prunings and hedge clippings, can be added, as long as they have been allowed to rot down first. Other material can be obtained from outside the garden: farmyard manure, old mushroom compost and composted bark are all invaluable.

SOIL CONDITIONERS

Chipped or composted bark – little nutritional value, but good mulch.
Farmyard manure – rich in nutrients, but often contains weed seed. Good conditioner.
Garden compost – composted garden waste. Good nutrient value and good conditioner.
Leaf mould – composted leaves. Good nutritional value. Excellent conditioner and mulch.
Peat – not very suitable as it breaks down too quickly and has little nutritional value.
Seaweed – rich in minerals. Good conditioner.
Spent hops – brewery waste. Some nutritional value, good mulch and conditioner.
Spent mushroom compost – good mulch. Contains chalk or lime.

MAKING A NEW BED

1 Choose the site of the bed and mark out its shape. This can be done with a hosepipe (garden hose), moving it around until you have the shape you want. Then dig around it with a spade, lawn edger or hoe.

2 For a circular bed, place a post in the centre of the proposed circle and tie a piece of string to it. Attach a sharp stick or tool at the radius (half the diameter) of the circle and, with the string pulled taut, scribe a circle around the central post. An alternative is to tie a bottle filled with sand to the string and allow the sand to trickle out as you move the bottle round the circle.

3 If the grass contains pernicious and persistent weeds, remove them before digging. The only sure way is to kill them with a herbicide. If the surrounding grass is full of such weeds, these should also be killed or they will soon encroach on the bed.

4 With many lawn grasses it will not be necessary to use herbicide; simply skim off the surface grass and dig out any roots that remain.

5 Dig the soil, removing any weeds and stones. If possible, double dig the soil, breaking up the lower spit (spade's depth) but not bringing this soil to the surface.

6 Mix plenty of organic material into both layers of the soil, but especially the bottom layer, to encourage the roots to grow deeply.

7 If possible, leave the bed to weather for a few months after digging; then remove any residual weeds that have appeared. When you are ready to plant, add some well-rotted compost or ready-prepared soil conditioner to the soil and lightly fork it in. The weather should have broken the soil down to a certain extent, but the rain will also have compacted it. Lightly fork it over to loosen the soil, break down any lumps and work in any soil conditioner.

8 Rake over the soil, to give it its final tilth, creating an even level over the bed but with a channel round the edge to facilitate trimming the edge of the lawn.

Right: Escallonia *'Gwendolyn Anley' covered in flower. To grow healthy plants that are both vigorous and floriferous all weeds should be removed and the condition of the soil should be improved.*

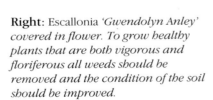

Choosing Plants

Before making the journey to select plants for your garden make sure you have a clear idea of where you are going to plant them, the type of soil and the aspect of your garden. Read the label and examine the plant before you buy it to make sure it is right for the spot you have in mind. Buying the wrong plant could waste a whole growing season.

USE AND SEASON OF INTEREST

Before buying a plant, it is worth considering where it is to go in the garden – especially if it is an impulse buy. It is said that a keen gardener can always find room for one more plant, but that does rather depend on the size of the plant in question.

Always check the plant's label for information about final height and spread – and how many years it will take to grow to full size – and ask for help if the label doesn't tell you. Then consider the situation you have in mind for the plant and whether the fully grown specimen will be in scale and in keeping with its surroundings.

Be sure to check when the main season of interest is, or whether it has the added bonus of a second one. The plant has not yet been discovered which can be interesting in all four seasons of the year, but many evergreen variegated plants, such as *Elaeagnus* x *ebbingei* 'Gilt Edge', do come close to it. This shrub has bright golden-yellow markings on leaves which are retained on the plant throughout the year and do not easily succumb to weather damage. *Cotinus coggygria*

'Royal Purple' is a tall, handsome shrub that, though leafless during the winter, has fluffy pink flowers in summer and rich plum-purple leaves throughout the spring and summer, which turn a dazzling red colour in autumn before they fall. The small, upright flowering cherry tree, *Prunus* 'Amanogawa', produces masses of soft pink flowers in spring and a spectacular show of colour in autumn, as the leaves turn to fiery reds, oranges and yellows, making the tree resemble a bright flame.

It is important that any plant earns its keep, but nowhere more so than in a smaller garden, where space is at a premium.

Adding organic matter to the soil will encourage earthworms, which will improve the condition of the soil.

SITE PREFERENCES

Every plant has a preference for the ideal conditions it needs in order to grow well, whether it is hot or shady, acid or alkaline, dry or damp, and most will have the greatest of difficulty growing in the wrong position.

Many conditions can be modified, at least to some extent, to extend the range of plants which can be grown. Improve the drainage of a localized wet spot, for example, by incorporating sharp sand or gravel into the soil, and by adding organic matter, such as well-rotted farmyard manure, to encourage worm activity. Dry areas will also benefit from the addition of organic matter,

Coarse grit incorporated into a localized wet area will improve drainage.

which will hold moisture during the vital summer months, and also from the use of a mulch over the surface, to reduce the amount of moisture lost by evaporation and reduce competition from weeds.

Acidic conditions can be modified by the addition of ground limestone or chalk, to raise the pH. It is difficult to lower the pH if the soil is alkaline, however. Flowers of sulphur will have some effect on alkalinity but the difference is only very slight and you will have to repeat the treatment every year. On the whole, it is better to choose plants that will thrive in your soil rather than labouring to change its pH, which may involve a lot of effort for little reward; a great range of plants will not mind a slight alkalinity. You will have to settle for growing acid-lovers in containers, and this is very successful and suitable for many of them. Many fascinating and attractive plants also enjoy growing in acidic conditions, so choose wisely and watch your plants thrive.

SIZE AND SHAPE

In the days when plants were grown and sold by the nurseryman, it was easy to ask advice about the plant being bought and its ultimate dimensions. These days, most plants are bought from large, impersonal garden centres (supply stores), and so the label that accompanies them is all-important.

There are very few truly small trees, although there are many that can be classified as "slow-growing" and that may take 50 years to reach a size that causes difficulties.

Right: *Dwarf conifers are a good choice in a small garden as they will mature without becoming a danger to nearby buildings.*

Feeding Plants

Giving plants sufficient nutrients will ensure strong growth, abundant flowering and fruit production, and make them healthy enough to withstand pests and diseases.

BALANCED NUTRIENTS

In common with all living things, plants need a balanced intake of nutrients to survive. These take the form of minerals and trace elements. In their natural environment these would be available in the soil, to be taken up, along with water, by the roots. They are then transported within the plant to supply the leaf cells, where the process of photosynthesis manufactures sugars and starches from the sunlight. As the plant grows, flowers and eventually dies, the decaying material then releases nutrients back into the soil.

In the garden, where far more plants are grown closely together than would happen in nature, the competition for nutrients becomes intense; this is exacerbated if the plant is in a container, where the roots cannot grow into new areas in search of extra food.

Seaweed

TYPES OF FERTILIZER

There are two groups of fertilizer: organic and inorganic. The organic ones are derived from natural ingredients, such as other plants (seaweed or nettles), blood, fish or bone, and generally last longer, although they become available to the plant slowly after application.

Growmore

Inorganic fertilizers are mineral-based and break down more quickly after application. The rate at which the fertilizer is released into the soil usually depends on temperature, soil-organism activity, the fertilizer's solubility in water and its size (the finer the particles, the more fast-acting it will be). Some fertilizers are "slow-release", meaning the particles are sur-rounded by a special coating which slowly breaks down. The nutrients are released only when the temperature is high enough for growth.

Liquid seaweed

Blood, fish and bone

Those fertilizers which are applied as a liquid are absorbed quickly and are useful as a fast-acting tonic if a plant is looking ill. This is especially true of foliar feeds, which are applied directly to the leaves rather than the soil around the roots, and are absorbed straight into the plant's system. These can have an effect within 3–4 days, compared with up to 21 days for a general granular fertilizer applied around the roots.

Nitro phosphate

Nitro chalk

The three most important elements contained in fertilizer are: nitrogen (N), phosphorus (P) and potassium (K). Nitrogen promotes healthy growth of leaves and shoots, phosphorus is needed for healthy root development and potassium improves flowering and fruit production. Put simply, N:P:K equals shoots:roots:fruits. The ratio is given on the pack because certain plants need some elements in a greater quantity than others – a foliage plant, for instance, will need more nitrogen and less potassium, as it produces leaves but not a great show of flowers or fruit, whereas ripening tomatoes need huge quantities of potassium to give a good yield. It is often necessary to change the fertilizer through the season, particularly for heavy feeders like vegetables. Apply more nitrogen and phosphorus in the spring to promote growth, and increase potassium as the season progresses, in order to produce a good show of flowers or fruit.

Fishmeal

Sulphate of ammonia

FEEDING SHRUBS

If you mulch regularly, you probably won't need to feed any further. A light sprinkling of an organic, slow-acting fertilizer, such as bonemeal, may be all that is required. However, when there is regular watering, such as to a shrub in a container, the soil can become drained of its nutrients and you will need to replace them. This can be done by adding a dry mixture by hand or by adding a liquid feed.

Roses, in particular, benefit from an annual feed, applied in spring or early summer after the dormant season of winter is over. Whenever possible, choose a slow-release or controlled-release fertilizer which will feed the plant throughout the summer.

Right: Rosa *'Alba Maxima'*. *Climbing roses tolerate most soil types, although careful cultivation will ensure each shrub gives of its best. Adding organic matter in the form of garden compost or farmyard manure will improve soil structure.*

LIQUID FERTILIZERS

An alternative method of feeding is to use a liquid feed. This is most useful for shrubs in containers. Add the fertilizer to one of the waterings; in the case of container shrubs, this could be once every three weeks, but it would not be required so frequently in the open soil – once every three months or as recommended by the manufacturer.

Regular watering and feeding helps to keep plants at their best as the healthy foliage of this Spiraea japonica *'Goldflame' shows.*

Applying Fertilizer

Feeding really does pay dividends. If you see a garden with particularly lush and healthy-looking plants, the chances are they have been well fed.

Feeding used to be a job that had to be tackled several times during the course of a season, and some enthusiasts still feed their plants once a week or even more frequently. If you use modern slow-release and controlled-release fertilizers, however, feeding is something you can do just a couple of times a year.

Liquid feeds, nevertheless, are more instant in effect and still have a use, being invaluable when plants need a quick pick-me-up.

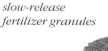

slow-release fertilizer granules

slow-release fertilizer pellets

slow-release fertilizer sachet

FEEDING CONTAINERS
Container plants require supplementary nutrients to keep them in good health.

1 A controlled- or slow-release fertilizer added to the potting soil at planting time will keep most containers blooming well all summer. Follow the instructions for application rates.

SLOW- AND CONTROLLED-RELEASE
Some fertilizers are described as slow-release and controlled-release. Both allow the nutrients to seep out into the soil over a period of months, but controlled-release fertilizers are affected by soil temperature. Nutrients are only released when the soil is warm enough for growth in most plants.

2 If you find it more convenient, you can place sachets of slow-release fertilizer beneath the plants when you plant them.

3 If you can buy pellets of slow-release fertilizer like this, place them beneath individual plants at planting time.

FEEDING THE LAWN
There are several ways to do this, all take relatively little time.

1 The quickest way to feed your lawn is with a wheeled spreader like this. Although individual models vary, you can usually adjust the delivery rate. Test the rate on a measured area of path first, then sweep up the fertilizer and weigh it to make sure the application rate is right.

2 An easy way to give your lawn a liquid boost is to use a sprinkler system into which you can introduce special fertilizer pellets. It will feed the lawn as it waters, and you don't have to stand there holding the hose.

3 A hose-end dilutor like this is a good way to apply a soluble fertilizer for a quick response. It is much quicker than mixing it in watering-cans to apply. You can use this type of hose-end dilutor for beds and borders as well as for the lawn.

BEDS AND BORDERS
An annual feed will keep the most demanding plants happy.

1 Most established plants, but especially demanding ones such as roses, benefit from annual feeding. Apply a slow- or controlled-release fertilizer in spring or early summer, sprinkling it around the bushes. Sprinkle the fertilizer in the root area away from the stem.

2 Hoe it into the surface so that it penetrates the root area more quickly.

3 Unless rain is expected, water it in. This will make the fertilizer active more quickly in dry conditions.

soluble fertilizer

Sheet Mulches

Mulches fall into two main groups: the mainly inorganic sheet mulches made from various forms of plastic or rubber sheets, and loose ones such as garden compost, and chipped bark that will eventually rot down and add to the humus content of the soil.

You may want to add one of the more decorative loose mulches to make a sheet mulch visually more acceptable. This can be more cost-effective than using a loose mulch alone, which has to be applied at least 5cm (2in) thick to be an effective weed control.

MULCHING WITH A SHEET
Use this method for low-maintenance shrub beds and newly planted trees.

1 Sheet mulches are most useful in shrub beds that can be left undisturbed for some years, and are best used when the bed or border is newly planted. Always prepare the ground as thoroughly as you would if not using a mulching sheet.

Make a slit around the edge of the bed with a spade, and push the sheet into this. For a vegetable plot you can use special plastic pegs, but these are too conspicuous for an ornamental position.

2 Make cross-shaped planting slits in the sheet with a knife or scissors. If planting a shrub you will probably have to make slits large enough to take a spade for planting. This won't matter as the sheet can be folded back into place.

3 Small plants can be planted with a trowel, but for shrubs you will need to use a spade. Provided the ground has been well prepared before the sheet was laid, it should be easy to dig out the planting hole.

4 Sheet mulches are very useful around newly planted trees and shrubs. The best way to apply the sheet is to cut a square or circle to size, then make a single slit from the centre. Place it around the tree or shrub – and the stake if there is one – and simply fold it back into place. It won't matter if the join is not perfect as you can hide it with a decorative mulch.

5 Although most of the sheet mulch will be hidden as the plants grow, it will be very conspicuous initially. A layer of a decorative mulch such as chipped bark or gravel will make it much more acceptable.

Black plastic sheeting is inexpensive and widely available. It does not allow water to penetrate, so it's best used in narrow strips, alongside a hedge.

Although more expensive than plastic sheeting, woven plastic mulches allow water to seep through while keeping out light.

Butyl rubber is a very long-lasting waterproof mulch. It is expensive, but you only require a thin gauge. It is more suitable for the area immediately around trees than as cover for a large area.

Some sheet mulches are made from degradable materials such as wool waste. This is a good option if you want a sheet mulch that will eventually disappear as it rots.

Below: *Established plants are more difficult to mulch with a sheet, but trees and hedges can be mulched this way very satisfactorily. If you want to control weeds along a young hedge, lay black plastic sheeting in two strips, one either side of the hedge.*

PRACTICAL POINTS
- Always prepare the soil thoroughly before laying the sheet.
- Enrich the soil with plenty of organic material such as rotted manure or garden compost (soil mix) – you won't have an opportunity later.
- Add fertilizer and water it in thoroughly – only liquid feeds are practical once the sheet is in position.
- Soak the ground before applying the sheet.

Sheet mulches can look unattractive in the ornamental garden. They are better covered with a shallow layer of a decorative mulch too.

Loose Mulches

Most loose mulches are visually acceptable, and the organic ones become integrated into the soil by insect life and worm activity, thus helping to improve soil structure and fertility. Loose mulches have to be thick to suppress weeds well.

APPLYING A LOOSE MULCH

1 Prepare the ground thoroughly, digging it over and working in plenty of organic material such as rotted manure or garden compost if the soil is impoverished.

2 Loose mulches will control annual weeds and prevent new perennial ones getting a foothold. You must dig up deep-rooted perennial weeds, otherwise they could grow through the mulch.

3 Water the ground thoroughly before applying the mulch. Do not apply a mulch to dry ground.

4 Spread the mulch thickly. This is bark mulch, but there are other decorative mulches that you could choose from.

chipped bark

gravel

peat

Material

Chipped bark

Cocoa shells

Garden compost

Gravel

Peat

Rotted manure

Sawdust

Spent hops

Spent mushroom compost

Advantages	Disadvantages
Very ornamental, and lasts for a long time before it needs replacing	Can be relatively expensive. May take some nitrogen from the soil as it rots down
Light to handle. Attractive colour and pleasant smell when handling. Lasts for a long time	Can be relatively expensive. Sometimes can encourage growth of superficial moulds
Excellent soil conditioner. High level of nutrients. Free if you make your own	Soon breaks down, which enriches the soil but means you need to keep topping up. Not visually attractive
Visually pleasing. Long-lasting	Contains no nutrients. Individual pieces may be a problem if they get onto the lawn
Visually pleasing and pleasant to handle. Very useful for plants that require acid conditions	Relatively expensive. Low in nutrients. Many people prefer to avoid its use because its extraction depletes peat reserves and peat bog habitats
Excellent soil conditional. Useful nutrient levels. Can be inexpensive if you have a local source	Soon breaks down, which enriches the soil but means you need to keep topping up. Not visually attractive, and can smell if not thoroughly rotted
Usually cheap if you have access to a plentiful supply. Usually slow to decay	Can temporarily deplete the soil of nitrogen when rotting down. Can be visually pleasing when newly applied but soon looks unattractive
Usually quite inexpensive if you live in an area where they are readily available. Easy and pleasant to handle	Can be difficult to obtain, especially in small quantities
Usually relatively inexpensive. Should contain animal manure and straw, which will improve the soil	Normally contains lime, so should be avoided on alkaline soils or where acid-loving plants are grown

Weed Out

Weeds are persistent, clever and successful – they reproduce quickly, competing with choice plants and shrubs for water, nutrients and light. These unwelcome additions to the garden must be kept under control, since they disperse seeds that are capable of surviving in the ground for many years.

Two types of weed exist – annuals which are short lived; and perennials, which establish a strong root system and need digging out by hand.

PERENNIAL WEEDS
These are by far the most difficult to get rid of, since many can re-grow from just the tiniest amount of root left in the soil.

Nettle
Two types of nettle exist. The smaller one lives for only a short time and has white roots, while the larger one, which has yellow roots, lives for several years and has spreading stems that creep along the soil. Both sting!

Bindweed
Bindweed climbs with twining stems that choke the plants it twines around.

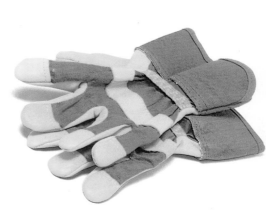

Alkanet
This weed has pretty blue flowers but will eventually take over the flower bed. It has a long, thick tap root like a dandelion so is difficult to dig out.

Dandelion
Dandelions have long tap roots that are difficult to dig out.

SHORT-LIVED WEEDS

Many of these can be pulled out by hand or using a hoe by chopping off the roots and leaving the tops to shrivel and die. These are weeds spread by seed, so catch them before they flower and do more damage.

Ocalis

This has pretty flowers, but don't be fooled, it is one of the most difficult weeds to get rid of. It grows from small bulbils growing underground which must be dug up and destroyed. Don't put them on the compost heap.

Mercury

Another weed that quickly seeds itself almost anywhere, but it can easily be pulled out.

Sow thistle

Pull it up from vegetable and flower beds. The seeds are very light and have a plume of hairs which carries them in the wind.

Groundsel

This weed grows everywhere. Easy to pull up. Catch it before the seeds spread.

Plantain

Often found in lawns where its large, flat rosettes hug the ground andescape the lawnmower's blades. It is quite tough, but can be pulled out by hand.

Shepherd's purse

A little weed that is quick-growing. It has triangular seeds which are sticky when wet and can be carried on boots and tools. Each plant can produce up to 4,000 seeds in one year that can survive in the soil for up to 30 years.

Controlling Weeds

The only place where weeds are acceptable is in a wildlife corner, although some people find daisies in the lawn a very attractive feature. Generally, however, weeds have to be controlled, and pulling them up by hand is a tedious and time-consuming job that few of us enjoy. It's even more frustrating if they grow again within days.

There are two main weapons if you want to cut down on weeding: mulching, which uses no chemicals, and herbicides – or weed-killers if you prefer to use a more descriptive term!

KILLING WEEDS IN BEDS AND BORDERS

Although there are weed-killers that will kill some problem grasses growing among broad-leaved plants, generally you can't use selective weed-killers in beds and borders. Most weed-killers will kill or damage whatever they come into contact with, but there are ways in which you can use herbicides around ornamental plants to minimize the amount of hand weeding necessary.

2 You may be able to treat areas in a shrub border with a watered-on weed-killer simply by shielding the cultivated plants. If deep-rooted perennials are not a problem you can use a contact weed-killer that will act rather like a chemical hoe (a real hoe may be an easier alternative to mixing and applying a weed-killer if the area is small).

1 Deep-rooted perennial "problem" weeds, such as bindweed, are best treated by painting on a translocated weed-killer such as one based on glyphosate. Ordinary contact weed-killers may not kill all the roots, but this chemical is moved by the plant to all parts. Even so you may have to treat really difficult weeds a number of times. Use a gel formulation to paint on where watering on the weed-killers may cause damage to adjacent ornamentals.

3 Once the ground is clear, if you don't want to use a mulch, try applying a weed-killer intended to prevent new weed seedlings emerging. These are only suitable for certain shrubs and fruit crops, but they remain near the surface above root level and only act on seedlings that try to germinate. These should suppress most new weeds for many months.

WEED-FREE PATHS

Paths can easily be kept weed-free for a season using one of the products sold for the purpose. Most of these contain a cocktail of chemicals, some of which act quickly to kill existing weeds and others that prevent the growth of new ones for many months. A single application will keep the path clear for a long time.

Use an improvized shield to prevent the weed-killer being blown onto the flowerbeds.

WORDS OF WARNING

Weed-killers are extremely useful aids, but they can be disastrous if you use the wrong ones, or are careless in their application.

- Always check to see whether it is a total or selective weed-killer.
- If selective, make sure it will kill your problem weeds – and make sure it is suitable for applying to the area you have in mind. Lawn weed-killers should only ever be used on lawns.
- Don't apply liquid weed-killers on a windy day.
- For greater control, use a dribble bar rather than an ordinary rose on your watering-can.
- Keep a special watering-can for weed-killers, otherwise residues may harm your plants.
- Avoid run-off onto flowerbeds, and if necessary use a shield while applying a weed-killer.

Right: *Paths can be marred by weeds. Make sure the joints are mortared between, or use a path weed-killer to keep them smart.*

Weed-free Lawns

A weedy lawn will mar your garden, but with modern weedkillers, it's quite easy to eliminate weeds to leave your grass looking like a lawn rather than a mown wild-flower meadow.

KILLING WEEDS IN LAWNS
This method ensures a weed-free lawn with as little as one application a year.

A lawn like this is the result of regular weeding and feeding. Once weeds have been eliminated, however, the grass should hold its own against new weeds.

1 Weeds in lawns are best controlled by a selective hormone weed-killer, ideally applied in mid- or late spring. These are usually applied as a liquid, using a dribble bar attached to a watering-can. To ensure even application you should mark out lines with string, spacing them the width of the dribble bar apart.

2 Always mix and apply the weed-killer as recommended by the manufacturer. There are a number of different plant hormones used, some killing certain weeds better than others, so always check that it is recommended for the weeds you most want to control. When mixed, simply walk along each strip slowly enough for the droplets from the dribble bar to cover the area evenly.

3 If your lawn also needs feeding, you can save time by using a combined weed and feed. The most efficient way to apply these – which are likely to be granular rather than liquid – is with a fertilizer spreader.

4 If you have just a few troublesome weeds in a small area, it is a waste of time and money treating the whole lawn. For this job a spot weeder that you dab or wipe onto the offending weed will work well.

Above: *A weed-free lawn leads the eye to a distant patio.*

Right: *The few weeds in this lawn are probably not worth worrying about, but you can easily spot treat an area if you don't want to waste time treating the whole lawn.*

DEALING WITH MOSS

Moss is much more difficult to control than ordinary lawn weeds, and hand weeding is simply not a practical option. Use a moss-killer – some you water on; others are sprinkled on. Ask your garden centre (supply store) for advice about which is best for your circumstances.

Once the moss has been killed, it is worth trying to avoid the conditions that encourage it: shade and poor drainage.

Common Pests

VINE WEEVILS (above)
These white grubs are a real problem. The first sign of an infestation is the sudden collapse of the plant, which has died as a result of the weevil eating its roots. Systemic insecticides or natural predators can be used as a preventative, but once a plant has been attacked it is usually too late. Never re-use the soil from an affected plant.

CATERPILLARS (above)
The occasional caterpillar can be simply picked off the plant and disposed of as you see fit, but a major infestation can strip a plant before your eyes. Contact insecticides are usually very effective in these cases.

SLUGS AND SNAILS
As a preventative measure, smear a circle of petroleum jelly below the rim of the pot as the slugs and snails will not cross this. If there is a already a problem with slugs in the pot, slug pellets should deal with any resident pests.

SCALE INSECTS
These can be very troublesome on container-grown plants, particularly on those with waxy leaves, such as bay, Ficus and Stephanotis. The first sign is often a sticky substance on the leaves. If you look under the leaves and at the leaf joints you may be able to spot the scales. A serious infestation will be indicated by a black sooty mould. The scale insect's waxy coating makes it resistant to contact insecticides, so use of a systemic insecticide is essential. As scale insects develop over quite a long period it is important to treat regularly for a couple of months.

WHITEFLY (above)
As their name indicates, these are tiny white flies which flutter in clouds when disturbed from their feeding places on the undersides of leaves. Whitefly are particularly troublesome in conservatories where a dry atmosphere will encourage them to breed. Keep the air as moist as possible. Contact insecticides will need more than one application to deal with an infestation, but a systemic insecticide will protect the plant for weeks.

Insecticides

There are two main types of insecticide available to combat common pests.

CONTACT INSECTICIDES

These must be sprayed directly onto the insects to be effective. Most organic insecticides work this way, but they generally kill all insects, even beneficial ones, such as hover flies and ladybirds. Try to remove these before spraying the infected plant.

MEALY BUGS

These look like spots of white mould. Like scale insects they are hard to shift and regular treatment with a systemic insecticide is the best solution.

GREENFLY

One of the most common plant pests. These green sap-sucking insects feed on the tender growing tips of plants. Most insecticides are effective against greenfly. Choose one that will not harm ladybirds as greenfly are a favourite food of theirs.

RED SPIDER MITE (above)

This is another insect that thrives indoors in dry conditions. Constant humidity will reduce the chance of an infestation. The spider mite is barely visible to the human eye, but infestation is indicated by the presence of fine webs and mottling of the plant's leaves. To treat an infestation, it is best to move the plant outdoors if the weather is suitable, spray with an insecticide and allow the plant time to recover before bringing it back indoors.

SYSTEMIC INSECTICIDES

These work by being absorbed by the plant's root or leaf system and killing the insects that come into contact with the plant. This will work for difficult pest such as vine weevils which are hidden in the soil, and scale insects, which protect themselves from above with a scaly cover.

BIOLOGICAL CONTROL

Commercial growers now use biological control in their glasshouses, which means natural predators are introduced to eat the best population. Although not all are suitable for the amateur gardener, they can be used in conservatories for dealing with pests such as whitefly.

Automatic Watering

An automatic watering system will save you time and is better for the plants, which are less likely to suffer water stress. Some garden hoses, sprinklers and timing devices are described on the following pages, but these are just some of the systems that you can buy. Look at garden centres (supply stores) and in magazine advertisements to see which appear to be the most appropriate for your needs.

PLANNING THE SYSTEM

Work out the layout of your self-watering system first, and decide the number and kind of delivery devices (such as drip heads) you need. Kits are a useful start, but are unlikely to contain the exact number of components that you need. Check that the master unit or flow-reducer will support the number of drips required.

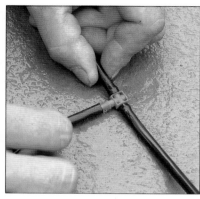

Most automatic watering systems are fitted with a suitable control system to reduce the pressure, and act as a filter. Designs vary, and either screw onto the outside tap or are inserted into the hose system. If the tap does not have a non-return valve fitted to prevent back-siphonage, make sure the master unit has one.

Drip-feed systems are versatile enough to be used for plants in beds, borders or in containers. Use a T-joint to run branches or tubes for individual drip heads.

Some automatic systems are controlled by the moisture level in the soil, but most operate on a continuous drip basis. Even if you can control the drip rate, too much water may be delivered if operated continuously. A timing device will turn your watering system on and off automatically, yet can easily be deactivated if the weather is wet. This one, operated by a battery, can be set to water your garden up to six times a day.

Unless your garden is extremely small, it's best to install a pipeline buried just beneath the ground surface, then you can "plug in" various watering devices as necessary. With this particular system a sprinkler can simply be pushed onto the fitting set flush with the lawn or soil surface.

Push the head onto the hose, and if necessary hold the delivery tube in position with a pipe peg. If the rate of delivery can be adjusted, the instructions that come with the kit will explain how this is done.

An automatic watering device will keep your garden lush throughout the summer.

Watering Aids

You may find the choice of watering aids bewildering, but decide what you want to water, then choose the kind of fitting that will do the job. You can avoid watering altogether if you choose drought-resistant plants, abandon containers, and don't mind a brown lawn in a dry summer. However, if you want lush, green grass and lots of colourful containers without the twice-daily chore of watering, some kind of automatic watering system is essential.

This type of drip feed is left connected continuously, through a flow-reducer provided, and the water-filled ceramic cone detects whether the soil is moist enough. Dry soil creates a partial vacuum, which then allows water to flow through the thin tubing, and the rate of flow can be adjusted. This system can be used in beds and borders but is ideal for troughs, tubs, and window-boxes. Like many drip systems, this one can also be fed from a reservoir or tank instead of being connected to the mains water supply.

Hanging baskets and other containers such as pots and window boxes can be kept in top condition with minimum effort on the part of the gardener, if you use an automatic watering system.

Left: *Leaky-pipe and perforated hose systems are suitable for beds and borders or the kitchen garden. The special hoses are either porous or have many fine fine holes, and water gradually seeps through them. You can bury them beneath the surface or lay them on top of the soil (useful where you might want to move the hose around).*

Watering

Too much water is as bad as too little – get the balance right and let your plants thrive.

1 The best way to avoid over-watering a plant is to stand the pot in a saucer and water into the saucer. The plant's roots can then take up moisture as needed.

2 Most plants are quite happy to be watered from above, as here. This is not recommended for plants with velvety leaves such as African violets. They should be watered in the saucer.

3 Houseplants enjoy being sprayed with water, but in hard water areas you should use rain water or bottled water.

Water-retaining Gel

One of the main problems for most container gardeners is the amount of water required to keep plants thriving. Adding water-retaining gels to compost (soil mix) will help reduce this task. Sachets of gel are available from garden centres.

1 Pour the recommended amount of water into a bowl.

2 Scatter the gel over the surface, stirring occasionally until it has absorbed the water.

3 Add to the compost (soil mix) at the recommended rate.

4 Mix the gel in thoroughly before using it for planting.

Dealing with Weather Problems

Weather, in particular winter weather, can cause problems for the gardener. Throughout the year, winds can break branches. If boughs or stems do break, cut them neatly back to a convenient point. If the wind is a constant problem, it becomes necessary to create a windbreak of some sort or plants will become permanently damaged.

PROTECTING AGAINST THE ELEMENTS

Frost can cause a lot of damage, especially late or early frosts, which can catch new growth and flowers unexpectedly. General cold during the winter can be dealt with more easily, because it is relatively predictable: either cover the plants or plant them next to a wall, which will provide warmth and shelter.

Drought can be a problem, especially if it is not expected. Defend against drought when preparing the bed by incorporating plenty of moisture-retaining organic material. Once planted, plants benefit from a thick mulch, which will help hold the moisture in.

There are some plants that do not tolerate wet weather. Most plants with silver leaves, such as *Convolvulus cneorum* and lavenders prefer to grow in fairly dry conditions. Unfortunately there is little that can be done to protect such shrubs from the rain, although making their soil more free-draining by adding grit to the soil, or by growing them in well-drained containers helps.

Some plants prefer a shady position away from the sun. Many rhododendrons and azaleas, for example, prefer to be out of the hot sun. These can either be planted in the shade of a building or under trees or beneath taller shrubs.

WINDBREAKS

If there are perpetual problems with wind, it is essential to create some sort of windbreak. In the short term this can be plastic netting, but a more permanent solution is to create a living windbreak. A number of trees and shrubs can be used for this: *Leylandii* are often used, because they are one of the quickest-growing, but they are really best avoided for more suitable alternatives. They are thirsty and hungry plants that take a lot of the nutrients from the soil for some distance around their roots. They also continue growing rapidly past their required height.

It is best to get the windbreak established before the shrubs are planted but, if time is of the essence, plant them at the same time, shielding both from the winds with windbreak netting.

SHRUBS AND TREES FOR WINDBREAKS

Acer pseudoplatanus (sycamore)
Arundinaria japonica (syn. *Pseudosasa japonica*)
Berberis darwinii
Buxus sempervirens (box)
Carpinus betulus (hornbeam)
Corylus avellana (hazel)
Cotoneaster simonsii
Crataegus monogyma (hawthorn)
Elaeagnus x *ebbingei*
Escallonia macrantha
Euonymus japonicus
Fraxinus excelsior (ash)
Griselinia littoralis
Hippophaë rhamnoides (sea buckthorn)
Ilex (holly)
Ligustrum ovalifolium (privet)
Lonicera nitida (box-leaf honeysuckle)
Olearia ilicifolia
Picea sitchensis (sitka spruce)
Pinus sylvestris (Scots pine)
Prunus laurocerasus (cherry laurel)
Prunus lusitanica (Portuguese laurel)
Pyracantha (firethorn)
Rosmarinus officinalis (rosemary)
Sorbus aucuparia (rowan)
Tamarix (tamarisk)
Taxus baccata (yew)
Viburnum tinus (laurustinus)

Hedges are frequently used as windbreaks to protect the whole or specific parts of the garden. Whilst they are becoming established, they themselves may also need some protection, usually in the form of plastic netting. Here privet (Ligustrum) has been chosen.

PROTECTING FROM WINTER COLD

1 Many plants, like this bay (*Laurus nobilis*) need some degree of winter protection. The same principles can be applied to container plants as to free-standing ones. Insert a number of canes (stakes) around the edge of the plant, taking care not to damage the roots.

2 Cut a piece of fleece, hessian (burlap) or bubble polythene (plastic) to the necessary size, making sure you allow for an overlap over the plant and pot. Fleece can be bought as a sleeve, which is particularly handy for enveloping plants.

3 Wrap the protective cover around the plant, allowing a generous overlap. For particularly tender plants, use a double layer.

4 Tie the protective cover around the pot, or lightly around the plant if it is in the ground. Fleece can be tied at the top as moisture can penetrate through, but if using plastic, leave it open for ventilation and watering.

5 Protecting with hessian (burlap) or plastic shade netting should be enough for most plants, but if one should require extra protection, wrap it in straw and then hold this in place with hessian or shade netting.

Late frost can ruin the flowering of a bush. This azalea has been caught on the top by the frost, but the sides were sufficiently sheltered to be unaffected. A covering of fleece would have given it complete protection.

Right: *Lilac* (Syringa) *can be affected by late frosts which nip out the flowering buds preventing displays such as this.*

Multiplying Plants

Increasing your stock of plants from those already in your garden is the most economical way of filling beds and borders – although you may have to wait for complete ground cover.

Lifting and dividing "blind" or overcrowded clumps of Narcissus *in late summer will ensure a colourful display.*

1 Some shrubby ground cover plants that spread by underground runners or suckers – such as Pachysandra terminalis – can easily be divided into smaller pieces. A plant like this can easily be divided into 3 or 4 plants. Water first to make sure the potting soil is moist.

2 Knock the plant out of its pot. If it doesn't pull out easily, try tapping the edge of the pot on a hard surface.

3 Carefully pull the rootball apart, trying to keep as much compost (soil mix) on the roots as possible.

4 If you find the crown too tough to pull apart, try cutting through it with a knife. It is better to do this than damage the plant even more if it does not separate easily.

5 It has been possible to divide this plant into 8 smaller ones, but the number you will be able to achieve depends on the size of the original plant and the species.

6 Replant immediately if you don't mind small plants, otherwise pot up and grow on for a year before planting.

7 Pot up the plants if you want to grow them on, using a good compost mixture. Keep them in a sheltered but light position, and make sure they never go short of water.

8 If you don't have automatic watering, plunge the pots up to their rims in soil. They will dry out less quickly and watering will not be such a chore.

Propagating

Sowing seed is one of the easiest methods of propagation. It is also one of the most satisfying, turning what often looks like not much more than a speck of dust into a tall tree or soaring climber that scrambles up the side of a house or through tall trees – it gives a great sense of pleasure.

WHAT YOU WILL NEED
Sowing seed is not only a way of saving money by producing your own plants, but also one aspect of gardening that gives immense satisfaction. It is a way of producing new plants to replace ageing ones or to insure against accidental loss due to frosts or disease. It also allows the gardener to produce extra plants to give to friends or to sell. "Green fingers" are not essential – anyone can propagate from seed, as long as they follow a few well-tried principles.

There are a wide variety of different types of sowing composts (soil mixes) available and the majority of them are suitable for sowing seed of plants. Seeds for bedding plants can usually be started in seed trays. If you are sowing larger seeds, such as shrubs or climbers, a 9cm (3¹/₂in) pot is more suitable.

As well as having the right compost and seed, for successful growing you will also need a spare pot, fine grit and plant labels, if these are available. A greenhouse or heated propagator will give the seedlings the best possible start in life.

GROWING CLIMBERS FROM SEED

1 Fill the pot to the rim with compost (soil mix). Tap it on the bench or table so that it settles and then *lightly* press down with the base of another pot, so that the surface is level. Do not ram the compost down into the pot.

2 Space the seeds out evenly over the surface, leaving well-defined gaps between them. Small seed can be scattered but, again, make certain that the seeds are thinly spread.

3 Cover the seed with a thin layer of fine grit, unless the seed packet advises it should be sown on the surface. This will make it easier to water the pot evenly as well as facilitating the removal of any weeds and moss that grow.

4 Label the pot immediately; any delay may allow you to forget what seed is in which pot – all the pots tend to look the same after a few days! Put the name of the plant on the label, with the date of sowing. Keep the seed packet, if it contains any useful after-care and growing information.

5 Water the pot. Stand the pot in a sheltered position outside or in a greenhouse or a heated propagator for faster germination. Seasonal plants are usually raised under glass in late winter or early spring.

Pricking Out and Growing On Seedlings

Once the seedlings appear, it is important to keep them growing well. If you have lots of seedlings in one pot, they should not be left in their pot too long, or they will starve, which stunts their growth and makes them prone to disease. If they are overcrowded, moreover, they are likely to become drawn and spindly, so that they never develop into good healthy specimens. Use a good potting compost (soil mix) that does not contain too much fertilizer. You can use a stronger one when you pot them on at a later stage.

POTTING COMPOSTS (SOIL MIXES)

There is a baffling array of composts on offer. When all is said and done, most seem to do the job and ultimately it seems to come down to what the gardener prefers rather than the plant. The main division is between soilless and soil-based composts.

Soilless composts (growing mediums) are mainly based on fibrous material such as peat or a peat substitute such as coir. Sometimes they contain an absorbent mineral, such as perlite or vermiculite. They are light-weight, moisture-retentive, easy to over-water and yet difficult to re-wet if allowed to dry out.

Soil-based composts are heavier, well-drained, difficult to over-water, but absorb water easily when dry.

Most composts contain varying amounts of fertilizer. For seedlings, use those with the least amount of fertilizer; for fully-grown plants, use composts with the most. Ericaceous plants, such as rhododendrons, need a special lime-free compost.

1 Fill the bottom of enough clean pots with a good potting compost (soil mix). Remove the plants, still in the compost, from the old pot. Choose a good place to split the rootball and gently divide it into two. Ease a plant away from the ball, making certain not to tear the roots. Hold the seedling by its leaves, not by the stem or roots.

2 Still holding the seedling by its leaves (avoid touching the roots), suspend it over the centre of the pot and gently surround it with compost.

3 Tap the pot on the bench, to settle the compost, and lightly firm the compost with your fingers. Level off the top of the compost and add a thin layer of fine grit, so that the surface is completely covered. At this stage, make a label to identify the plant.

4 Immediately after pricking out, water the pot thoroughly, either with a watering can with a fine rose or by standing it in a bowl of water until the surface of the grit becomes wet. Place the pot in a shady place, preferably in a closed cold-frame.

Growing from Cuttings

While using seed to increase plants is a simple procedure, it has the disadvantage that the resulting plant may not be like its parent, because not all plants will come "true" from seed. Seed-raised plants may vary in flower or leaf colour, in the size of the plant and in many other ways. When propagating from cuttings, the resulting plant is identical to its parent (in effect a clone).

TAKING CUTTINGS

Taking cuttings is not difficult and many plants can easily be propagated in this way. It is not necessary to have expensive equipment, although, if you intend to produce a lot of new plants, a heated propagator will make things much easier.

The most satisfactory method of taking cuttings is to take them from semi-ripe wood, that is, from this year's growth that is firm to the touch but still flexible and not yet hard and woody. If the shoot feels soft and floppy, it is too early to take cuttings. The best time for taking such cuttings is usually from mid- to late summer.

When taking cuttings it is vital that you always choose shoots that are healthy: they should be free from diseases and pests and not be too long between nodes (leaf joints). This usually means taking the cuttings from the top of the climber, where it receives plenty of light.

Do not take cuttings from any suckers that may rise from the base of a tree or shrub; if the plant was grafted on to a different rootstock, you might find that you have propagated another plant entirely.

CHOOSING COMPOST (SOIL MIX)

Specialist cutting compost (soil mix) can be purchased from most garden centres and nurseries. However, it is very simple to make your own. A half and half mix, by volume, of peat (or peat substitute) and sharp sand is all that is required. Alternatively, instead of sharp sand, use vermiculite.

1 Choose a healthy shoot that is not too spindly. Avoid stems that carry a flower or bud, as these are difficult to root. Cut the shoot longer than is required and trim it to size later. Put the shoot in a polythene (plastic) bag, so that it does not wilt while waiting for your attention.

2 Remove the shoot from the bag when you are ready to deal with it. Cut at an angle just below a leaf joint (node). Use a sharp knife, so that the cut is clean and not ragged.

3 Trim off the rest of the stem just above a leaf, so that the cutting is typically about 10cm (4in) long, though the size of the cutting will depend on the plant – dwarf plants will produce smaller cuttings.

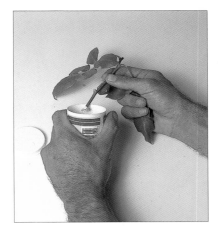

4 Trim off all leaves except the upper one or pair. Cut the leaves off right against the stem, so that there are no snags. However, be careful not to damage the stem. Dip the base of the cutting into a rooting compound, either powder or liquid. This will not only promote rooting but also help protect the cutting against fungal attack.

5 Fill a small pot with cutting compost (soil mix) and insert the cuttings round the edge. Pushing them into the compost removes the rooting powder and damages the stems, so make a hole with a small dibber or pencil. Several cuttings can be put into one pot but do not overcrowd. Tap the pot on the bench, to settle the compost. Water gently. Label the pot.

6 If a propagator is available, place the pot in it and close the lid so that fairly high humidity and temperature are maintained. A less expensive alternative is to put the pot into a polythene (plastic) bag, with its sides held away from the leaves. Put it in a warm, light, but not sunny, position.

7 After a few weeks, the base of the cutting will callus over and roots will begin to appear. Carefully invert the pot, while supporting the compost with your other hand. Remove the pot and examine the roots. Once the roots are well developed, pot the cuttings up individually. Put the pot back in the propagator if roots are only just beginning to appear.

INTERNODAL CUTTINGS
A few plants, of which clematis is the main example, are propagated from internodal cuttings. The procedure is similar to that for conventional cuttings, but the bottom cut is through the stem, between two pairs of leaves, rather than under the bottom pair.

Even large plants like this rambling rose can be grown from cuttings.

Layering

Layering is a simple technique, useful for propagating shrubs and climbers that are difficult to root from cuttings. It can be a slow process: occasionally, some plants can take several years to root. If one or two layers can be laid down at regular intervals, however, you should have a continuous supply of new plants at your disposal.

TIMING LAYERING

Layering can be carried out at any time of year. The time taken for roots to appear on the chosen stem depends on various factors and varies from one type of plant to another. Growth appearing from the area of the layer indicates that it has rooted and is ready for transplanting.

ACHIEVING SUCCESS

To increase the success rate with layering, make a short slit in the underside of the stem at its lowest point. This checks the flow of the sap at this point and promotes rooting. Alternatively, cut a notch or remove some of the bark.

1 Make a shallow depression in the soil and place the selected stem in it. If the soil is in poor condition, remove some of it and replace it with potting compost (soil mix).

2 Use a metal pin or a piece of bent wire to hold the stem in place, if necessary, so that it cannot move in the wind.

3 Cover the stem with good soil or potting compost, and water it.

4 If you haven't pinned the stem down, place a stone on the soil above the stem, to hold it in position.

5 Once growth starts – or the stem feels as if it is firmly rooted when gently pulled – cut it away from the parent plant, ensuring that the cut is on the parent-plant side. Dig up the new plant and transfer it to a pot filled with potting compost. Alternatively, replant it elsewhere in the garden.

6 An alternative method is to insert the layer directly into a pot of compost, which is buried in the ground. Once the stem has rooted, sever it from the parent as above and dig up the whole pot. This is a good technique for making tip layers, as with this fruit-bearing tayberry. Tip layers are made by inserting the tip of a stem, rather than a central section, in the ground, until it roots; it is a suitable propagation technique for fruiting climbers, such as blackberries.

Roses are just one of the types of climber that can be propagated by layering.

Perfect Pruning

Many gardeners approach pruning with a sense of trepidation, worried that injudicious action will stunt or kill the plant. If you follow the advice in this chapter, however, you will soon achieve pruning success without the stress. You can cut out the problems in ailing plants, encourage new growth, restrict the unwanted spread of prolific plants, increase the yield of foliage, flowers and fruit, and even influence the shape of your shrubs, hedges and trees.

Left: *Roses that have been pruned regularly and given attention will produce a good display of flowers.*

Above: *Pruning helps to shape shrubs as well as encouraging new growth.*

Pruning Principles

There are probably many different plants and shrubs in your garden, but the principles of pruning are relatively few, and easy to remember. If you grasp the fundamentals, you should be able to tackle your pruning with confidence – even if your plant looks nothing like the one in the picture.

MAKING A GOOD CUT

1 This is how you should prune. Leave a very short stump about 6mm (¼in) long above a bud, angled so that moisture runs away from the bud and not into it.

2 A cut like this could lead to trouble. The long stump will be starved of sap and is likely to rot back. The rot may spread back into the healthy shoot below the bud.

CONTROLLING SHAPE

You can influence the shape of a bush by where you prune. If the leaves, and therefore the buds that grow into shoots, are in opposite pairs, removing part of the shoot will stimulate each pair behind the cut to grow.

If the leaves are arranged alternately along the stem, just one shoot will take over the extension growth, which will be in the direction the bud below the cut is pointing towards.

The growing tip of a shoot produces an inhibitor which restricts the development of the buds behind it. When you prune, you remove the growing tip and the buds behind the cut are no longer inhibited and therefore grow into a replacement shoot or shoots. Bear this in mind when shaping a shrub.

BIG BRANCHES

If you have a large tree it is best to get a qualified professional to deal with it. If you want to remove a low branch from a small tree or from a large, old shrub follow the steps.

1 To avoid the weight of a large branch tearing the wood and perhaps damaging the main stem, cut it off in three stages. First make an upward saw cut about half way through the stem, or until the saw begins to bind.

3 Avoid cutting too close to the bud: physical damage may be caused or infection could be introduced.

4 Blunt secateurs (pruning shears) or careless use may bruise or tear the stem instead of cutting through it cleanly. This is an invitation for disease spores to enter. The stump is also too long.

5 If the cut slopes downwards towards the bud, the excessive moisture that may collect in the area could cause the stem to rot.

6 Shrubs with opposite leaves should be treated in a different way to those with leaves that form an alternate leaf arrangement. Cut straight across the stem, just above a strong pair of buds.

2 Next, saw downwards a short distance further out along the branch to remove it. If it does fall, the tear should not reach beyond the first cut.

3 Finally, saw right through the branch again at the point you want to cut back to. This will be a clean cut because there is no weight pulling on it.

NEW WOOD OR OLD?

Pruning instructions often refer to old or new wood. Although the appearance varies according to the time of year, you can usually tell whether wood is old or new by the colour as well as the thickness. New wood is paler and more supple. Old wood is darker and more rigid. Study the stems on a number of shrubs - you will begin to identify each year's growth by its appearance. This is easier to do in late summer when the differences are clearer.

This year's growth – greener and flexible. Last summer's growth – darker and less flexible. Two-year-old wood – darker, thicker, and more rigid.

Prune Out the Problems

Even if you do not prune to shape or restrict a plant, or to improve its flowering, it makes sense to prune out any potential problems. Rubbing or badly placed branches should be removed, as should signs of rot in a branch or shoot before the problem has a chance to spread to healthy parts. That seemingly harmless single green shoot on a variegated plant may, if left, gradually dominate the growth and the pretty variegated effect will be lost. This kind of pruning is best done as part of an annual check on all your shrubs, whether or not you usually prune them.

DEAD OR DYING SHOOTS

Shoots that are obviously dead or badly diseased on an otherwise healthy-looking plant should be cut out. They will not grow and will mar the beauty of the shrub. Leaving dead growth on the plant may also encourage or harbour diseases. Cut back to healthy wood, right back to the main stem if necessary.

BADLY CROSSING OR RUBBING SHOOTS

Cut these out while they are still young, otherwise friction will damage them and may let in disease spores. They may also make the bush look congested if not removed. Straggly old shoots should also be cut out if they are badly positioned.

REMOVE DIE-BACK

Die-back is a descriptive term. Shoots, often relatively young ones, start to die back from the end, slowly spreading towards healthy growth. To stop it spreading, cut back to just above a bud on a healthy, unaffected part of the stem.

STOP THE ROT

Other rots and diseases should be cut out. Whether the trouble appeared on live or dead wood, cut it out before it can spread.

MAKE GOOD WINTER DAMAGE

1 Shrubs of borderline hardiness may be damaged but not killed by a cold winter. Often it is biting winds rather than low temperatures alone that cause the damage, with the younger growth at the tips of the shoots browned or even killed.

2 In spring cut out cold-damaged shoots. Often you need to remove the affected tip only. This will improve the appearance and new growth will soon hide the gaps.

3 Once the damaged shoots have been removed, the shrub will soon recover.

DON'T BE A SUCKER

Remain alert to the problems that suckers can cause. These only affect plants grafted on to a different rootstock – roses and lilacs are common examples. A sucker is a shoot that arises from the rootstock, usually from below ground level; it will normally have leaves that look different (in the case of roses the colour may vary and there may be more leaflets), but with plants such as rhododendrons and lilacs you may not recognize a sucker until a shoot produces an inferior flower.

If you allow suckers to remain they will often dominate the plant over time, at the expense of the desirable variety. Cut them right back to their point of origin. This will involve pulling back some of the soil.

DON'T BE PLAIN

Check variegated plants to make sure they are not "reverting" (producing shoots with all-green leaves). If you leave these on the plant, they will gradually dominate it because they are normally more vigorous. Cut them back to their point of origin. With a few plants, such as Elaeagnus pungens 'Maculata', the variegation on new shoots only develops fully as the leaves age, so be careful not to be premature with your pruning.

Pruning for Colourful Stems

Winter colour is always valuable, and as flowers are scarce it makes sense to grow a selection of plants with bright and colourful stems. Dogwoods (*Cornus* 'Sibirica' and *C. alba* varieties for example) and some of the willows, like *Salix alba* 'Britzensis' (syn. *S. alba* 'Chermesina'), are widely used for this purpose. It is the young stems produced the previous summer that are the most colourful, so if you do not prune regularly the results can be dull and disappointing. This is a job to do annually in early spring or every other spring if you are not prepared to feed and mulch the plants annually.

1 This is what the shrub will look like if pruned the previous spring. If it has not been pruned for a few years, there will be thicker and duller older stems as well as the bright ones, but prune old and recent stems alike.

2 Pruning is simple but severe. Cut the stems back to within a few centimetres or inches of the stump of old wood, or to within 5–8cm (2–3in) of the ground if an old framework has not yet been established.

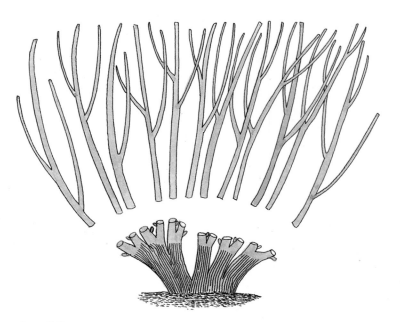

Cut off the most recent growth just above a bud, close to the stump of the old, thick woody base.

3 You do not have to be precise about the length of stem to leave, but aim for about 5cm (2in). The older wood will be darker, and the shoots produced the previous summer will be brighter. Cut back just above the old wood, to an outward-facing bud if possible to give the shrub a better shape.

4 The treatment may look alarming, but new shoots will probably start to grow within weeks and by the end of summer they will probably be 1.2–1.8m (4–6ft) long. It is a good idea to hoe in a fertilizer around the base of the plant, then water well if dry, and top with a thick mulch. This will encourage very strong growth.

SHRUBS TO TRY

Shrubs to cut back hard each spring or every second spring include:
Cornus alba varieties
Cornus stolonifera varieties
Salix alba 'Britzensis' (syn. *S. alba* 'Chermesina').

Right: Cornus stolonifera *'Flaviramea' is grown mainly for its colourful stems, which can be seen at their best in winter after the leaves have fallen.*

EARLY YEARS

Do not prune a young plant as severely as described here. Allow the plant to grow naturally for a season after planting, then the following spring prune to within 5cm (2in) of the ground. This will produce a bushy plant in future years, which can then be pruned as described.

Salix alba *'Britzensis' in full glory.*

POLLARDING

Pollarding is a form of coppicing, but on a short trunk usually 1.2–1.8m (4–6ft) tall.

1 Once a trunk of appropriate height has been created, a head like this can be formed. This is *Salix alba* 'Britzensis' (syn. *S. alba* 'Chermesina').

2 Cut back the stems to very short stubs, leaving perhaps one or two buds on each stem to grow. The treatment looks drastic, but a mass of new shoots will be produced during the summer. These will create a colourful effect during the winter. If possible, feed after pruning, and mulch if the tree is not growing in a grassed area.

Cutting Back to a Framework

If you've wondered why your butterfly bush, *Buddleja davidii*, has a few flowers far above head level on a tall, straggly plant, yet your neighbour has plentiful flowers on a compact plant which blooms at eye level, it is all because of the pruning. Shrubs that flower on shoots produced in the current year will become increasingly straggly year on year, with the blooms less accessible as the new growth on which they flower extends skywards. If you cut these shrubs back hard in early spring, they will still bloom, but on the new shoots produced closer to ground level. This is a really easy technique, so try it and see the improvement.

Prune back hard to just above the framework of old, darker and harder wood. This will encourage new shoots and compact growth.

1 These old stems show how much growth can be made in a season on a plant that was pruned the previous spring. Some of the dead flowerheads are still visible, showing how they flowered on compact plants.

2 Simply cut back all the previous summer's growth to within about 5cm (2in) of last year's stem. Do not worry if this seems drastic. The plant will soon produce vigorous new shoots to replace the ones you are cutting out.

3 Cut back to just above a bud. Keep to outward-facing buds as much as possible to give a bushier effect. Most of the shoots should be cut back to new growth, but if the bush is very old and congested, cut out one or two stems close to ground level. This will avoid the plant becoming too congested.

4 This is what a plant that has been cut back to a low framework of old stems looks like. Try to keep the height after pruning to about 90cm (3ft) or less.

Left: *You can create even shorter plants by cutting the old stems back close to the ground. The plants usually grow readily from new shoots produced at the base. They may already be visible if you delay pruning until early spring. The pruning can be done at any convenient time during the dormant season, but late winter and early spring are popular times.*

Below: *Buddleja in full glory. The new shoots grow fast, and within months they should be as tall as this and blooming prolifically. They are much more attractive than sparse flowers on a leggy plant.*

START YOUNG

It can be difficult to improve a very old and neglected plant, although you could try cutting it back to a few centimetres or inches above the ground to see whether it will shoot from the base. It is much more preferable, however, to start pruning a bush from an early age so that it never becomes too woody and neglected. You can start using the technique in the first spring after planting.

Below: Sambucus racemosa *'Plumosa Aurea' is grown mainly for its foliage. Harsh pruning in spring will result in a display like this by midsummer.*

SHRUBS TO TRY

Shrubs that respond well to this hard pruning are:
Buddleja davidii
Hydrangea paniculata
Sambucus racemosa
  'Plumosa Aurea'.

Cutting to the Ground

Even the most hesitant of pruners can use this technique with confidence. Simply cut everything down to the ground! The technique is used only for a few plants, notably those with cane-like shoots that rise from the ground. Some twiggy shrubs that flower on new growth, such as hardy fuchsias, can be treated this way.

SUITABLE SHRUBS
Groups of plants that can be treated in this way include ceratostigmas, hardy fuchsias and *Spiraea japonica* (syn. x *bumalda*). In mild areas, these plants form a woody framework of shoots that survive the winter but are often tidier if cut back. In cold areas the top growth may be killed, in which case the old shoots are cut back to ground level in spring. New shoots grow from the base and quickly produce a very bushy and compact plant.

1 *Rubus cockburnianus* is among the plants pruned using this technique. It is cut back to the ground annually to prevent the growth becoming an impenetrable tangle. The white bloom on the stems is also more pronounced on young stems, so the plant is more attractive if all the canes have been produced in the current year.

2 Simply cut the old canes to just above the ground. The height is not critical as new shoots will grow from the base. Although pruning does not come simpler than this, with this thorny plant it is not without hazards. Protect your hands by wearing strong gloves.

3 You may find it easier to use long-handled pruners (loppers). Do not worry about trying to cut back to a bud as new growth will come from the base.

4 Little will be visible, but if you prune in spring, new shoots will appear within weeks.

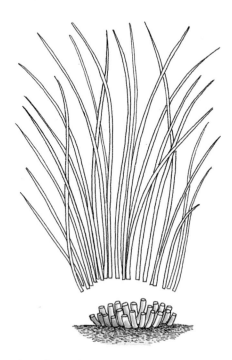

Cut back to just above the ground each spring.

By the end of the growing season, the new shoots will be as long as those removed in the spring. And because they are young, the white bloom will be particularly pronounced.

Deadheading with Shears

Deadheading (removing the old flowers that have died) can become a form of pruning. The technique is mainly used for heathers but, as you must avoid cutting into old wood, it is most effective if you adopt this method at an early stage. If you wait until the plants become old, straggly and woody, shearing them will not restore them to their former beauty.

1 When the flowers die trim them back with shears. Wait until spring, however, before you prune winter-flowering heathers.

2 Shear the dead heads off just below the bottom of the flower spike. Cut below the old flower head, but above old, hard wood. Heathers do not grow easily from hardened wood, so you may be left with bare or sparse patches if you cut into this.

Clip off the dead flowers, being careful not to cut back into dark, old wood.

3 The appearance will be improved as soon as the deadheading has been done, and as soon as new shoots start to grow the plant will look less manicured and more natural.

As long as you prune to keep the plants compact, with lots of new growth you should have a neat heather bed that will provide a carpet of colour.

SECATEURS (PRUNERS) OR HAND (HEDGE) SHEARS?
The advantage of using hand (hedge) shears is speed and convenience, especially if you have a whole bed of heathers. Pruning a bed of heathers with secateurs (pruners) can be extremely tiring, especially if you have to crouch down to do it. If, however, you have just a few heathers, it is a good idea to use secateurs because they leave the plants with a less "shaved" appearance.

Shaping with Shears

Lots of small-leaved evergreens can be clipped to shape. They will thrive without any regular pruning, but they can soon outgrow their allotted space. Trimming with shears leaves them looking formal but the natural shape returns quickly.

3 Trim off as much as necessary of the new growth, but avoid cutting back into the old, darker wood.

4 For a few weeks, the pruned shrub will look as though it has had a haircut, but in a surprisingly short time it will regain a more natural appearance.

1 Formally shaped plants should be clipped as soon as they look untidy, which may mean doing it more than once a year. If the plant simply needs restraining, the best time is from mid-summer onwards.

2 Clip the plant like a hedge if you want a formal shape, and less severely if you simply want to restrain its growth a little.

If you make sure the growth does not get out of hand, and the basic shape is retained, evergreens will always look good, even in a small garden.

Cut off new growth but do not cut back into the older wood.

SHRUBS TO TRY

Berberis (evergreen types)
Buxus sempervirens (box)
Ligustrum ovalifolium 'Aureum'
Lonicera nitida

Restraining Large-leaved Evergreens

Many evergreen shrubs grow happily without any routine pruning. However, if you have a small garden, you may want to restrict their size. Small-leaved evergreens can be clipped with hand (hedge) shears, but for large-leaved kinds use secateurs (pruners). Prune flowering kinds after flowering and non-flowering ones in spring.

3 If you find particularly badly placed stems crossing and rubbing against each other, cut one out.

Your shrub should not look radically different after its annual tidy up.

1 Most large-leaved evergreen shrubs only need pruning when they need restricting, or when diseased or dead wood is found.

2 Check all shrubs once a year, and cut back the remains of the old flower heads or dead shoots to healthy wood, or to the base if this is more appropriate.

DEADHEADING

Many rhododendrons set seed freely, and this diverts the plant's energy resources needlessly. Unless the seed is required, deadhead the plants as soon as the flowers fade.

1 The old flower truss should snap off easily between finger and thumb.

2 The developing flower bud may already be visible.

Large-leaved evergreens require little shaping, but it is worth checking the plants annually to remove dead or badly positioned branches. Removing flowerheads will also improve the appearance.

The "One Third Method"

This simple technique replaces a number of more complicated methods that can be used for a wide range of flowering plants. It is not necessarily any better, but it is a simple one to remember and easy to apply. And because no shoot is more than three years old, the method also ensures reasonably compact plants with vigorous, healthy growth that usually blooms best. Timing is easy to remember too: just do it as soon as possible after flowering is over.

1 The best time to prune using the one third method is soon after flowering has finished. This forsythia is ready for pruning and, because it is spring-flowering, plenty of replacement shoots will grow during the summer.

2 Count the number of main stems, then decide which third look the oldest (they will usually be the thickest and darkest). You do not have to follow the numeric formula slavishly, and one or two stems either way will make no difference.

Cut out one third of the oldest stems close to the base as soon as flowering has finished.

3 Cut back to just above the ground if the branches appear to rise from ground level, or to a stump near the base if your shrub forms a framework of thick old wood at the base. If possible, cut just above a new shoot arising from a position near the base of the plant. If there are few very old stems, make up the number to be thinned out by removing very weak ones or badly placed branches that are making the centre of the bush congested.

4 The bush will probably look a little sparse after pruning, but the basic shape and size will have been retained. Any apparent gaps within the bush will soon be filled in by new growth.

Kolkwitzia amabilis *can be pruned by the one third method after flowering if you want to keep the bush compact.*

SHRUBS TO TRY

Cornus (those grown for foliage effect, such as *C. alba* 'Elegantissima' and 'Spaethii')
Cotinus coggygria (for flowers and foliage)
Forsythia
Hypericum (border kinds grown for flowers)
Kerria japonica
Kolkwitzia

Leycesteria
Philadelphus
Potentilla (shrubby type)
Ribes sanguineum (flowering currant)
Spiraea (spring-flowering species such as *S.* 'Arguta' and summer-flowering kinds that bloom on old shoots such as *S.* x *vanhouttei*)

If you prune annually using this method, you will create a shrub that always has plenty of relatively young wood that will bloom well regardless of whether your shrub flowers on new wood or year-old shoots, and it should remain compact. Forsythias will remain compact and clothed with flowers from top to bottom.

DON'T START TOO YOUNG

Although the one third method of pruning is satisfactory for established shrubs, it is unsuitable for young plants. Wait until the shrub has been established for three years before you start using this technique.

Shorten New Growth

Brooms and genistas usually become too tall or leggy if you do not prune them regularly from an early age. Annual pruning once the flowers have faded will keep them looking good year after year.

Some plants, such as brooms, will become tall and leggy if you do not prune them annually, but they do not grow easily from old wood. Shorten the youngest, greenest lengths of shoot by about half, after flowering has finished.

1 The best time to prune brooms and genistas is as soon as possible after the flowers have faded. This allows plenty of time for the new growth to develop through the summer to flower next spring.

2 Shorten the growth that was formed last summer by about half. You should be able to identify last summer's growth easily because it will be paler and more supple than older wood.

3 Avoid cutting back into dark, older wood, as new shoots are seldom produced from this. Cut the most recent growth – that made last summer.

4 From a distance the difference after pruning will not be obvious, but it should be neater and more compact. The real benefit will be cumulative, however, as the plant will become less sparse and leggy over time.

START YOUNG

Do not wait until your broom is tall and woody before pruning. This method will only work if you start while the plant is still young. It is difficult to rejuvenate an old broom that is already tall and sparse. It is better to replant with a new one and care for it as described.

This is how a broom should be – well clothed with flowers over the whole shrub. If you don't prune to keep it like this, it will probably become bare at the base with the flowers high up on tall shoots.

Shorten Sideshoots

Some popular flowering shrubs, such as rock roses, Cistus, require a little pruning after flowering to encourage more flowering shoots to form for an even better show next year. From a distance, you will find the shrubs look little different after pruning, but you should see the benefits the following year.

Shrubs that flower on shoots that grew the previous year (yellow in this illustration) should produce more flowers if the flowered shoots are cut back by two thirds as soon as flowering is over.

I Prune once the flowers are over. Although the shrub will probably remain well shaped even if you don't prune, it will flower even more profusely next year if you can stimulate it to produce extra shoots.

2 Decide which shoots have to be shortened. Select those that have just borne flowers, which will be softer and paler than the older wood. Cut this section of the stem back by about two thirds.

Below: Kalmia latifolia.

3 Visually estimate a cutting point on the sideshoots that have flowered, about two thirds along the length of the young growth, then prune at that point. If there is 15cm (6in) of growth, make the cut about 10cm (4in) from the tip. Ignore the older, darker wood.

4 From a distance the pruned shrub will not look very different after pruning, because most of the cutting back will have been done to sideshoots and not the older main stems. But it will encourage the production of even more sideshoots, which will flower next year.

SHRUBS TO TRY

Cistus
Convolvulus cneorum
Kalmia latifolia

By careful pruning after flowering the previous summer, an abundance of new sideshoots that carry the flowers has been produced. Although it would have looked good without pruning, you should have a better show if you do prune.

Rejuvenating the Neglected

Often it is best to dig up old plants and replace them with new ones. Sometimes, however, even an old and unpromising shrub can be rejuvenated. The illustrations show how to improve neglected plants, and it is always worth trying similar techniques with any shrub that you want to save. If, after a season, there is no sign of new growth, then dig it up and replace it.

An old and neglected rhododendron can sometimes be rejuvenated by very hard pruning over a period of two or three years. This shows about one third of the branches cut back hard this year, a third that were cut back last year and are already producing new shoots close to the ground, and some branches not yet pruned. The unpruned branches will still be producing flowers, and by the time these are pruned next year some of the new growth from the pruned branches may be ready to flower.

STARTING AGAIN
If a shrub has become really overgrown, or simply neglected – perhaps with dying branches – be prepared to be drastic. Some shrubs will not survive cutting down close to the ground but others will. If you would have to remove the plant anyway, it is worth a try.

1 On this shrub one of the branches has partly broken off the main stem.

2 Cut out badly placed or unhealthy shoots back to their point of origin. Sometimes this, together with shortening over-long branches, may be sufficient.

3 If necessary, saw down the branches close to ground level. Some shrubs will not survive this, but others will grow again from the base.

4 To reduce the risk of infection after such drastic surgery, avoid leaving the wound ragged. Use a rasp or knife to smooth off the edges of the cut.

REMOVING SUCKERS

1 Some shrubs, such as rhododendrons and lilacs, are grown on a rootstock that is decoratively inferior to the variety that has been grafted on to it. Often, the rootstock will try to re-establish itself and suckers will appear. These grow from the base of the plant, often from beneath soil level. The leaves may look similar, but the flowers will be different.

2 Remove the suckers as close to the ground as possible. Finish off by trimming in closely with secateurs (pruning shears).

3 If you do not take out the suckers they will take over your shrub.

Taking out the suckers will ensure that the superior flowers of the grafted rhododendron will not be taken over by the rootstock.

Shrub Roses

The term shrub rose includes species of wild rose and old-fashioned varieties of bushy roses that pre-date hybrid teas and floribundas. Modern shrub roses are large bushy roses, raised in recent times but retaining many of the characteristics of the traditional old-fashioned types. Unlike modern floribundas and hybrid teas, shrub roses generally flower over a much shorter period. And most of them make bigger bushes too. They do not require such regular or intensive pruning but annual pruning will help to prevent the bushes becoming too large or too congested.

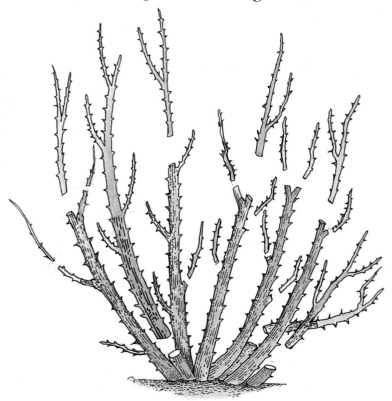

Shorten the main stems by between a quarter and a half, and the sideshoots by about two thirds. Badly positioned stems can be cut out completely.

1 Although a rose like this will continue to flower well, pruning will help to prevent it becoming too congested and improve its general appearance.

2 After some years there will be a lot of very old, and probably congested, stems at the base. Cut out one or two of the oldest stems from the base if they have become congested or look very old.

    The rose illustrated naturally produces a lot of cane-like stems from the base; others will have fewer but thicker stems, more like those on a hybrid tea. Cut out any dead or diseased wood at the same time.

3 Shorten the main shoots (those that arise from the base of the plant, not sideshoots) by between one quarter and one half. If the shoot is 1.2m (4ft) tall, cut off 30–60cm (1–2ft). If the rose you are pruning has also produced a lot of sideshoots (those growing off the main stems), shorten these by about two thirds. If the shoot is 30cm (1ft) long, cut back to about 10cm (4in).

4 Even when pruning has been done, you may be left with a substantial framework of stems. This is normal, as shrub roses usually make quite large bushes. With those that shoot freely from the base, like this one, you can be more drastic.

Shrub roses are usually quite large and bushy but they still benefit from pruning.

Standard Roses

Standard roses can appear confusing to prune if
you are unfamiliar with them. If you concentrate
on forming an attractive rounded head, however,
you will have no difficulty.

Weeping standards are dealt with differently.
These are pruned in summer – after flowering –
and not in spring like normal standards.

1 A standard before pruning can look
extremely confusing. Just concentrate on
achieving a nice rounded shape while
shortening the stems.

Below: *This is what a good
standard will look like if pruned
properly: a nice rounded head of
well-spaced shoots with masses of
flowers.*

2 During the dormant season (late
winter or early spring), shorten the main
stems in the head to about six buds,
more or less depending on the age of
the plant.

Do not prune too hard, otherwise
you may stimulate over-vigorous shoots
that could spoil the shape. Cut to an
outward-pointing bud, to encourage a
good shape.

Above left: *Prune a standard rose by shortening last summer's growth by
about half.*

Above right: *Prune a weeping standard by cutting back any old long shoots
to a point where there is a new one to replace it.*

3 Old plants may have areas of dead or diseased wood. Cut these back to a healthy bud.

4 Shorten sideshoots growing from the main stem to a couple of buds, to stop growth becoming too congested.

5 Aim to leave a rounded head of reasonably evenly spaced branches. Although the rose looks unattractive at this stage, visualize it with the summer's growth from this framework.

WEEPING STANDARDS

Weeping standards, which sometimes have their shoots trained over an umbrella-like frame, are really rambling roses grafted on to a single stem. For that reason they are pruned in summer or early autumn, when flowering has finished, and not in the dormant season.

If you do not prune annually the growth can become congested and tangled and the head top-heavy. While you are pruning, take the opportunity to check the stake is sound and the ties are not too tight.

1 Prune each shoot that has flowered, cutting it back to a position where there is a vigorous new shoot to replace it. This is not a measuring task, as each variety and each plant will be different. Just try to visualize where a new shoot could replace the one you are cutting back. If you can't find a suitable replacement shoot, do not prune the main stem. Instead, shorten the sideshoots on the flowered stem to two buds.

Although you should have a good idea of the shape of the head after pruning, it is difficult to predict the vigour of the replacement shoots. If the growth seems uneven by spring, cut back the longest shoots to create a more balanced effect.

Climbing Roses

This loose term covers plants with a wide range of characteristics, from rampant plants which will climb through a tree to restrained beauties which require coaxing over a pergola. Decide which group is relevant, then prune accordingly.

Left: Once-flowering climbing rose in full bloom.

ONCE-FLOWERING CLIMBERS

These have a permanent framework of woody stems, usually with very few new shoots growing from the base. Prune in summer.

1 Because these climbers have a stable framework of woody shoots, and are pruned in summer after flowering, they can often be intimidating to prune. Fortunately they usually flower even with minimal pruning, provided you keep the plant free of dead and diseased wood.

2 Try to cut out one or two of the oldest stems each year, to increase the amount of new growth. If you can find a young replacement shoot near the base, cut the old stem off just above this. Tie in the new shoot to replace the old one. Sometimes the replacement shoot starts perhaps 30–60cm (1–2ft) up the stem, in which case cut back to just above this higher level. Do not remove more than a third of the stems, otherwise flowering will suffer next year.

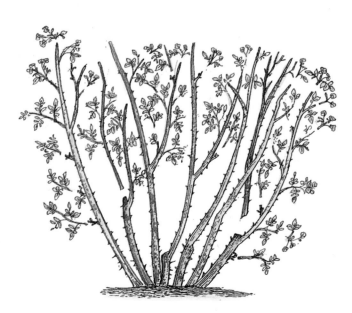

Cut out one or two of the oldest stems to a point just above a new young shoot close to the base; otherwise to a point higher up the plant where there is a replacement shoot. Deadhead at the same time.

3 If there are strong young replacement shoots higher up the plant, prune back a proportion of stems that have flowered to just above the newer growth. Tie in if necessary.

4 Go along the remaining stems and shorten the sideshoots, pruning back to leave two or three buds.

VERY VIGOROUS CLIMBERS

The climbing wild species such as *Rosa filipes* and very vigorous varieties like 'Wedding Day' are not suitable for routine pruning to control their growth. Just let them have their head with a suitably robust support, such as a tree or large ropes strung between poles. In the latter case you may have to prune out some of the shoots periodically if the rose outgrows its space.

REPEAT-FLOWERING CLIMBERS

Repeat-flowering climbers generally bloom from mid-summer though to mid-autumn, although after the first flush the flowers may be fewer and more sporadic. The terms perpetual-flowering, remontant or recurring may also be used to describe these roses. They flower on new wood but, as relatively few new main shoots are produced, little pruning is required. It is best done in two stages: in summer and winter.

1 When you first look at a repeat-flowering climbing rose with a view to winter pruning, do not be surprised if it seems difficult to know where to start. You will be pruning the ends of the shoots that flowered last summer. Fundamental shaping and training should not be necessary.

2 Shorten the tips if they have flowered, then go along each stem in turn to identify which sideshoots flowered in the summer, and prune each one back to two or three buds. Thin shoots that are badly positioned are also best cut out.

If the plant is a large one, you may not notice a lot of difference from a distance, but the pruning will encourage production of new growth that will increase the flowering capacity of the plant in the long term.

3 Cut out any dead or diseased wood. The basic outline of your rose may not look very different after the winter pruning, but it will encourage plenty of flowers in future years.

4 Deadhead as the flowers fade in summer, unless the plant is too large for this to be practical. Cut back to the nearest leaf.

Clematis: Which to Prune When

Clematis are not difficult to prune. Indeed some are just cut down almost to ground level at the end of winter, others are not routinely pruned at all. The problem is knowing which one to prune and how. If you get it wrong you may end up pruning out your next flush of flowers. For pruning purposes, clematis fall into three groups. You may be able to identify which group your plant belongs to from the descriptions below. If you are still not sure, see if you can find the variety in the checklist on this page. Only a selection of the hundreds of different clematis can be included here; if yours is not listed, ask a clematis expert or specialist nursery.

WHICH GROUP?

Does it flower in spring or early summer and have relatively small flowers?
YES = It is probably Group 1.
NO = Go to next question.

Does it bloom in early or midsummer, possibly with a few flowers later, and are the flowers large?
YES = It is probably Group 2.
NO = Go to next question.

Does it flower from mid- or late summer and into autumn?
YES = It is probably Group 3.
NO = There is an area of doubt, so consult a clematis expert or specialist nursery if you cannot find the variety listed on this page.

GROUP CHECK

This table contains some of the most popular species and varieties. If yours appears in this list it will tell you how best to prune it.

Species or variety	Group 1	Group 2	Group 3
C. alpina	o		
'Barbara Dibley'		o	
'Barbara Jackman'		o	
'Bee's Jubilee'		o	
'Belle of Woking'		o	
'Comtesse de Bouchaud'			o
'Duchess of Albany'			o
'Duchess of Edinburgh'		o	
'Ernest Markham'			o
'Etoile Violette'		o	
'Gipsy Queen'			o
'Hagley Hybrid'			o
'Jackmanii'			o
'Jackmanii Superba'			o
'Lasurstern'		o	
C. macropetala	o		
'Marie Boisselot'		o	
C. montana	o		
'Mrs Cholmondeley'		o	
'Nelly Moser'		o	
'Niobe'		o	
C. orientalis			o
'Perle d'Azure'			o
C. tangutica			o
'Ville de Lyon'			o
C. viticella		o	

Group 1 Clematis

These flower in spring or early summer on the shoots produced the previous year. One of the most widely planted of all clematis, *C. montana*, belongs to this group.

Group 1 clematis only need pruning when they outgrow their space. Just cut out sufficient branches to reduce congestion, and take those that encroach beyond their space back to their point of origin.

1 Retain plenty of vigorous young growth like this. Concentrate on cutting out any dead, damaged or diseased shoots. Cut back to a strong bud or shoot.

2 Cut back any stems that have outgrown their space to their point of origin. Then thin out any very congested growth.

3 After pruning, the plant will look neater at the edges, especially where shoots had been encroaching, but overall relatively few shoots will have been removed. The more you managed to leave, the bigger the show of flowers next year. When thinning out congested growth, always keep an eye on the overall appearance, and try to avoid creating large gaps in the growth.

Many of the clematis in this group can be left to their own devices for many years, especially vigorous species such as C. montana. *In a confined area, perhaps where the plant is trained along a fence or over a trellis, pruning may be required simply to improve its overall appearance and limit its spread.*

Group 2 Clematis

This group of clematis flower mainly in early or midsummer, although with some varieties, flowering may continue into autumn. Many of the popular large-flowered hybrids are in this group. The flowers are produced on shoots that grew the previous summer. Although some pruning – to thin out the growth – can be done immediately after the main flush of flowers, late winter or early spring is the best time to prune as without the foliage you can see what you are doing more easily. Pruning should not be a routine task, do it only if the plant is beginning to outgrow its allotted space.

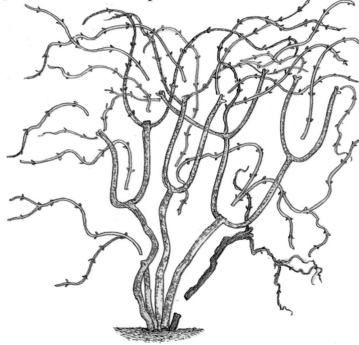

Prune when the plant has become congested and overgrown. Remove dead and damaged stems, weak and spindly shoots, and shoots that are simply making the plant too congested.

1 Group 2 clematis will not require pruning every year, but once the growth begins to look congested some thinning can be beneficial.

2 Prune out any dead or damaged stems, and any of last year's shoots that look very weak and spindly.

REJUVENATING A NEGLECTED PLANT

A neglected or very overgrown plant can be pruned back very hard, like a Group 3 plant. Although you will lose flowers for a season, the plant should bloom beautifully the following year. And if you have trained the shoots to a suitable support, the plant will look much tidier.

3 Do not remove too many shoots. If you want the plant to cover a large area it may still be worth thinning a new plant like this, but then respacing the shoots in a fan-like formation to form a framework.

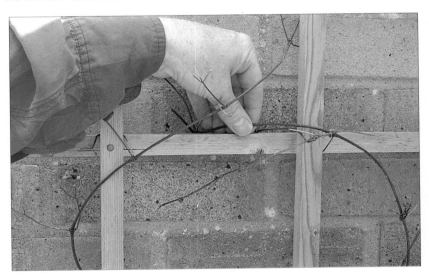

4 After pruning is a good time to respace shoots to fill in the gaps. These shoots are still young but they will thicken to form a basic framework over the years. New young growth will then fill in vacant spaces.

Prune plants in this group only when they outgrow their space or begin to look congested. If they are still pleasing and within bounds, leave them alone.

Group 3 Clematis

Clematis in this group flower late on shoots produced in the current year, making them the easiest of all to prune. You can make a fresh start each year by pruning back severely, and the plants will be more compact and better for it.

1 Most of this growth has been made since the previous spring, and if the plant is not pruned, this year's flowers will be an extension to growth already here. This is a recipe for a congested plant — with flowers high up while the base is bare. To keep a Group 3 clematis looking good and flowering well, prune in late winter or early spring, ideally before the new leaves emerge.

2 In winter prune all the shoots back to between 23–60cm (9–24in) above the ground. This will stimulate the production of plenty of new shoots that will flower well in late summer.

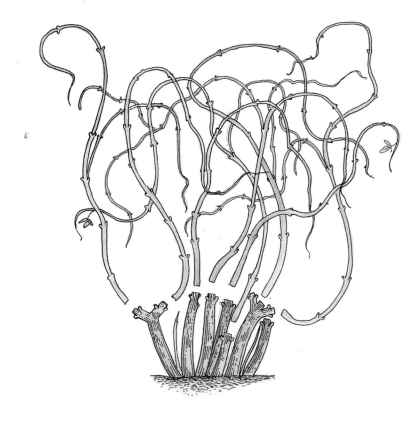

Be harsh with clematis that flower late on shoots produced in the spring and summer. In late winter, cut them back to between 23–60cm (9–24in) above the ground.

3 Make a straight cut just above a pair of promising buds. Although the pruning height is not critical, aim for 23–30cm (9–12in) above the ground. It will not matter if you leave old stems longer, but the flowers may be that much higher.

4 Pruning Group 3 plants seems very drastic, but by early summer the new shoots will be growing fast and you should have a compact plant covered with flowers by late summer or early autumn. This plant has not been pruned back as far as some gardeners may prefer, but it will grow just as well although the flowers will be just that bit higher. On a pergola you may want the flowering stems to grow tall.

Clematis 'Jackmanii Superba' is one of the clematis that flower on wood produced in the current season, and so benefits from hard pruning in late winter.

Vines and Creepers

Ornamental vines, such as *Vitis coignetiae* and *V. vinifera* 'Purpurea', are often grown over a pergola or a rustic framework. Unless you adopt a methodical pruning method they will become tangled and difficult to manage as the years go by. It is best to train them to create a framework of permanent branches that run along the top of the pergola or rustic frame or trellis, then prune them annually for a curtain of summer growth.

1 A well-trained climber growing against a wall will already have its framework of branches well spaced out in a spreading fan.

2 Prune last summer's growth back to about two buds from the old woody branches that form the framework.

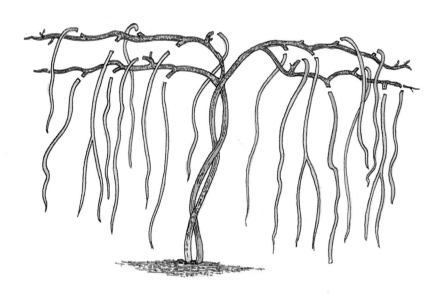

If you train a climber over a pergola or similar support, the new growth will cascade down like a curtain. Prune these long new shoots back to short spurs (stubs) each year, when the plants are dormant.

3 Cut sideshoots from the stumps left by earlier pruning back to one or two buds, choosing one pointing in an appropriate direction.

4 After pruning, the basic framework of old, thick branches will be left, with the other shoots shortened to stump-like spurs (stubs). Although the climber will look rather bare straight after pruning, within a few months there will be plenty of new growth.

Ornamental vines put on a lot of growth each summer. If you prune them and space out the branches, they will look neater.

PERGOLA PLANTS

If the main shoots are trained along the top of the horizontal support until they reach the required length, subsequent pruning will be simplified. Each winter, cut the previous summer's growth back to within one or two buds of its point of origin, to keep the plant tidy and restrained, as shown in the picture.

Over the years short spurs (stubs) will form along the main framework of branches. By cutting back to these each winter, you will have a fresh curtain of new shoots each summer without the tangled growth that would otherwise develop. If the spur system becomes too congested, cut out some of the spurs to reduce the number of summer shoots.

SELF-CLINGING CLIMBERS

Some vigorous climbers, such as ivies and parthenocissus, may need annual constraint if they have reached the limit of their acceptable growth, for instance once they start to clog gutters, penetrate under tiles, cover windows, or spread onto walls that you want to keep clear.

1 Vigorous self-clingers such as ivies and parthenocissus can reach great heights if planted against a tall wall, but pruning is usually restricted to keeping the exploring new shoots clear of windows or areas where they can cause damage, such as blocking gutters or loosening roof tiles. They will also spread to adjoining walls if their growth is not restricted annually.

2 The actual pruning, best done in early spring, is very simple, but you may require ladders to reach the offending shoots. If necessary, pull the stems clear of the wall or support (this may require some force as they can cling tenaciously), so that you can use the secateurs (pruning shears) freely. Simply cut back far enough to allow for this year's growth. This will depend on the plant and its position, but you should have a good idea of growth rate from previous experience.

3 Although it will be obvious that some cutting-back has taken place, new growth in spring and early summer will soon soften the effect. On this wall a hard edge after pruning is acceptable, but around windows you may prefer to cut the shoots back by different amounts to avoid a clipped or straight-line appearance.

Formal Hedges

Formal hedges (those neatly clipped to a regular shape) can make or break a garden. If they are well shaped and neatly trimmed they give a garden that well-manicured look. If they are uneven and poorly clipped, they will be a constant source of irritation to the perfectionist, detracting from the garden within.

Cutting a hedge seems such a natural thing that many gardeners are surprised that there is anything to explain, yet using the right techniques will make your hedge look smarter, probably enable the job to be done more quickly with less effort, and, if you use a powered hedge trimmer (shears), probably more safely too.

I The beauty of a formal hedge lies in its crisp outline. If you neglect trimming, attention will be drawn to it for the wrong reasons. Quick-growing hedges will require trimming several times a year, but many evergreens remain respectable with one or two cuts during the year. If you are in doubt about when to trim, consult a specialist book for the best times, although you will not go far wrong if you trim whenever the hedge begins to look untidy between spring and autumn.

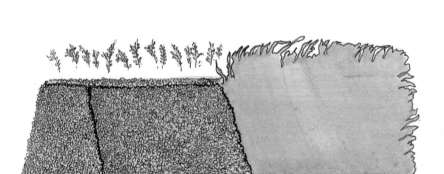

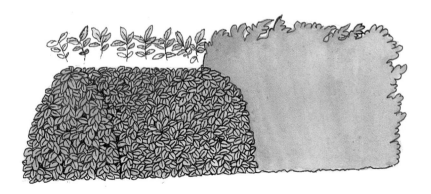

5 Try to hold the blades flat and horizontal when cutting the top. This may mean standing on steps or a raised plank.

Top: *Try to cut the sides so that they slope to the top. A flat top is easier than a curved one.*

Bottom: *A rounded top can look attractive, but you need a good eye to keep it even.*

6 Powered tools speed the job and ease the effort, but they must be used carefully. Use protective glasses or goggles, gardening gloves, and ideally ear protectors. If using mains electricity, make sure the cable is always well away from the blades, and protect the circuit, and yourself, with a residual current device (RCD). Use the trimmer with a wide, sweeping motion, keeping the blade parallel to the hedge.

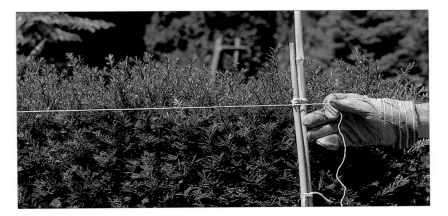

2 The clippings will be easier to cope with if you lay a plastic sheet along the base of the hedge to catch them. You will be able to pick up most of them quickly and easily simply by gathering up the sheet.

3 If using hand (hedge) shears, try to keep the blades flat against the side of the hedge. If you cut with a stabbing motion the finish is likely to be uneven.

4 The difficult part of cutting a hedge is achieving a level top. Unless you have a very good eye for this, or have lots of experience, there is likely to be a dip somewhere or a slope from one end to the other. Often you can only see this when you stand back from the hedge. The taller the hedge, the more difficult it is to achieve a level top without an aid. The higher you have to reach, the greater the tendency to create dips. String stretched taut between two canes (stakes) could make all the difference. Remember to have your guideline low enough to allow for growth. It will depend on the plant used, but 30cm (1ft) below the required final height might not be too much.

7 Some conifers produce stray vigorous sideshoots, and simply nipping these off with secateurs (pruning shears) may be enough to improve the appearance between proper trims.

This carefully clipped yew shows all the graceful formality of a carefully maintained hedge.

ROUNDING AND TAPERING
A hedge that tapers towards the top is less likely to be spoilt by heavy snowfall. If you live in an area where heavy snowfalls are common, it is worth creating a pointed or rounded top. This is best achieved over a period of time as the hedge matures. If you try to do it with an established hedge, there will probably be unattractive areas of sparse growth for some time. It is also a good idea to taper the sides, even if the top is flat. There is marginally less trimming to do (because the top is narrower) but the main benefits are to the hedge itself because more light reaches the lower parts.

Informal Hedges

Informal hedges are usually flowering hedges, so timing can be critical. If you prune at the wrong time you may cut out the flowering shoots. There is much more flexibility in the way an informal hedge is pruned, however. As a crisp outline is not expected, pruning should be aimed mainly at restricting size.

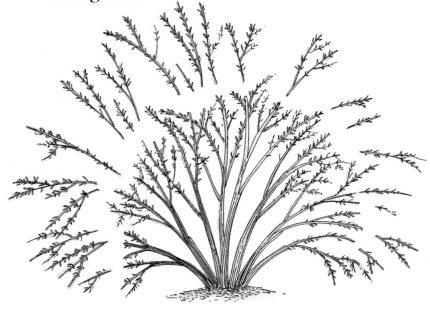

Informal flowering hedges are usually best pruned after flowering has just finished. Don't clip to a formal shape, but shorten the shoots that have grown since the last pruning to maintain compact plants with a neat outline.

1 Most flowering hedges are best trimmed when the flowers have finished. Exceptions are where attractive fruits or berries will follow, such as *Rosa rugosa*.

4 Simply shortening long shoots each year will keep most informal hedges looking good. It restrains the size and stimulates plenty of sideshoots that give the hedge a denser appearance. An informal hedge should not look tightly clipped, so avoid trimming the whole plant uniformly.

5 Lavender is best trimmed with hand (hedge) shears in early or mid-spring, or after flowering. Shear off the old flower heads (if not already done) together with about 2.5cm (1in) of last summer's foliage. Do not cut back into older, harder wood. Rosemary can be clipped in a similar way, but wait until the flowers have finished.

2 If you have a large informal hedge, the simplest and quickest way to prune is with hand (hedge) shears or a powered hedge trimmer (shears). Only do this with small-leaved plants, such as berberis, though. Trim to size rather than attempt a smooth, even finish like a formal hedge.

3 Although more time-consuming, secateurs (pruners) will do a better job, especially with large-leaved plants. To restrict size, cut back over-long shoots to a position where there is a suitable replacement shoot. If there is no replacement shoot you can usually cut it out entirely. The loose structure of this type of hedge is very forgiving. Alternatively, just shorten the shoot as shown in the next step.

6 The kind of shrub rose usually used for a hedge will not require heavy pruning like those used in rose beds. If they are becoming congested and very woody, cut out some of the oldest and thickest stems close to the base.

Escallonias are sometimes clipped as formal hedges; however, if you do not clip them tightly but allow plenty of growth to remain, an informal flowering effect can be achieved. Prune when flowering has finished.

Good Plant Guide

Good planting is the result of good planning. There is a range of plants for every situation, be it dry or wet, hot or cold, sunny or shady. With a little thought, it will usually be possible to find plants to provide colour or interest for every month of the year, so that the garden need never look dull.

Left: *Although your attention is drawn to the beautiful colours of the flowers, it is the foliage which creates the backdrop.*

Above: *This cottage garden style border is a balance of careful planning and happy accidents.*

Although effective planning and well-designed hard-landscaping are vital in creating a garden, it is of course the plants you choose which will ultimately determine its overall look. It is impossible to give many planting suggestions for beds and borders in a book of this size, and in any case you should try to include mainly those plants that appeal to you rather than follow another person's preferences.

Most garden centres now have well-labelled plants, often with a picture of the mature plant as well as notes about its height, spread, soil preferences and the aspect it prefers, and a good plant encyclopedia will fill in most of the gaps.

The vast majority of plants will grow well in most gardens, tolerating a wide pH range (a measure of how acid or alkaline the soil is), and doing well in sun or partial shade. It is only where your soil is extreme in some way, or the aspect particularly unfavourable (very shady, exposed and windy, or very acid or alkaline, for example), that you will have to consider whether the plant will thrive.

This section of the book tells you which plants should be suitable for a range of problem sites, so you know which ones to consider when you are browsing through catalogues or looking around the garden centres.

There are also suggestions for other groups of plants for which ideas are usually welcome, such as those that make a good focal point, and plants to grow for wildlife, or for fragrance.

Bear in mind that these short lists are only a selection of the many plants that may be appropriate. But they are all dependable plants, and are well worth including as, at least, a starting point.

Focal Point Plants

The majority of these plants look good in borders, but most of them are particularly striking as individual specimens, or in a position where they stand out above the rest of the plants in the border. They are plants that will catch the eye, even from a distance, and in many cases serve a similar purpose to a garden ornament.

BORDER PERENNIALS

Acanthus spinosus (bear's breeches) Above: Large, divided, spiny-looking leaves, topped by 1.2m (4ft) spikes of unusual purple and white flowers in summer.

Agapanthus hybrids (African lily) Above: Large, rounded heads of blue flowers on stiff stems about 60–75cm (2–2½ft) tall, make an excellent focal point when grown in a large container.

Allium giganteum (giant onion) Ball-like heads about 10cm (4in) across containing masses of small, mauve flowers on stiff stems about 1.2m (4ft) tall.

Crambe cordifolia (colewort) Above: Huge, dark green leaves and cloud-like masses of small, white flowers in early summer on stems about 1.8m (6ft) tall.

Eremurus robustus (foxtail lily)
Above: Tall, rocket-like flower spikes often 2.4m (8ft) tall in late spring and early summer. This species has peach-coloured flowers.

Gunnera manicata
Enormous leaves like a giant rhubarb, on plants up to 3m (10ft) tall. It requires very moist soil.

Kniphofia (red hot poker)
Above: Stiff, blade-like leaves and poker-like spikes of usually red and yellow flowers, 1–1.8m (3–6ft) tall.

Phormium tenax (New Zealand flax)
Above: Clumps of broad strap-like leaves, green, purple or variegated, according to species or variety; most are 1–1.8m (3–6ft) tall.

GRASSES

Arundo donax
A large grass, up to 2.4m (8ft) with long, drooping, blue-green leaves. 'Variegatus', banded white, is only about half this height.

Cortaderia selloana (pampas grass)
Above: Large grass with 1.8m (6ft) long, silvery-white flower plumes in autumn. Evergreen. For a small garden use 'Pumila' – 1.2m (4ft).

SHRUBS AND TREES

Cordyline australis (cabbage palm)
Above: Palm that is hardy except in cold areas. Strap-shaped leaves (on tall stems on mature plants). Can reach tree-like size.

Fatsia japonica
(false castor oil plant)
Above: Hand-shaped, large, glossy green leaves. White, ball-shaped flower head in autumn on mature plants. 1.8m (6ft) or more tall.

Garrya elliptica (silk tassel bush)
Evergreen of undistinguished appearance most of year, but spectacular long catkins in winter.

Mahonia* x *media 'Charity'
Evergreen with stiff, upright growth and large, divided leaves. Sprays of yellow flowers in winter. Grows up to 2.4m (8ft) or more.

Paulownia tomentosa (coppiced)
If pruned to just above ground level each spring, this tree can be grown as a tall shrub with leaves 60cm (2ft) or more across.

Trachycarpus fortunei
(Chusan palm)
Above: Clusters of large, fan-shaped leaves on a tall stem. Only hardy in areas where winters are mild.

Yucca gloriosa (and *Y. filamentosa*)
Above: Stiff, sword-like evergreen leaves (on a stout stem in the case of *Y. gloriosa*), with imposing spike of creamy-white bells.

Sun or Shade?

In every garden, there will be parts that are sunnier or shadier than others. This is influenced by overhanging trees, tall buildings and high walls and by the direction of the garden.

WISE DECISIONS

Putting a plant in the wrong place for its growing preferences will cause it to become stressed, slowing down the growth, reducing the flowering and, ultimately, killing it. Garden centres (supply stores) today are filled with plants from all over the world, from the hottest areas to the coolest, so there will definitely be a range of plants for any situation.

The plants that enjoy being in a hot place often hail from Mediterranean regions, and have silver or blue leaves to reflect the light. This is one of the many ways in which plants can adapt to live in particular conditions. Other adaptations include having leaves that are rolled or covered with a waxy coating, to reduce the amount of moisture lost through the leaf-pores, or leaves that are reduced to spines.

Plants growing in shady areas, evolve large, soft leaves in order to absorb the maximum amount of available light, and they tend to be dark green with chlorophyll, to be as efficient at producing food as possible.

PLANTS FOR SHADY AREAS

Astrantia (moist shade)
Astilbe (moist shade)
Aucuba japonica (dry shade)
Camellia (moist shade)
Dicentra spectabilis (moist shade)
Fatsia japonica (moist shade)
Hamamelis mollis (moist shade)
Helleborus (moist shade)
Hosta (moist shade)
Ilex (dry shade)
Mahonia (moist shade)
Pachysandra terminalis (dry shade)
Rhododendron (moist shade)
Rodgersia (moist shade)
Sarcococca (moist shade)
Skimmia (dry shade)
Viburnum davidii (moist shade)
Vinca (dry shade)

Above: *Ferns enjoy moist shade and will add lush greenery to your garden scheme.*

Opposite: *Most gardens are a combination of sunny and shady areas, although some may be predominantly one or the other. Choose plants accordingly for garden success.*

Above: *The summer-flowering* Hemerocallis *is easy to grow in sun or partial shade.*

Left: Monarda *'Squaw' is enjoyed for its aromatic foliage and flowers. It requires moist soil.*

PLANTS FOR SUNNY AREAS

Agapanthus
Achillea filipendulina
Caryopteris x *clandonensis*
Cistus
Convolvulus cneorum
Cytisus
Echinops vitro
Helianthemum nummularium
Iris germanica hybrids
Kniphofia hybrids
Monarda
Pelargonium
Santolina chamaecyparissus
Senecio
Verbascum
Yucca

Plants for Shady Areas

Shade-tolerant plants are among the most useful in the garden as they can make the most of those unpromising areas that are usually dull and uninteresting. A few well-chosen, attractive shade plants can transform those parts of the garden that receive little direct sun into a lush and lovely area that you will not want to avoid.

BORDER PERENNIALS FOR DRY SHADE

Anemone japonica (A. x *hybrida*)
White or pink, single or double flowers about 5cm (2in) across in late summer and autumn, on stems 1–1.2m (3–4ft) tall.

Bergenia (elephant ears)
Above: Large, rounded, glossy leathery leaves (sometimes purplish in winter). Flowers – mostly pink – in spring. 30–45cm (1–1½ft).

Brunnera macrophylla
Loose heads of blue, forget-me-not-like flowers in spring, but taller at about 45cm (1½ft). Avoid dry soil.

Euphorbia (spurge)
There are many kinds, but for shade look for *E. amygdaloides*, *E. griffithii* and *E. robbiae* (one of the best for shade).

Liriope muscari (lilyturf)
Grass-like tufts of foliage, with spikes of blue, bead-like flowers in autumn. 30–45cm (1–1½ft).

Pulmonaria (lungwort)
There are many species and varieties, most with silver-splashed leaves. The spring flowers are in shades of blue and pink.

BORDER PERENNIALS FOR MOIST SHADE

Astilbe hybrids
Above: Deeply cut foliage, topped with plumes of pink, red or white summer flowers. 60–75cm (2–2½ft).

Astrantia (masterwort)
White to pink flowers with papery bracts, on slender stems, in summer. 60–75cm (2–2½ft).

Dicentra spectabilis (bleeding heart)
Fern-like foliage, topped by arching sprays of pendulous pink or white flowers in spring. 60cm (2ft).

Helleborus (hellebore)
The most popular species are *H. niger* (winter) and *H. orientalis* (spring), but there are other species and hybrids to try.

Hosta (plantain lily)
These popular foliage plants come in many variations, so choose species or varieties with leaves that particularly appeal to you.

Rodgersia
Large, bold, divided or lobed leaves (there are several species) and plumes of white or pink flowers in summer. 1–1.5m (3–5ft).

SHRUBS FOR DRY SHADE

Aucuba japonica (spotted laurel)
Above: Large, glossy evergreen leaves, splashed yellow or gold. Flowers insignificant, occasionally red berries. 1.5m (5ft).

Ilex (holly)
There are dozens of excellent hollies, many attractively variegated. If you want berries, check that you are buying a female variety.

Mahonia
There are many species and hybrids, all with large, divided leaves and yellow flowers in winter or spring.

Pachysandra terminalis
A low-growing ground cover about 30cm (1ft) tall, with white, insignificant flowers. 'Variegata' is a more attractive plant.

Skimmia
Glossy-leaved evergreens, with red berries (if you buy a female variety or one that has flowers of both sexes). About 1m (3ft).

Vinca (periwinkle)
A rather untidy, spreading ground cover, but useful for its usually blue flowers all summer long. There are variegated forms.

SHRUBS FOR MOIST SHADE

Camellia
Above: Large flowers in spring, set against glossy, evergreen leaves. There are many different kinds.

Fatsia japonica
(false castor oil plant)
A bold foliage plant with large, hand-shaped leaves. Grows to about 1.8m (6ft).

Hamamelis mollis (witch hazel)
A large shrub to 3m (10ft) or more, grown for its spidery-looking, yellow, fragrant flowers in winter.

Rhododendron
Popular flowering woodland plants. There are hundreds of widely available varieties to choose from.

Sarcococca (sweet box)
Glossy, evergreen foliage and white, winter flowers that are small but very fragrant. About 1m (3ft).

Viburnum davidii
Low-growing evergreen with conspicuously veined leathery leaves. Turquoise fruits on female plants.

Plants for Sunny and Dry Areas

Few plants object to sunshine, but the dry soil that sometimes goes with a shallow or sandy soil in a sun-baked situation is a more demanding environment. For a position like this, choose plants that are naturally adapted to such conditions and will thrive in them.

SHRUBS

Caryopteris x *clandonensis*
(blue spiraea)
Clusters of bright blue flowers in late summer and early autumn. Grey, aromatic leaves. Height about 1m (3ft).

Cistus (rock rose)
Above: Large, single flowers between late spring and mid-summer. Mainly pinks and white, and often blotched. 45–90cm (1½–3ft).

Convolvulus cneorum
A leafy evergreen with a silvery appearance. Funnel-shaped, white flowers in summer, on a plant that grows to about 60cm (2ft).

Cytisus (broom)
There are many species and hybrids to choose from, mainly with bright, pea-type flowers.

Helianthemum nummularium
(rock rose)
Above: Low-growing shrubs to about 30cm (1ft), with masses of single or double pink, red, yellow or white flowers in early summer.

Santolina chamaecyparissus
(cotton lavender)
Finely divided, stem-hugging grey leaves that create a silvery mound about 60cm (2ft) tall. Button-like, yellow flowers in summer.

Senecio
Above: *S. greyi* and *S.* 'Sunshine' are similar plants with grey leaves on bushy plants about 1m (3ft) tall. Yellow daisy flowers in summer.

Yucca
Any of the hardy yuccas make imposing plants, with spiky leaves and bold spikes of white, bell-like flowers in summer.

BORDER PERENNIALS

Achillea filipendulina (yarrow)
Above: Flat, yellow flower heads over fern-like foliage, flowering at intervals between early summer and mid-autumn. 1.2m (4ft).

Agapanthus (African lily)
Large, rounded heads of blue flowers on stiff stems about 60–75cm (2–2½ft) tall. Not suitable for cold winter areas.

Echinops ritro (globe thistle)
Above: Globular, steely-blue flower heads in mid- and late summer, on plants about 1m (3ft) tall with grey-green, deeply lobed leaves.

Geranium (cranesbill)
Above: There are many species of these summer-flowering border plants, with pink or blue flowers, most 30–60cm (1–2ft) tall.

Iris germanica hybrids (flag)
The border flag irises, which flower in early summer, come in many colours. Most grow to about 60–90cm (2–3ft) tall.

Kniphofia hybrids (red hot poker)
Stiff, blade-like leaves and imposing poker-like spikes of usually red and yellow flowers. 1–1.8m (3–6ft) tall.

Nepeta mussinii (*N.* x *faassenii*)
(catmint)
Above: Massed spikes of blue flowers in summer, backed by grey-green leaves. Grows up to 30–60cm (1–2ft) according to variety.

Verbascum (mullein)
There are several good hybrids for the border, but they tend to be short-lived. Tall spikes of pink, yellow or white flowers.

Dry Areas

Most gardens have patches where there is less moisture than elsewhere. This is especially a problem in front gardens, which are often overhung by structures that create "rain shadows". If you improve the soil and select plants that enjoy dry conditions, this need not be a problem. Factors that can influence the amount of moisture within the garden include rainfall, sunshine, soil type, drainage, surrounding structures and the plants already in position.

RETAINING MOISTURE

Rainfall varies considerably within small areas depending on local topographical conditions; this can result in dramatically different amounts of water reaching the soil in different parts of the garden. The direction in which the garden faces can affect the water it receives if the house is positioned as a shield. Even though plenty of rain falls, it may not be falling where it is needed.

How long the moisture is held within the soil, and therefore how long it is available for use by the plants, is affected by both the amount of sun and shade and the soil type. A light, sandy soil loses its moisture quickly, because there are large air spaces between the particles, allowing rapid drainage. A heavy, clay soil, on the other hand, has tiny air spaces, because the soil particles are much smaller. The water is slower to drain away and is available to the plants for a longer time.

In a flat area of the garden drainage will take longer than in a garden that slopes.

Having large, established specimens already *in situ* can mean that there is less water available for new plants. An older plant will have sent roots down to the lower levels within the soil, to take advantage of all the moisture it can, leaving little for the new plant. A five-year-old tree, for example, may drink in excess of 4 litres (1 gallon) of water a day.

If the garden does not receive enough rainfall to support plants with this kind of requirement, you may have to consider plants that need a lower intake. You can improve moisture by adding a mulch around the base of the plants. This keeps the soil moist by slowing down evaporation.

Salvia officinalis *will grow successfully in dry soil.*

Above: *Gardening in containers is one way to overcome less-than-perfect soil types, and will allow you to grow certain species that might not normally flourish in your garden.*

PLANTS FOR DRY SITUATIONS

Agapanthus
Buddleja alternifolia
Campanula persicifolia
Cistus
Convolvulus cneorum
Cortaderia selloana
Corylus avellana 'Contorta'
Cytisus battandieri
Eryngium bourgatii
Escallonia 'Slieve Donard'
x *Halimiocistus*
Helianthemum
Lavandula
Liriope muscari
Osteospermum
Papaver orientale
Perovskia
Rosmarinus
Salvia officinalis
'Sunshine'
Yucca filamentosa

Above: Lavandula *'Hidcote' prefers dry soil.*

Right: *Containers add instant and moveable colour to the garden.*

Plants for Alkaline Soil

Alkaline soils – predominantly those that are in chalky areas – pose a problem for many plants. The high pH (alkalinity) can cause various nutrients and trace elements to become locked into a form unavailable to the plants, which then grow poorly and often have yellowing leaves. You can overcome some of these problems with cultural techniques and the use of special chemicals, but it is easier to concentrate on those plants that grow well on chalky soils.

SHRUBS

Buddleja davidii (butterfly bush)
Annual pruning ensures sprays of white, mauve or purple flowers on bushes about 1.8m (6ft) tall.

Clematis
Above and top: There are many species and hybrids of these popular climbers to be grown, all of which should thrive on chalky soils.

Cotoneaster
Choose from the many kinds of cotoneaster, deciduous or evergreen, ground-huggers or tall shrubs. All tolerate chalky soil.

Helianthemum nummularium (rock rose)
Low-growing shrubs to about 30cm (1ft), with masses of single or double pink, red, yellow or white flowers in early summer.

Lavandula (lavender)
Above: Lavender, blue, pink or white flowers between mid-summer and early autumn. Usually grey-green, aromatic foliage.

Paeonia suffruticosa (tree peony)
Above: Very large flowers – often 15cm (6in) across – in shades of pink or red, as well as white, in late spring. 1.5–1.8m (5–6ft).

Pyracantha (firethorn)
Small, white flowers in early summer, followed by red, orange or yellow berries. Grow against a wall or free-standing.

Syringa (lilac)
Above: *S. vulgaris* (common lilac) and other species of these popular and fragrant shrubs will all thrive on chalky soils.

BORDER PERENNIALS

Dianthus (carnations, pinks)
Above: Border carnations and pinks of all kinds will do well on chalky soils. Your garden centre should have a good selection.

Doronicum (leopard's bane)
Above: Bright yellow, single, daisy-type flowers, or doubles, in late spring and early summer. Most grow to about 60cm (2ft).

Gypsophila paniculata (baby's breath)
Masses of small white or pink flowers in summer, on a loose plant to about 1m (3ft). The lax stems benefit from a support.

Helleborus
The most popular species are *H. niger* (winter) and *H. orientalis* (spring), but there are other species and hybrids to try.

Paeonia (peony)
Above: Large single or double flowers about 12cm (5in) across, in late spring or early summer, mainly pinks and reds, 60–75cm (2–2½ft).

Scabiosa (scabious)
Above: *S. caucasica* (blue flowers from summer to autumn) is the popular border species, but other scabious will also thrive on chalk.

Verbascum (mullein)
There are several good hybrids for the border, but they tend to be short-lived. Tall spikes of pink, yellow or white flowers.

Plants for Acid Soil

Acid soils are generally less of a problem than alkaline ones. Most plants that tolerate a wide range of soil will do well on reasonably acid soils, especially if you add lime to neutralize the effect. The plants listed here not only thrive in acid soils but are also particularly reluctant to grow in alkaline conditions – so also use this list as an indication of what to avoid for chalky soils.

SHRUBS

Azalea
Above: There are evergreen and semi-evergreen azaleas, ranging in size from dwarfs for the rock garden to large woodland plants.

Calluna vulgaris (heather)
There are hundreds of varieties, some grown for foliage colour. Most flower late summer and autumn. 30–45cm (1–1½ft).

Camellia
Above: Large, rose-like flowers in spring, set against evergreen leaves. There are many different kinds.

Corylopsis pauciflora (winter hazel)
Spreading growth and slender branches with pale yellow catkin flowers in spring. Grows to about 1.8m (6ft).

Daboecia (Irish heath)
Above: Heather-like plant with pink or white bell-like flowers on bushy plants about 60cm (2ft) tall. Flowers from summer to autumn.

Gaultheria procumbens (winter green)
Above: A creeping plant with small evergreen leaves, useful for ground cover. Grown mainly for its red berries. 15cm (6in).

Halesia carolina (snowdrop tree)
A large, spreading shrub growing to more than 3m (10ft). Pendulous, bell-shaped white flowers appear in late spring.

Kalmia latifolia (calico bush)
Above: Evergreen with glossy green leaves and pink flowers in early summer. Grows to about 1.8m (6ft).

Pernettya Gaultheria mucronata
Above: An evergreen grown mainly for its berries on female plants: shades of red, pink, purple or white according to variety.

Pieris
Above: There are many good species and varieties, grown for their white flowers and red-flushed young leaves. About 1.8m (6ft).

Rhododendrons
Above: There are rhododendrons to suit all sizes of garden, and catalogues and garden centres offer hundreds of them.

Skimmia
Glossy-leaved evergreens, with red berries (if you buy a female variety or one that has flowers of both sexes). About 1m (3ft).

Ground-cover Plants

Ground-cover plants will help to suppress weeds, and if used over a large area will add a sense of texture to the garden floor. Remember, however, that until they become well established, ground-cover plants are as vulnerable to dry soil and competition as most other plants.

SHRUBS

Cotoneaster dammeri
Ground-hugging shrub to about 15cm (6in). The stems root as they spread to about 1m (3ft). Red berries in autumn.

Erica carnea (heather)
Above: Most varieties make a mound of growth about 30cm (1ft) high, covered with pink, red or white flowers in winter and spring.

Euonymus fortunei (wintercreeper)
A tough evergreen about 30–45cm (1–1½ft) tall with a spread of 60cm (2ft) or more. Grow the bright variegated varieties.

Hedera (ivy)
Above: Both small-leaved and large-leaved types of ivy can be used for ground cover.

Hypericum calycinum
(rose of Sharon)
Above: A semi-evergreen about 30cm (1ft) tall, with large, yellow flowers and a prominent boss of stamens. A rampant spreader.

Juniperus horizontalis
(creeping juniper)
A ground-hugging conifer with a spread of 1.2m (4ft) or more. There are several good varieties varying mainly in foliage colour.

Lonicera pileata
An evergreen with horizontally spreading branches and small, bright green leaves. Grows to about 60cm (2ft) by 1.2m (4ft).

Pachysandra terminalis
Above: A low-growing ground cover about 30cm (1ft) tall, with white insignificant flowers. 'Variegata' is a more attractive plant.

Polygonum affine (knotweed)
Above: Forms a creeping mat of bright green foliage to about 15cm (6in), with small, pink, poker-like flowers. Bronze leaves in winter.

Rosa (rose)
Above: Modern ground-cover roses are very compact and ideal where you need summer colour for a sunny site.

Thymus serpyllum (creeping thyme)
Above: A ground-hugging plant with aromatic foliage and clusters of tiny, purple, white, pink or red flowers in summer.

Vinca (periwinkle)
Above: A rather untidy spreading ground cover, but useful for its usually blue flowers all summer long. There are also variegated forms.

BORDER PERENNIALS

Acaena (New Zealand burr)
Above: A colonizing carpeter with small, fern-like leaves, to about 5–8cm (2–3in) high. Brownish-red burrs follow summer flowers.

Ajuga reptans (bugle)
Grown primarily for foliage effect. There are purple and variegated varieties that form a carpet 5–10cm (2–4in) high.

Bergenia (elephant ears)
Above: Large, rounded, glossy green, leathery leaves. Flowers – mostly pink – in spring. 30–45cm (1–1½ft).

Cotula squalida (brass buttons)
An evergreen carpeter with fern-like foliage, growing to about 5cm (2in). Small yellow flowers appear in mid-summer.

Epimedium (barrenwort)
There are various species, grown mainly for foliage effect. Pale green leaves sometimes flushed brown or bronze. About 23cm (9in).

Geranium endressii (cranesbill)
Above: Deeply lobed foliage topped with pale pink flowers from early to late summer. Dies down in winter but summer cover is dense.

Hosta
Above: These popular foliage plants come in many variations, so choose species or varieties with leaves that particularly appeal to you.

Lamium maculatum (deadnettle)
A loose carpeter about 23cm (9in) tall. Choose a variety with silvery or attractively mottled foliage. White or purple flowers.

Lysimachia nummularia (creeping Jenny)
Top: Small, rounded leaves, yellow in 'Aurea', and yellow flowers. Needs moist soil, and only retains leaves in winter in mild areas.

Pulmonaria (lungwort)
There are many species and varieties, often with silver-splashed leaves. The spring flowers are in shades of blue and pink.

Stachys byzantina
(syn. *S. lanata*) (lamb's tongue)
Above: A grey evergreen with narrow, woolly leaves. Foliage height about 15cm (6in) but purple flower spikes grow to 45cm (1½ft).

Tiarella cordifolia (foamflower)
Above: A carpeter about 10cm (4in) tall with lobed, hairy leaves, topped with small spikes of white flowers in spring and early summer.

Waldsteinia ternata
Above: Evergreen about 10cm (4in) tall, spreading rapidly by creeping, rooting stems. Yellow flowers in spring and early summer.

Planting for Wildlife

Wildlife will be encouraged into your garden by features such as water, bird tables and nest boxes, and plenty of borders to provide shelter and protection. But if you want to encourage bees, birds and butterflies, you also need shrubs to provide the necessary protection and plants that are rich in nectar or have a plentiful supply of berries or seeds that birds like to eat.

SHRUBS

Buddleja davidii (butterfly bush)
The flowers attract birds, butterflies, bees and many other insects.

Cotoneaster species
Above: The flowers attract insects, the berries bring the birds.

Ilex (holly)
Above: Holly berries are very attractive to birds, but be sure to plant a female variety otherwise you will not have any berries.

Lavandula (lavender)
Useful for attracting butterflies.

Leycesteria (pheasant berry)
Above: Birds love the juicy berries.

Pyracantha (firethorn)
Above: Bees and other insects are attracted to the flowers, and birds eat the berries that follow.

BORDER PLANTS

Aster (Michaelmas daisy)
Above: Butterflies, bees and other insects are attracted to this shrub.

Aubrietia
Above: This shrub attracts butterflies, bees and other insects.

Centranthus
Attracts a wide range of insects.

Erigeron (fleabane)
Butterflies, bees and other insects.

Helenium (sneezeweed)
Butterflies, bees and other insects.

Scabiosa (scabious)
Butterflies, bees and other insects.

Sedum spectabile (ice-plant)
Above: Butterflies, bees and other insects.

Solidago (golden rod)
Butterflies and insects.

ANNUALS

Iberis (candytuft)
Above: Butterflies and other insects.

Centaurea cyanus (cornflower)
Butterflies and other insects.

Tagetes patula (French marigold)
Above: Butterflies and other insects.

Heliotropium (heliotrope)
Butterflies and other insects.

Reseda (mignonette)
Butterflies and other insects.

Limnanthes douglasii
(poached egg flower)
Above: Butterflies and other insects.

Helianthus (sunflower)
Birds are attracted by the seeds.

Lobularia maritima
(sweet alyssum)
Butterflies and other insects.

Dipsacus (teasel)
Birds are attracted by the seeds.

Cheiranthus (wallflower)
Butterflies and other insects.

Planting for Scent

Scent adds another dimension to the garden, so plant with it in mind. Most people think first of fragrant flowers, but fragrant foliage will remain a feature for a much longer period.

SHRUBS

Chimonanthus praecox (wintersweet)
Yellow, claw-like flowers in mid- or late winter. Needs a sheltered position and best near the shelter of a wall.

Choisya ternata (Mexican orange blossom)
Above: Evergreen, aromatic leaves, yellow in the variety 'Sundance'. Fragrant white flowers in late spring and into summer.

Cytisus battandieri (Moroccan broom)
Above: Small spikes of yellow flowers in summer, with strong pineapple scent. Requires a sheltered position, perhaps near a wall.

Daphne mezereum (mezereon)
Dense clusters of highly fragrant, purple-red flowers in late winter and early spring, followed by scarlet berries.

Jasminum officinale (common jasmine)
A vigorous, twining climber with sweetly scented white flowers, pink in bud, in summer.

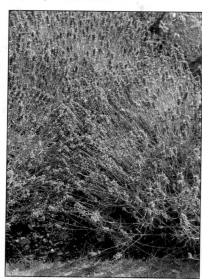

Lavandula (lavender)
Above: Blue, pink or white flowers between mid-summer and early autumn. Usually grey-green aromatic foliage.

Lonicera fragrantissima (shrubby honeysuckle)
A twiggy shrub with creamy-white, bell-shaped flowers in mid- and late winter. The scent is strong.

Lonicera periclymenum (honeysuckle)
Above: A popular, scented climber. The flowers are a combination of rose-purple and yellow. Early to late summer, depending on variety.

Philadelphus (mock orange)
Above: There are many good species and varieties, all with white, very fragrant flowers in mid- and late summer.

Rosa (rose)
Above: Roses need no introduction, but the strength of their scent varies, so consult a good catalogue if in doubt on this point.

Sarcococca (sweet box)
Clump-forming shrub with glossy, evergreen foliage and white, winter flowers that are small but very fragrant. About 1m (3ft).

Spartium junceum (Spanish broom)
Almost leafless, rush-like stems with pea-shaped, golden yellow flowers all summer. Sweet honey scent.

Syringa (lilac)
S. vulgaris (common lilac) and other species of these popular and fragrant shrubs, blooming in late spring and early summer.

Viburnum x bodnantense
A winter-flowering shrub with small clusters of fragrant pink flowers on bare stems in winter.

Viburnum carlesii
Top: Sweet-scented white or pink flowers, pink in bud, in spring. Foliage usually has good autumn tints.

Wisteria sinensis
Above: A very popular, large climber with cascades of sweet-scented mauve to purple-lilac flowers in late spring and early summer.

Aspect

The aspect is something you don't have any choice about. Whichever direction the garden faces, though, there will be a range of plants suitable for growing in it; selecting the right plants will produce a wonderful show of colour throughout the year.

KNOW YOUR PLANTS

The direction the garden faces will have a strong influence on the plants likely to thrive in it. If a plant originally hails from the warm, dry and sunny countries, it is unlikely to grow well in a damp, shady corner, and, similarly, a bog plant from a northern moors will not enjoy being placed between a south-facing wall and a path. One of the basic keys to successful gardening is to match the position and the plant as closely as possible. Doing this when the plant is first acquired will save both time and money, because the plant will not have to be dug up later when it has failed to thrive and most of the growing season has been lost. A good nursery is invaluable for advice, but most plants will be labelled.

PLANTS FOR POSITIONS WITH MORNING SUN

Berberis darwinii
Bergenia cordifolia
Chaenomeles x *superba*
Clematis montana
Clematis tangutica
Cotoneaster horizontalis
Deutzia scabra
Euphorbia griffithii
Forsythia suspensa
Fuschia
Galanthus nivalis (snowdrop)
Hamamelis mollis
  (witch hazel)
Helleborus foetidus
Hypericum 'Hidcote'
Lonicera periclymenum
Pyracantha 'Golden Glow'
Rosa rugosa
Vinca major (periwinkle)

PLANTS FOR POSITIONS WITH NO SUN

Akebia quinata
Aucuba japonica
Berberis x *stenophylla*
Camellia japonica
Camellia x *williamsii*
Clematis alpina
Clematis 'Nelly Moser'
Choisya ternata
Crinodendron hookerianum
Euonymus fortunei
Garrya elliptica
Hedera colchica
Hedera helix
Hydrangea petiolaris
Ilex
Jasminum nudiflorum
Kerria japonica 'Pleniflora'
Mahonia japonica
Parthenocissus
Piptanthus laburnifolius
Tropaeolum speciosum

Above: Choisya ternata *'Sundance'.*

Right: Parthenocissus *is suitable for a garden that receives little sun. A good nursery will give advice on the best plants for your garden.*

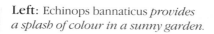

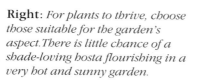

Left: Echinops bannaticus *provides a splash of colour in a sunny garden.*

Right: *For plants to thrive, choose those suitable for the garden's aspect. There is little chance of a shade-loving hosta flourishing in a very hot and sunny garden.*

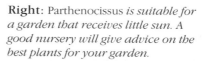

PLANTS FOR VERY SUNNY POSITIONS

Aethionema grandiflorum
Brachyglottis (syn. *Senecio*)
Campsis
Canna indica
Carpenteria californica
Cistus
Dianthus
Eccremocarpus scaber
Echinacea purpurea
Echinops ritro
Fritillaria imperialis

=*Geranium cinereum*
  'Ballerina'
Helenium
Helianthemum nummularium
Moluccella laevis
Osteospermum
Paeonia fruiticosa
Reseda odorata
Rosa
Salvia officinalis
Sempervivum

PLANTS FOR WEST-FACING POSITIONS

Abelia x *grandiflora*
Campsis
Ceanothus 'Gloire de Versailles'
Ceanothus impressus
Crocosmia
Deutzia scabra 'Plena'
Eccremocarpus scaber
Fremontodendron
  'California Glory'
Geranium
Helichrysum italicum
Humulus lupulus 'Aureus'

Ipomoea hederacea
Jasminum nudiflorum
Lavandula angustifolia
Lavandula stoechas
Papaver orientale
Penstemon
Potentilla fruiticosa
Rosmarinus officinalis
  (rosemary)
Spirea
Vitis coignetiae
Wiegela

Ideal for sunny gardens, Helenium *'Waldraut' will also tolerate very alkaline soil.*

Campsis radicans *is a good screening plant.*

Right: *Growing plants in pots will allow you to move them into full sun or shade easily.*

Choosing Plants to Cope with Pollution

Pollution is a problem in all areas but town gardens are particularly exposed to its effects. In this battle between our need for the peace and tranquillity of nature and the necessities of economic activity, the front garden is the front line. Some plants can cope with the problems of pollution, while others cannot, but with thoughtful planting, the garden need look no less beautiful in a town than in the countryside.

POLLUTION-TOLERANT PLANTS

Amelanchier canadensis	*Garrya* (all)
Aucuba japonica	*Ilex aquifolium*
Berberis (all)	*Leycesteria formosa*
Buddleja davidii	*Ligustrum ovalifolium*
Ceratostigma willmottianum	*Olearia* x *haastii*
Chaenomeles (all)	x *Osmarea burkwoodii*
Cotoneaster (most)	*Philadelphus* (all)
Elaeagnus x *ebbingei*	*Syringa* (all)
Elaeagnus pungens	*Tamarix pentrandra*
Forsythia (all)	*Weigela florida*

PROBLEM SITES

Any substance in the atmosphere that is not beneficial can constitute pollution, whether it is air-borne, water-borne or deposited directly. Some plants are more tolerant of pollution than others and it is worth knowing which these are.

The most obvious site at risk from pollution is next to a busy main road, where traffic is constantly streaming past or snarled up in slow-moving jams. Not only does the deposit from the vehicle exhausts settle on the leaves throughout the year but, if the road is salted in winter, it is splashed on to the nearest plants as the traffic passes. The solution may be as simple as a hedge of plants that can tolerate this kind of treatment, planted along the most vulnerable part of the garden to protect the more delicate species behind it.

Environmental pollution is a much more general problem to the garden. In an area with such difficulties it is worth choosing a selection of plants that are known to be tolerant of a range of unfavourable conditions. Careful selection will provide a varied collection of both evergreen and deciduous plants, for flowers and foliage, that will provide interest throughout the year.

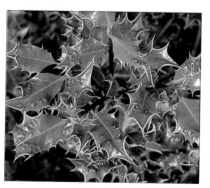

Left: Ilex *(holly) will tolerate most urban conditions.*

Right: Berberis *can be planted to shield more delicate plants.*

Opposite: *Plants at the front of the house often have to contend with car exhaust. By choosing plants that are tolerant of such conditions, you can achieve gardening success.*

Security

In the absence of a drawbridge, it is difficult to avoid having trespassers on the garden, whether they have two legs or four. Measures can be taken to make the garden a less inviting prospect for invaders, without spoiling its overall appearance.

ANIMALS AND INSECTS

Neither animals nor insects recognize human boundaries, and if something looks or smells interesting to them, they will investigate. This can result in damage to plants. Although there isn't an instant solution, there are steps that you can take without resorting to chemicals.

Certain plants may attract certain animals; they are usually plants with strong odours, such as *Nepeta* x *faassenii* (catmint), so avoiding these will reduce the attraction of your garden.

Ants are a particular nuisance because, they tunnel through the soil along the lines already created by plant roots, causing the root to lose contact with the soil and dry out. If this happens along enough roots, the plant can no longer take up the water it needs to live, and it will die. Higher up on the plant, ants "farm" aphids (greenfly), which feed on sap from the leaves causing distorted foliage and poor growth, in order to take advantage of the sweet honeydew aphids excrete. Ant-repellant plants such as pennyroyal (*Mentha pulegium*) is said to be around the base of subjects which are particularly prone to attack.

Once the garden is established, the best means of controlling insect pests is to encourage other insects that act as predators.

Above: *Climbing roses are a decorative and practical way to discourage unwelcome visitors from scaling fences to gain access to the garden.*

Below left: *Prickly plants will deter both human and animal visitors to the garden.*

PRACTICAL WAYS TO PREVENT THEFT AND DAMAGE

- Put bricks in the base of a container, making it too heavy to move easily.

- Use a tree anchor (saves using a stake).

- Fit small hanging-basket locks to protect your baskets.

- Install security lighting.

- Photograph and make an identifying mark on valuable ornaments

PRICKLY OR THORNY PLANTS

Aralia spinosus
Berberis julianae
Berberis x *stenophylla*
Chaenomeles speciosa
Colletia spinosissima
Crataegus monogyna
Elaeagnus angustifolia
Hippophane rhamnoides
Ilex x *altaclarensis*
Ilex aquifolium
    'Ferox argentea'
Ilex aquifolium
Mahonia aquifolium
Mahonia x *media* 'Charity'
Osmanthus heterophyllus
Poncirus trifoliata
Pyracantha 'Mohave'
Ribes speciosum
Rosa rugosa
Rubus tricolor
Ruscus aculeatus
Ulex europueus
Yucca gloriosa

PROBLEMS WITH HUMAN VISITORS

People visit the garden for many reasons and tailoring the design in response to these reasons will welcome those who visit for pleasure, help those who visit through necessity and discourage those who have less beneficent motives.

People can cause damage to the garden in many ways, often without even realizing it. Simply walking across a frost-covered lawn will damage the frozen cells of the grass plants, leaving a trail of brown footprints which will take most of the spring to fade. This can be overcome by using the planting to guide the visitor to the proper point of access – a hedge, even a low one, acts as a physical barrier and will cause people to detour around it.

Less easy to deal with is the visitor with less than honest intentions, but remember that most theft is opportunistic rather than premeditated, and reducing the number of easily-carried-away items on view should have an effect on this. Tools, for instance, should be tidied away if the garden is left unattended. Prickly or thorny plants are an effective deterrent near a potential point of entry, perhaps against a wall that could be scaled, but don't plant anything large enough to screen the door as this may allow someone enough time to try the lock. To this end, security lighting which comes on automatically is also effective.

Right: *Tall fences maintain privacy and discourage access to the garden and can be softened with climbing plants.*

Reducing Noise

While it is difficult to eliminate an annoying noise completely, it is possible to use plants to filter it down to a more acceptable level. Plants near the house are more attractive than sound-proofing.

HEDGES AS SCREENING

In built-up areas it is difficult to get away from noise. To an extent, noise becomes so familiar that it barely registers, but there are occasions when it is preferable to do something about it. At the front of a house, a particularly persistent noise may interfere with sleeping, for instance, and here it may be useful to install plants to act as a baffle to the noise and to try to deflect it up over the building.

Hedges, particularly when they consist of broad-leaved evergreen plants such as *Prunus laurocerasus*, *Aucuba japonica* or *Elaeagnus* x *ebbingei*, are effective at reducing noise, because they form a dense barrier throughout the year. The higher the hedge, the higher it will deflect the noise.

In a very small garden, this may not be an option, because hedges do take up quite a lot of space, so the strategic positioning of a single upright or small-sized tree may be necessary. Both *Prunus* 'Amanogawa' (upright) and *Prunus* x *subhirtella* 'Autumnalis' (a small tree bearing flowers throughout the autumn and winter) are deciduous trees suitable for small gardens.

Above: *A dense planting of tall shrubs can act as an effective screen against noise, as well as providing privacy from nearby houses or roads.*

INDEX

ACKNOWLEDGEMENTS

Special photography by John Freeman, Jonathan Buckley, Marie O' Hara and Janine Hosegood.

The publishers would like to thank the following picture libraries and photographers for allowing reproduction of their photographs:

A–Z Botanical: pages 300br, 301l (© Simon Butcher), 301r (© Moira Newman).

Camera Press: pages 85 (© Linda Burgess), 300.

David Way: page 145.

Debbie Patterson: pages 40tr, 126bl, 257.

Derek St Romaine: pages 149, 153, 155, 160, 161, 162.

Garden Picture Library: pages 40bl, 44tr, 289tr, 290t (© Steven Wooster), 295 and 298 (© Friedrich Strauss), 300tr (© Ron Sutherland), 385.

Jenny Harpur Garden Picture Library: pages 11bl, 14br, 36, 37, 39r, 46, 49, 57l, 59, 61, 62, 63, 90t, 91b, 115tl, 123l, 124t, 131l and br, 133, 144, 152, 154, 239l.

John Freeman 42bl, 256, 294, 296, 302.

Jonathan Buckley: pages 100, 101, 179br, 196, 210l, 216bl, 217r, 218bl, 222tl, 224tl, 225tl, 290bl and br, 298bl, 382bl and c, 389l and r, 398bl, br, c and r, 399tl, 400.

Juliette Wade: pages 41, 42t and r, 43, 45, 80, 81, 96, 97, 112tr, 113, 126tr, 127bl, 128, 129, 255, 384tr, 398br, 399br, 402bl, 403, 404.

Michelle Garrett: page 127t.

Peter McHoy: pages 10, 11tl, 13, 14t, 15, 17, 25, 28, 31, 39tl and bl, 51br, 55, 56, 57tr, 58, 60, 67l, 70t and br, 71t, 72t, 74, 75, 78bl, 79, 86l, 87, 90b, 91b, 95, 104, 105, 115tr and bl, 116, 119, 121bl, 122, 123tr, 125, 132, 134, 135, 140, 159, 164bl and tr, 165, 188tr and br, 189tr, 211b, 214tr, 219bl, 222b, 223r, 224br, 225bl, 228bl, 229r, 231, 233, 235, 237, 238, 239tr, 241, 243, 247t, 251, 305, 315t, 323, 324, 325l, 327, 328t, 331br, 344br, 347br, 349bl, 350b, 351br, 352br, 355b, 357b, 364b, 365b, 370, 371, 372tr and br, 373r, 378br, 382, 383, 386, 387, 390, 391, 392, 393, 394, 395, 396, 406, 411.

Richard Bird: page 337br.

key t = top, b = bottom, c = centre, l = left, r = right